Standard Cataloging
for School and Public Libraries

Fourth Edition

SHEILA S. INTNER
Professor Emerita
Simmons College Graduate School of Library and Information Science
at Mount Holyoke College
South Hadley, Massachusetts

and

JEAN WEIHS
Technical Services Group
Toronto, Ontario

D1451082

A Member of the Greenwood Publishing Group

Westport, Connecticut • London

Library of Congress Cataloging-in-Publication Data

Intner, Sheila S.
   Standard cataloging for school and public libraries / Sheila Intner and Jean Weihs.—4th ed.
      p. cm.
   Includes bibliographical references and index.
   ISBN-13: 978–1–59158–378–3 (alk. paper)
   1. Cataloging.   2. School libraries.   3. Public libraries.   I. Weihs, Jean Riddle.   II. Title.
   Z693.I56 2007
   025.3—dc22 2007009009

British Library Cataloguing in Publication Data is available.

Library of Congress Catalog Card Number: 2007009009
ISBN-13: 978–1–59158–378–3

First published in 2007

Libraries Unlimited, 88 Post Road West, Westport, CT 06881
A Member of the Greenwood Publishing Group, Inc.
www.lu.com

Printed in the United States of America

The paper used in this book complies with the
Permanent Paper Standard issued by the National
Information Standards Organization (Z39.48–1984).

10 9 8 7 6 5 4 3

Contents

Preface

Only a few years of the twenty-first century have passed, but the world of cataloging and classification stands at a crossroads. As this book is being written, much soul-searching is going on within the cataloging community about the future of the specialty. Perhaps it is inevitable that this should be happening. Librarianship and media services themselves have been going through a similar transition for the last dozen years as library and media center collections and services have automated. Patrons no longer must travel to library buildings and search card catalogs located there. Instead, catalogs are available on the Internet and can be searched by all people with the proper computer connections who wish to do so. Interlibrary loan requests facilitated by bibliographic networks now number in the millions per month and show no likelihood of diminishing. National and international exchange of bibliographic data is not merely a dream for tomorrow, but the reality of today. The twenty-first-century library functions in a brave, new world.

Two developments are currently in progress: changes in the descriptive cataloging code and changes in the way the Library of Congress interprets its mission regarding bibliographic control. Both will have substantial impacts on the ways in which local libraries organize their collections. The first will result in the publication of new rules for creating bibliographic records, now expected in 2009, which might take some time to be absorbed into catalogers' daily routines. However, despite the code's new name—*Resource Description and Access* (RDA)—and its new approach—rules are organized by descriptive element, not by medium—most observers expect that the adoption and understanding of the new code will proceed smoothly and that the resulting catalog entries will not look radically different from those created using current rules.

The second development is more worrisome, because its outcome is less clear. For more than 100 years, the U.S. Library of Congress (LC) has been the undisputed leader of the American cataloging community, setting the standards for the nation and, indirectly, through its leadership role in international circles, for the world. Since the turn of the twentieth century, U.S. catalogers have become increasingly dependent on LC for catalog records (first on cards, now in electronic form) as well as for original cataloging tools: subject headings, classification numbers, descriptive cataloging rule interpretations, subject analysis policies, name and title authorities, and, most recently, computer encoding protocols. The classic joke is "How many catalogers does it take to change a lightbulb?" The answer: "Only one, but she has to wait to see how LC does it."

In 2006, while this book was being written, LC announced it was considering how best to accomplish its mission as it moves further into the new millennium. It also declared that its catalogers are discontinuing the practice of establishing new series authority records. Catalogers responded with great concern as well as no little dismay at the possibility that LC may be considering more changes of a similar nature. Although many, including the authors of this book, believe LC will always play a leadership role both at home and abroad, no one knows the kinds of responsibilities it might relinquish or to whom they might be bequeathed.

Thus, the bottom line is that catalogers working in local libraries and media centers can anticipate taking more, not less, responsibility for organizing their materials. They may also be expected to assume a larger share of the work on standards and policies in a new multi-institutional model of leadership in cataloging and classification. In a distributed leadership environment, knowledgeable librarians and media specialists at the grassroots level will be especially important.

In that spirit, this book has been written to convey knowledge about standard methods of cataloging and classifying library materials in a manner that students and beginning catalogers can use. It is intended as an introduction and does not attempt to be exhaustive, mainly because an exhaustive book would be many times the size of this one and would go far beyond a beginner's world. Several chapters offer exercises so readers can practice what has been covered. Many chapters end with reading lists that provide more information for readers who wish to pursue a topic further. Time-sensitive details are as accurate as the authors could make them as of January 2007. Nevertheless, we accept full responsibility, with profound apologies, for all errors on these pages. Nothing is more exasperating than errors that mislead readers of an introductory text.

The authors believe that doing good-quality cataloging and classification results in better service for patrons, and that giving patrons the best possible service is our readers' goal. We sincerely hope this book speeds readers toward the goal. *Excelsior*!

Acknowledgments

The authors wish to acknowledge the assistance and advice of the following friends, colleagues, and family members who generously contributed their time and knowledge to the writing of this book:

Diane Boehr, National Library of Medicine

Christel Bullen, Manager, Cataloguing & Processing, S&B Books

Joe Cox and the Inforum staff at the Faculty of Information Studies, University of Toronto

Trudy Downs, Rutgers University, Graduate School of Communications, Information, and Library Studies

Joanna Fountain, University of Texas, Austin, Texas Library Connection Database

Deborah A. Fritz, The MARC of Quality

Jonathan S. Intner, Novartis

Mathew Intner, retired

Bruce Chris Johnson, Library of Congress

Peggy Johnson, University of Minnesota

Judith Klavans, University of Maryland, College of Information Studies

Susan S. Lazinger, Hebrew University of Jerusalem

Jennifer Levere and Sue Meggs-Becker, Montcrest School Library, who allowed access to their nonbook collection

Joan Lussky, Catholic University of America, School of Library and Information Studies

Karen Markey, University of Michigan, School of Information

James M. Matarazzo, Simmons College, Graduate School of Library and Information Science

David Miller, Curry College

Roger Miller, Ohio Library Council

Ingrid Parent, Library and Archives Canada

Glenn Patton, OCLC Online Computer Library Center, Inc.

Wayne Piper, Ohio Library Council

Cameron Riddle, computer consultant

Tony Stankus, College of the Holy Cross

Margaret Stewart, Library and Archives Canada

Verna Urbanski, University of North Florida

Linda Watkins, Simmons College, Graduate School of Library and Information Science

David Weisbrod, Rutgers University, School of Communication, Information and Library Studies

Nancy Williamson, University of Toronto Faculty of Information Studies

1

Introduction

Many things have changed in the years since *Standard Cataloging for School and Public Libraries* was first published, but one constant is the dynamic nature of the rules and standards used for library cataloging and classification. Those responsible for standards call the process by which they are kept up-to-date "dynamic revision," and it truly never ends. Because of dynamic revision, books such as this one must be updated regularly to keep the details of the standards it describes accurate and relevant.

At the same time, the principles on which cataloging and classification are based are enduring. Even as their implementation through descriptive cataloging, subject cataloging, classification, and encoding changes, the goal of identifying library materials and empowering patrons to find them, select what they want, and retrieve their selections remains the same.

Since the third edition of this text was published in 2001, public library and school library media center collections have continued to grow and change. The definition of a small collection, which once might have encompassed a few thousand titles, now refers to up to 20,000 titles. Whereas large collections once were defined as holding several hundred thousand titles, in the twenty-first century they are more likely to approach, equal, or exceed 1,000,000 titles.

The composition of collections has also changed over recent decades. Once they included primarily paper-and-print-based materials such as books, magazines, and journals, augmented by an array of nonbook objects such as sound recordings on cassette or disc, music, maps, motion pictures, videorecordings, filmstrips, flash cards, posters, photographs, microfilms and microfiche, kits, and so on. Today, although collections in some places may remain bibliocentric (meaning consisting mainly of books) and most of the previously enumerated nonbook materials are still being collected, an important and growing number of materials are not objects in the traditional sense. Instead, new items are transmitted as digital signals via computer. These materials, called "electronic resources" by librarians and media specialists, cannot be found by scanning library and media center shelves. They must be located through the public catalog, which lets patrons see what electronic titles are available via computer in the library or elsewhere, helps them select what they need, and enables them to obtain it.

At the end of the day, the public catalog is still the most important tool patrons can use to find out what the library has in both its local and remote access collections. Public catalogs can enable searchers to see what materials are available by particular authors or on particular subjects as well as what versions and editions of a title can be found in the collections.

Functions of the Catalog

Charles Ammi Cutter, one of America's most distinguished and innovative librarians, who published America's first book of rules for cataloging materials in 1876, established the purpose of catalogs as follows:

1. To enable a person to find a book when one of the following is known:
    a) The author
    b) The title
    c) The subject

2. To show what the library has
    d) By a given author
    e) On a given subject
    f) In a given kind of literature

3. To assist in the choice of a book
    g) As to the edition (bibliographically)
    h) As to its character (literary or topical)[1]

Cutter called these purposes "the objects of the catalog." They have been valid for more than 130 years and they continue to express what current catalogs try to achieve.

Cutter's objects describe two distinct functions for the catalog: a finding list function and a collocation (gathering) function. Patrons who approach the catalog with a known item in mind are served by the finding list function. When they search for the item, the presence or absence of a record for it in the catalog informs them whether it is part of the collection. If patrons are not sure of an exact item, but want to select an item from among the works of an author, or find a particular edition of a work, or locate materials on a subject, the collocation function gathers all the records that match a chosen search term and helps to answer their queries. All the publications of an author are filed in one place under the heading for the author's name, all the editions of a work are filed together under the heading for the title, and all the publications on a subject are gathered under the headings for that subject. Searchers can scan the set of records gathered under their search terms (name, title, or subject) and select what they want.

Regarding collocation by literary genre headings: they may have been assigned in Cutter's day and are currently considered appropriate, though optional, but standard practice for much of the twentieth century was not to assign them. Library and media center collections of fiction, poetry, drama, and other literary genres are so large that the resulting sets of retrieved records could be enormous. Most searchers are not willing to scan huge numbers of records, negating the value of genre headings.

Cutter's objects sound simple but they are not. Cataloging rules that promote identification, such as transcribing titles and other bibliographic elements exactly as they appear on materials being cataloged, may work against collocation, and vice versa. For example, when different editions of the same work spell title words differently or use different wordings for the title, transcribing titles exactly does not collocate. Consider philosopher David Hume's *An Enquiry into Human Understanding*. An American publisher chooses to spell it *An Inquiry into Human Understanding.* The two editions contain the same work, but the first title files in the E's; the second in the I's. Or, consider Lewis Carroll's *Alice in Wonderland.* One publisher uses that familiar title, but another calls it *Alice's Adventures in Wonderland*; a third publisher chooses to emphasize the illustrations, calling its edition *The Illustrated Alice in Wonderland.* All are titles for the same story, but they file in different places in the catalog.

Current cataloging rules serve both functions by mandating both strict transcription in bibliographic descriptions for identification purposes and the construction of one authorized heading form for each heading for collocation purposes. Catalog records for the three editions of Carroll's *Alice* mentioned in the last paragraph would not only have three different titles transcribed as they appear on the books, called *titles proper*, in the bibliographic descriptions, but also bear identical constructed authorized title headings, called *uniform titles.* When both titles proper and uniform titles are searchable headings, patrons can find what they want by requesting a known edition directly via its title proper heading, using the catalog as a finding list; or if they do not have a particular edition in mind, they can select one from the group gathered under the uniform title, using the catalog as a selection tool.

Searching Beyond Local Catalogs

One reason public librarians and school library media specialists should be concerned about Cutter's second object, the collocation function, becomes very clear when local catalogs are linked with the catalogs of other information agencies in bibliographic networks. Good cataloging and classification not only enables local catalogs to perform better locally but also makes it possible for them to link more effectively with the catalogs of peer libraries and media centers as well as those of colleges and universities, special libraries, state and provincial libraries, and national libraries, belonging to the same bibliographic network. The ultimate goal is to make any title owned anywhere in the world available to a person with a need for that material.

Development of national and international computer-based bibliographic networks such as OCLC, Inc. (Online Computer Library Center) based in Dublin, Ohio, is turning the goal of universal bibliographic availability of all library materials into a reality. OCLC's tens of thousands of members share many millions of catalog records representing real materials, and cooperative arrangements for interlibrary borrowing and lending make a great many obtainable far beyond their local jurisdictions. More than 12 million interlibrary loan transactions are transmitted among OCLC's members annually, and most requests are satisfied promptly. This is reason enough for local institutions to think beyond cataloging solely for their own collections to the enormous possibilities of linking with a global partnership, along with the challenges partnerships bring with them. In the twenty-first century, local library and media center catalogs are more than just keys to the collections housed within local schools and community buildings. They are also gateways to the world that lies beyond school and town, with all of its rich intellectual resources.

Rewards of Good Cataloging

Good cataloging has rewards that resonate within the local borders of villages, towns, and cities, and schools at all grade levels. Small collections can be explored and used more effectively when local catalogs contain good-quality information. The point of buying materials for local collections is for them to be used. Good cataloging contributes to the use of materials by making it easier for people searching the catalog to find what they want and need. A catalog containing high-quality standardized information gives better responses to searchers' queries. Standard methods can be applied to all types of information resources in all kinds of physical forms. Using a good-quality catalog in their local public libraries and school media centers helps to prepare searchers for encounters with catalogs and collections in college, university, and corporate libraries.

This book is dedicated to the proposition that standardized cataloging is the key that opens the door of better access to local materials—resources that can satisfy patrons' information, recreation, and education needs. The chapters that follow cover each component of the cataloging process: description and access; subject headings; classification and call numbers; and computer encoding. Each component is first discussed generally and then followed by one or more chapters describing individual standard tools used in practice. Each chapter contains many illustrations and a selected bibliography of helpful manuals to assist readers in continuing to add to their knowledge.

A Word About the Figures and Examples

The figures in this book that represent bibliographic records are designed to highlight a student's progress in learning to catalog. The figures in Chapter 2 and Chapters 4 through 12 that highlight cataloging rules are done in the format used in cataloging-in-publication (CIP) records usually found on the versos of title pages, because CIP is frequently the basis on which catalog records are built and because it is easier to demonstrate cataloging principles without the distraction of computer encoding. The figures in Chapters 2 and 4 do not include "tracings"; that is, the subject headings and additional descriptive headings that are added to the records in the course of normal cataloging procedures. As the student progresses to the subject heading chapters, tracings for appropriate subject headings are included in the bibliographic record. Similarly, when classification numbers are discussed, the figures include appropriate classification. In Chapter 12, "Computer Encoding," illustrative catalog records contain standard MARC (MAchine Readable Cataloging) coding. The subfield codes in these records have been separated from the terms following by a space to make the coding more understandable to the beginning cataloger.

Although no textbook can supply all the practice students might want or need to polish their cataloging and classification skills, the authors have provided exercises at the end of selected chapters to enable readers to apply the tools discussed within those chapters. The MARC exercises in this book do not require students and novice catalogers to code many of the fixed fields, because fixed fields are handled differently by various databanks. (See Figure 12.2 on page 210.) A graduate cataloger will learn the needs of a library's system on the job. Answers to the examples in the exercises can be found in Appendix B at the end of the book. The authors believe it is not difficult to do high-quality standard cataloging. It just takes the right knowledge, a little confidence, and practice.

In the next chapter, cataloging policy decisions are explored. These decisions form the basis for all practices followed by a library or media center catalog department.

Note

1.   Charles A. Cutter, *Rules for a Dictionary Catalog*, 4th ed. (Washington, DC: Government Printing Office, 1904), 12.

2

DECISIONS

The most important policy decision catalogers can make in connection with local library and media center operations is to conform (at least, generally) to standard practices. The next most important decision is to accept the fact that the tools used in standard practices do not remain static. Adopting them means committing the catalog department to do a certain amount of updating in both products and procedures, as needed, when changes occur. Although small changes are approved from time to time, when a standard tool is published in a new edition or version, it may contain a larger number of changes—modifications that produce bigger and more important differences in the resulting catalog records. Decisions about how to handle these matters are discussed in some detail in this chapter.

It might seem that conforming to standards limits catalogers to only one way of doing things, but this is not so. Cataloging consists of four components: description and access, subject cataloging, classification, and encoding. Two components—subject cataloging and classification—can be implemented with the adoption of several possible tools. The other two—description and access, and encoding—require adopting only one tool for each component, but the tools themselves offer options in the ways they can be implemented.

This chapter explores the policy decisions that need to be made for each component in turn. First, however, use of standard catalog records originating at the Library of Congress, the Library and Archives Canada, and the British Library that appear within published materials, called cataloging-in-publication (CIP, pronounced "sip"), is explored. Currently, CIP is an important resource for all types of libraries and media centers, and its use helps to ensure that standard cataloging practice is followed in libraries that do not have access to major bibliographic networks. At this writing, however, the program is undergoing evaluation and reconsideration, and it is not clear what changes may be implemented in the future.

Cataloging-in-Publication

CIP records are created before publication when the items they represent, mainly books and some nonbook materials, are not yet complete. As they approach completion, participating publishers send copies of the bibliographic information, such as the title pages and tables of contents of books (or the equivalent sources from other materials), to the national library, which does as much cataloging as possible from the data in hand and returns preliminary catalog records to be printed in the finished items. The national library catalogers perform all necessary research on CIP records' access points and call numbers, and enter them into national bibliographic databases and networks with identifying tags to show they are not full or complete. Information, such as the number of pages in books, is left out of the record because at the point of CIP cataloging it is unknown. Sometimes, information in CIP records has to be corrected to reflect changes made by publishers after CIP cataloging is done. The changes can be as far reaching as giving a different title to a book or as minor as adding a foreword or a frontispiece.

In books, CIP records usually appear on the back of the title page (called the *verso*) or, occasionally, at the back of the book (called the *colophon*). After checking to be sure that the bibliographic data on the item in hand match the elements given in the CIP record, the work done by national library catalogers in establishing call numbers, name headings, and subject descriptors can be used by local librarians and media specialists to select headings, determine titles proper, assign call numbers, and complete accurate bibliographic descriptions.

The catalogers at the national libraries do not see the content of the items they catalog for CIP and must rely on the publishers to provide such information. Before the previous three editions of this book were published, the authors of this book examined the CIP and found, in each case, that the subject headings were incorrect and requested that the Library of Congress change them. Most authors, not being knowledgeable about cataloging, would be unaware of discrepancies.

Occasionally, a totally incorrect CIP appears on the verso (see Figure 5.1 on page 65). Catalogers should be particularly careful in checking the CIP for older books that are being added to the collection because rules for descriptive cataloging, subject heading terms, and classification numbers may have changed since the books were published. (See Figure 11.3 on pages 191–192 where the subject heading terminology for African Americans has changed since the book was published.)

Catalogers should also be aware of the differences in the CIP produced by different national libraries. For example, in Figure 2.1 different call numbers are given to the same book by the Library of Congress and the Library and Archives of Canada.

Despite these discrepancies, to which good catalogers must be alert, CIP is usually reliable, trustworthy work, performed carefully and thoroughly by some of the best catalogers in each nation. Local libraries can have one of three policies on CIP:

- Accept and use CIP records as given.

- Use CIP after checking the items in hand and making corrections when necessary.

- Ignore CIP, generally because other sources of bibliographic information are available.

The decision should be based on the agency's need for accuracy and the availability of alternative information sources as well as the expertise of the cataloging staff in improving the CIP records.

Descriptive Cataloging

The *Anglo-American Cataloguing Rules* (AACR2) is the only code of rules currently accepted as a standard for descriptive cataloging. Having said this, however, readers can anticipate a major update to AACR2 now in progress that will supersede AACR2 when it is published, known at this time as *Resource Description and Access* (RDA).[1] RDA is discussed

FIGURE 2.1

This example is an illustration of:
- compiled work entered under title
- two compilers
- additional words added to statement of responsibility to enhance meaning
- publishing date not listed, copyright date given
- contents (index) note
- two ISBDs listed on verso; one given relates to the library's copy
- ISBN qualified
- Library of Congress subject heading and Canadian subject heading the same
- added entries for compilers
- comparison between Library of Congress classification and Library and Archives Canada classification
- Library and Archives Canada CIP data

2nd level cataloging

First drafts : eyewitness accounts from our past / [compiled by] J.L. Granatstein [&] Norman Hillmer. -- Toronto : Thomas Allen, c2004.
    486 p. ; 22 cm.

    Includes index.
    ISBN 0-088762-135-X (pbk.).

    1. Canada -- History -- Sources. I. Granatstein, J.L.
II. Hillmer, Norman.

Recommended LCC classification: F1026

Recommended LAC classification: FC176

Author's note: The CIP record has "&" inserted between the compilers' names. This is not on the title page and it is properly placed in square brackets.

Fig. 2.1—Continues

briefly in Chapter 3. Nonetheless, an understanding of the decisions catalogers make in connection with AACR2's options not only is needed for the period of time until RDA appears but also is likely to be helpful in understanding how RDA operates in practice. Two types of decisions are covered here: AACR2 levels of description and rule options. The national libraries provide standard choices for the catalogers in their nations, which are described as well as the implications for making different decisions.

Levels of Description: In response to a call from librarians for a flexible standard that acknowledges libraries differ in the need for detail in catalog records, AACR2 offers three choices for description. Level 1 is the simplest and least detailed level, and is considered appropriate for libraries with small collections serving people doing uncomplicated searches

FIGURE 2.1 *(continued)*

(chief source of information)

(title page)

J. L. Granatstein

Norman Hillmer

FIRST DRAFTS

Eyewitness Accounts

from Our Past

Thomas Allen Publishers

Toronto

(information on verso)

National Library of Canada Cataloguing in Publication

Main entry under title

First drafts : eyewitness accounts from our past /
    [compiled by] J. L. Granatstein & Norman Hillmer.

Includes index.

ISBN 0-88762-113-9 (bound). — ISBN 088762-135-x (pbk.)

1. Canada—History—Sources. I. Granatstein, J. L., 1939–
II. Hillmer, Norman, 1942–

FC176.F47 2002   971   C2002-902551-6
F1026.F57 2002

Editor: Patrick Crean
Cover design: Gordon Robertson
Cover image: Canada Science and Technology Museum, CSTM/CN Collection, no. 1485

Page 467 constitutes a continuation of this copyright page.

Every reasonable effort has been made to locate the copyright holders of material found in this book. In the event that any material has not been correctly sourced, the publisher will gladly receive correspondence in efforts to rectify the citation in future printings.

Published by Thomas Allen Publishers,
a division of Thomas Allen & Son Limited,
145 Front Street East, Suite 209,
Toronto, Ontario M5A 1E3 Canada

www.thomas-allen.com

  Canada Council
for the Arts

The publisher gratefully acknowledges the support of the Ontario Arts Council for its publishing program.

We acknowledge the support of the Canada Council for the Arts, which last year invested $21.7 million in writing and publishing throughout Canada.

We acknowledge the Government of Ontario through the Ontario Media Development Corporation's Ontario Book Initiative.

08 07 06 05 04   1 2 3 4 5
Printed and bound in Canada

(see the level 1 description in Figure 2.2 on page 9). Level 1 descriptions do not include information about single authors that appears in headings, omit subtitles and series titles, and require only the extent of an item be given (for example, the number of pages in a book, but not the presence of illustrations or its size). However, libraries can add information normally omitted from a level 1 record if that piece of information is considered useful for their clientele. This is called enhanced level 1.

Level 2 is a middle-ground level that includes more detail than level 1 (see the level 2 description in Figure 2.2). It is the standard level of description selected by the national libraries and bibliographic networks for "full-level" cataloging.[2] Level 2 descriptions are considered sufficient to serve the needs of scholarly researchers using large collections of materials. In addition to all the information required by level 1, level 2 requires the inclusion of subtitles and other title information, statements of responsibility, additional physical details, and series statements. This level of detail helps to distinguish different works with

FIGURE 2.2

This example is an illustration of:
- other title information (in 2nd level description)
- edition statement (in 2nd level description)
- publishing date not listed, copyright date given
- contents (glossary and index) notes (in 2nd level description)
- two ISBNs
- two levels of cataloging

1st level cataloging

```
Randall, Lisa.
  Warped passages. -- Ecco, c2005.
  xi, 499 p.

  ISBN 10: 0-06-053108-8. -- ISBN 13: 978-0-06-053108-9.
```

2nd level cataloging

```
Randall, Lisa.
  Warped passages : unraveling the mysteries of the universe's
hidden dimensions / Lisa Randall. -- 1st ed. -- New York : Ecco,
c2005.
  xi, 499 p. : ill. ; 24 cm.

  Glossary: p. 459-471.
  Includes index.
  ISBN 10: 0-06-053108-8. -- ISBN 13: 978-0-06-053108-9.
```

Fig. 2.2—Continues

similar titles and different editions of the same title, and facilitates the selection of items with specific characteristics desired by searchers.

Level 3 is the most detailed level. It requires the inclusion of every detail mandated by the rules that is applicable to the items being cataloged. Level 3 descriptions are, by definition, the most thorough work possible. Such work is likely to be desired primarily for special collections serving the needs of specialized clients.

Rule Options: AACR2 has optional rules as well as choices in the way some of the mandated rules are applied. One well-known optional rule is rule 1.1C3, which specifies inserting general material designations (gmds) immediately after the main titles of items being cataloged to alert searchers about their physical forms. Not only is the entire rule optional, but if a library chooses to exercise the option, it must decide between two lists of gmds, one intended for British libraries, the other for North American libraries.[3] A second example is the mandatory rule for giving edition statements (1.2B). Giving the statements as they appear on items being cataloged is not optional; yet when no statements appear but catalogers know items differ from other editions, an option is offered to make up the statements and give them in square brackets in catalog records.

At the time AACR2 was first published and implemented, its national library participants—LC, LAC, and the British Library (BL)—made decisions on all the options that ap-

FIGURE 2.2 *(continued)*

(chief source of information)

(title page)

LISA RANDALL

Warped Passages

Unraveling the Mysteries of the
Universe's Hidden Dimensions

(information on verso)

WARPED PASSAGES. Copyright © 2005 by Lisa Randall.
All rights reserved. Printed in the United States of America.
No part of this book may be used or reproduced in any manner
whatsoever without written permission except in the case of brief
quotations embodied in critical articles and reviews.
For information, address HarperCollins Publishers,
10 East 53rd Street, New York, NY 10022.

HarperCollins books may be purchased for educational, business,
or sales promotional use. For information, please write:
Special Markets Department, HarperCollins Publishers,
10 East 53rd Street, New York, NY 10022.

FIRST EDITION

Library of Congress Cataloging-in-Publication Data
has been applied for.

ISBN-10: 0-06-053108-8
ISBN-13: 978-0-06-053108-9

05 06 07 08 09 ❖/QWF 10 9 8 7 6 5 4 3 2 1

ecco

An Imprint of HarperCollinsPublishers

———————

plied to their cataloging. They disseminated the decisions throughout their cataloging communities by both publishing them and leading workshops on AACR2 implementation in which the decisions were explained and taught to practicing catalogers. The decisions about options made by each national library are the standard for its nation. As a result, *LC Rule Interpretations*[4] are the standard for the United States and *LAC Rule Interpretations*[5] are the standard for Canada. For example, LAC follows the rules in AACR2 for microforms, whereas LC's rule interpretation mandates that the original document be cataloged with the microform described in a note (see Figure 2.3).

FIGURE 2.3

Descriptive cataloging taken from an AMICUS record demonstrating LAC's decision to follow the rules in AACR2.

```
100 1  $a Osberg, Lars.
245 10 $a Schooling literacy and individual earnings $h [microform] /
       $c Lars Osberg.
260    $a [Toronto] : $b Micromedia, $c [2000]
300    $a 1 microfiche ; $c 11 x 15 cm.
500    $ a Issued also in French under title: Scolarité alphabétisme et
       gains personnels.
500    $a Title from original t.p.
534    $p Original version: $c Ottawa : Statistics Canada, 2000.
       $n International adult literacy survey. $n Co-published by: Human
       Resources Development Canada and National Literacy Secretariat.
```

Descriptive cataloguing for this item following LC's rule interpretation for microform reproductions of previously published materials.

```
100 1  $a Osberg, Lars.
245 10 $a Schooling literacy and individual earnings / $cLars Osberg.
260    $a Ottawa : $b Statistics Canada, co-published by Human
       Resources Development Canada and National Literacy Secretariat, $c 2000.
300    $a 34 p.: $b ill.; $c 28 cm.
440    $a International adult literacy survey
500    $a Issued also in French under title: Scolarité alphabétisme et
       gains personnels.
533    $a Microform. $b [Toronto] : $c Micromedia, $d [2000]. $e 1 microfiche ; $c 11 x
       15 cm.
```

On the other hand, LC follows AACR2 rules for dimensions whereas LAC uses optional metric measurements (Figure 2.4) because the Canadian government mandates the use of metric measurements for all government operations.

Choosing Different Options: Supposing a library or media center wishes to implement rule options that its national library does differently. What then? No arm will reach out of the sky to pluck the catalog records bearing nonstandard data out of local catalogs. No visit from the Catalog Police to the agency will ensue. The library that opts to exercise nonstandard decisions accepts total responsibility for monitoring their use and ensuring that records produced using them do not contravene the provisions of contracts the libraries have with their networks and other cataloging partners. This may sound trivial, but the impact may be substantial. "Going it alone" can be costly and time consuming, and the results should be deemed very important to justify the costs.

Incorporating Rule Changes into Local Cataloging: Because cataloging rules are constantly undergoing review and being updated, important policy decisions cover how to incorporate the changes into local work flow and into the local catalog. Regarding work flow, rule changes can be accepted and adopted immediately as they occur (they are announced online on national library websites) or ignored until a designated time (for example, the beginning

FIGURE 2.4

Example of physical description area for sound recordings in LC records

```
1 sound cassette (60 min.) : analog, 3 3/4 ips, mono. ; 7 1/4 x 3 1/2
in.
```

LAC rule interpretation for 1.5 Physical description area

```
As allowed by rule 0.28, Library and Archives Canada uses metric
measurements in recording the extent of item, other physical details
and dimensions data of the item described.

In accordance with metric writing conventions, all units of measurement
are symbols and are not followed by a period (contrary to an
abbreviation) unless it is standard punctuation prescribed by 1.0C.

1 sound cassette (60 min.) : analog, 9.5 cm/s, mono. ; 19 x 9 cm.
```

of a new year) when a shift to new rules is made at once for all changes occurring within the period of time. A good many libraries opt for the latter, waiting until a new edition of the rules is published before altering their practices. The problem in waiting for a new edition is that the sheer volume of changes causes confusion until the staff learns them all. Adopting the changes one at a time may seem to be a nuisance, but it minimizes the learning process when a new edition appears. It is unwise to ignore changed cataloging rules entirely, because the catalog department's products depart more and more from standard practice, eventually creating problems that are costly to resolve.

Deciding what to do about existing catalog records—whether to allow them to remain static or change them to conform to new rules—is a more complicated issue. Libraries typically do not update existing catalog records, opting to ignore the differences until or unless they cause serious problems for searchers. When the rule changes are profound, as happened when AACR2 was first published in 1978, the impact on catalog departments can be enormous.

In the 1970s and 1980s, many libraries simply closed their old catalogs and began new ones in which catalog records followed the new rules. Because this coincided with the initial implementation of library automation and new computer-based catalogs were in the planning stages, rule changes were folded into the automation process. Far from making the changes easier and simpler to adopt, AACR2 was blamed, at least in part, for the disruptions and costs of computerizing libraries. However unfair this might have been, changes that had to be made directly to materials on the shelves (new call numbers, shifts of materials) were difficult and costly, and these were the direct result of AACR2's changed rules for access points. As a result of this experience, the experts responsible for rule changes are more sensitive to the practical impact of their decisions. Now, they consider practical impact along with other factors when rule changes are made.

Knowing that rule changes are a fact of professional life, local libraries and media centers should establish policies regarding whether, how, and when they will be adopted in advance of facing a crisis such as that attributed to AACR2. Incremental adoption on an ongoing basis seems to be the least disruptive and costly, and bears serious consideration.

Subject Cataloging

Each item given original cataloging must be assigned subject headings. Subject headings can and should be selected from a standardized list of authorized subject headings, because such headings can be shared via network cataloging with other libraries. At the same time, headings assigned by network partners can be adopted by the local agency. The vast majority of general libraries and media centers in the United States and Canada follows one of two published lists of subject headings, along with its Canadian counterpart: *Library of Congress Subject Headings* (LCSH) and *Canadian Subject Headings* (CSH), or *Sears List of Subject Headings* (Sears) and *Sears List of Subject Headings: Canadian Companion* (Sears CC).[6] Specialized libraries often choose to use alternative lists for their specialized materials; for example, medical libraries often utilize the National Library of Medicine's *Medical Subject Headings,* and art libraries often use the Getty Art History Information Project's *Art & Architecture Thesaurus.*[7] These libraries may also employ one of the two general lists for materials for cataloging the balance of their materials covering nonspecialized subjects.

LCSH is popular with large libraries, because its hundreds of thousands of headings and cross-references enable finer distinctions to be made among materials on similar, but not identical, subjects. Sears's much smaller list totals several thousand headings, most of which are broader than LCSH headings for the same subjects. Sears is appropriate for general collections numbering fewer than 20,000 volumes, because its headings gather materials that LCSH's more specific headings would separate. Searchers in a small library or media center requesting materials on a topic such as "American painting," for example, would retrieve titles assigned more specific headings in an LCSH catalog. Media centers that are part of large school districts and small public libraries participating with larger partners in cooperatives, however, might opt to adopt LCSH in order to conform to a common standard. Thus, the initial decision to adopt one of the two lists should be made very carefully, and subsequent decisions to change from one list to the other should be made only after examining all the consequences.

The aim of the subject catalog is to bring together enough materials in a subject area to satisfy the needs of searchers looking for materials on the subject, but not overload them with marginally useful titles having only small amounts of relevant information. To make a decision about which list to adopt, catalogers should ask which one brings together a "better" number of titles in response to typical searches done by patrons using the catalog. The definition of "better" is subjective, but can be specified, for example, as greater than zero and fewer than fifty. (Catalogers must choose some number of titles retrieved as the maximum desirable total. In this example, fifty has been chosen arbitrarily as the maximum number of desired retrievals.) If assigning Sears headings routinely retrieves many more than fifty titles in most subject areas, one can conclude the collection is too large to use the list successfully.

Other differences between LCSH and Sears need to be considered as well, among them the nature of the terminology of the list in relation to the knowledge and language of the patrons using the catalog. LCSH tends to use technical and scientific terminology suitable for scholars, not searchers new to subjects who are likely to use popular terminology for them. A media center serving an elementary school might prefer Sears's simpler vocabulary, whereas a secondary school or public library serving a well-educated population might prefer LCSH. No one list is ideal for a mixed service population, some of whom are knowledgeable and some beginners, but librarians and media specialists can assist those who need help in navigating the chosen system. What would be extremely confusing, however, is for both lists to be used simultaneously in the same local catalog. This should not be done.

To summarize, criteria for deciding to adopt Sears or LCSH include the following, given in order of their importance in terms of service to local patrons:

1.   Total numbers of retrievals, greater than zero but smaller than a chosen maximum for typical subject searches

2.   Relevance of the vocabulary of the list for most of the patrons using the catalog

3.   Consistency with the standard used by partners sharing the catalog and its related systems

Both LCSH and Sears are continuously undergoing review and amendment, adding new headings and altering or deleting existing headings. Heading changes appear in new editions of the publishers' printed lists, annually for LCSH[8] and approximately every five or six years for Sears.[9] Decisions about how to implement the changed headings must be made by every library using one of the two tools.

Some of the possible strategies for implementing subject heading changes include the following:

1.   Implement all the affected headings at once, both in new cataloging and existing catalog records. This is the ideal solution, but it demands effort on the part of the catalog department. Existing records must be revised by employing a global change function, if one is available, or by revising each occurrence of changed headings one at a time and adding cross-references from the previous headings.

2.   Implement all the changes in new cataloging at once, but make changes to existing catalog records over a specified length of time. This takes just as much effort on the part of the catalog department, but distributes the workload for revising existing catalog records over time.

3.   Implement all the changes in new cataloging at once, but make only selected changes to existing catalog records. This lessens the workload for the catalog department, but means discrepancies in heading forms are bound to occur and increase over time.

4.   Implement selected changes in both new cataloging and existing records, and ignore the rest. This strategy requires revising new records that bear changed headings the agency did not select for updating in order to display the old headings instead. Over time, the number of such revisions can be expected to grow.

5.   Ignore changes to existing catalog records, but implement all the changes in new cataloging and add "see also" cross-references to old headings. This seems to be an attractive compromise, but it shifts the burden of dealing with the changes from the catalog department to patrons, who must do multiple searches using both old and new subject headings for materials on the subjects involved.

No solution is without its advantages, disadvantages, and costs. The best way to handle subject heading changes is to make them incrementally, as they occur, and not to wait for the publication of new editions of the subject heading list mandating numerous changes at once, in the same manner it is recommended to implement changes in descriptive cataloging rules. The basic principle underlying these decisions, however, ought to consider how much of the burden of change should be shouldered by the catalog department and how much should be passed on to the patrons searching the catalog.

Classification and Call Number Assignment

Another important decision concerns the choice of classification system and shelf marks to be used in arranging materials on the library's or media center's shelves. Two standard classification systems dominate in North America: the Dewey Decimal Classification (DDC) and the Library of Congress Classification (LCC).[10] In both the United States and Canada, DDC is the favorite choice of schools and public libraries regardless of size, although there are exceptions (for example, Boston Public Library and a number of smaller Massachusetts public libraries that follow its practices use LCC). In Canada, the United Kingdom, and many other Commonwealth countries, national libraries also use DDC for shelving their collections and arranging their national bibliographies.

In the United States, LC uses LCC, the scheme it developed at the beginning of the twentieth century for arranging its collections. Many North American colleges and universities, particularly those that are members of the OCLC network, use LCC. Some that had been using DDC adopted LCC when they began participating in the computerized network, because a large proportion of OCLC cataloging at that time contained only LCC call numbers. Today, LC's own cataloging includes both DDC and LCC numbers, as well as the shelf marks assigned for LC's own use. The shelf marks (everything in call numbers except for the classification number) can be copied by libraries that use DDC, if they wish to do so, although LC's records do not add them to the assigned DDC numbers.

Shelf marks, explained more fully in Chapter 9, are usually assigned locally and serve local needs. Small collections may not bother to add many shelf marks, because it is not difficult to distinguish small numbers of titles in the same classification number. Large collections tend to add more, because they need to distinguish large numbers of similar titles on the same subject. Briefly, shelf marks can include one or more of the following: cutter numbers or cutter letters, title marks, dates, volume numbers, and copy numbers. Small libraries and media centers might be able to shelve materials successfully using only a simple cutter letter in addition to the classification number. Catalogers should not add more shelf marks than are actually needed for easy shelving, because everything that must be assigned, tracked, and recorded takes staff time to do properly, and staff time is costly.

Once materials are classified and call numbers assigned, they may be placed on the library's shelves (or, if they are computer-based materials, stored in databases and/or digital libraries). A decision must be made concerning the way they are shelved: all in one sequence or in different sequences based on their physical formats. Studies show that all materials get more use when they are shelved together in one sequence, probably because patrons browsing the shelves are able to see and select from everything pertaining to a subject or genre of literature.[11] Therefore, intershelving is recommended for your consideration. Doing so, however, requires creative thinking about making it possible to keep materials together that have different shapes and sizes.[12] When materials are shelved by physical format in multiple sequences, searches must be repeated over and over, depending on how many sequences a library or media center maintains simultaneously.

An important set of decisions relates to how changes in classification numbers are implemented in the local library. The possible strategies are similar to those enumerated above for changed subject headings. As a practical matter, however, making changes for materials shelved in library stacks also involves physical work: revising the markings on the materials and shifting them to new positions on the shelves. When large numbers of materials are involved, this can be a disruptive, costly, and physically taxing task, requiring more staff than normal.

Shifts of materials are so unwelcome that some librarians believe it is better to dispose of materials than to revise their markings and shift them, whereas others think they can just ignore the changes. Neither strategy provides good service. Changed classification numbers cannot be ignored indefinitely, nor is it acceptable to remove useful items simply because their classification numbers have changed. Instead, other options should be weighed carefully and the chosen strategy implemented as promptly as possible, so that patron service is not degraded or disrupted more than absolutely necessary. It is recommended that changed numbers be implemented over a reasonable period of time and that high-priority subject areas are tackled first. A schedule that divides the entire collection into manageable parts should be followed, with added staffing provided as needed to do the heavy lifting.

Decisions about how to shelve books, videos, sound recordings, maps, and other materials do not follow any mandated standard. It is entirely up to the local library to decide what works best for its staff and provides the best service for its patrons.

Encoding for Computer Entry

At this writing, the MARC format is the only standard tool for encoding cataloging data. If a library or media center wishes to join a bibliographic network and share its cataloging with other agencies, use source data from the network (or regional, state, or local networks derived from them), and take advantage of standard library computer systems for catalogs and related functions (orders, circulation control, serials management, etc.), it must encode its cataloging according to the MARC format, explained in more detail in Chapter 12. Thus, the policy decision is clear; to conform to standards, libraries and media centers that use computerized catalogs or cataloging systems must adopt the MARC format for encoding catalog records.

The decision to use the MARC format is a necessary step in joining a bibliographic network. Once a member, the network mandates standard methods for encoding, which the library or media center must follow. Changes to the protocols are administered by the network, which sends notices of the changes it adopts to its members. Members are expected to adopt the revisions and implement new practices by set deadlines or, in some instances, are only told that the network is implementing them and their practice must change to conform to network requirements.

Encoding of electronic resources, called metadata, presents more choices, also described in Chapter 12. The MARC format is one type of metadata schema, but not the only one that can be used for materials gathered into collections called digital libraries. MARC is a very complex schema, mandating not only the encoding but also the content of each field. Other metadata standards, such as Dublin Core, merely mandate how to encode fields, but not what to put in the fields. For digital library cataloging, the MARC format is one possible choice, but others can and should be explored, based on the generally accepted standard of digital library partners and the majority of the members of the service community.

Conclusion

This chapter has described and discussed the decisions that must be made in order to organize materials collected by libraries and media centers as well as to provide retrievable catalog records representing those materials. Written policies help ensure that uniform practices are followed regardless of who performs the work, and they make it possible for all members of the library or media center community to see the way things are done. The authors recommend maintaining a policy manual for the agency that is regularly reviewed and amended as necessary, documenting these decisions and helping new staff members become familiar with them.

In the next three chapters, descriptive cataloging practices that follow current standard rules are described and explained.

Recommended Reading

Carpenter, Michael, and Elaine Svenonius, eds. *Foundations of Cataloging: A Sourcebook.* Littleton, CO: Libraries Unlimited, 1985. [An anthology of landmark writings about description and access, standards, and theory. With its companion volume, *Theory of Subject Analysis*, listed below, provides background material useful in understanding today's rules, tools, and practices.]

Chan, Lois Mai, et al., eds. *Theory of Subject Analysis: A Sourcebook.* Littleton, CO: Libraries Unlimited, 1985.

Intner, Sheila S., et al., eds. *Cataloging Correctly for Kids: An Introduction to the Tools,* 4th ed. Chicago: American Library Association, 2006.

Kaplan, Allison G., and Ann Marlow Riedling. *Catalog It: A Guide to Cataloging School Library Materials*, 2nd ed. Worthington, OH: Linworth, 2006.

Taylor, Arlene. *The Organization of Information*, 2nd ed. Westport, CT: Libraries Unlimited, 2004.

Notes

1.   Several cataloging experts, who asked not to be named, assured the authors when questioned that cataloging produced using RDA is unlikely to differ significantly from cataloging produced using the current edition of AACR2. The language employed by RDA in articulating the rules, however, is expected to differ considerably.

2.   Level 2 descriptions are mandated for the cataloging of monographic materials. Full-level cataloging of continuing resources is mandated at level 1 in most instances, although many institutions choose to enrich level 1 data with optional details.

3.   Using both lists would confuse searchers, because multiple terms apply to the same medium; for example, art reproductions could be given "graphic" from list 1 or "art reproduction" from list 2. Searchers would not know whether the sets they retrieve using one term included all, some, or none of the titles bearing an alternative term.

4.   LCRIs are available as part of *Cataloger's Desktop*, which can be purchased from LC's Cataloging Distribution Service.

5.   LACRIs are available at http://collectionscanada.ca/6/18/index-e.html

6.   Library of Congress, Subject Cataloging Division, *Library of Congress Subject Headings*, 29th ed. (Washington, DC: Library of Congress, 2006); *Canadian Subject Headings*, http://collectionscanada.ca/csh/index-e.html; *Sears List of Subject Headings*, 17th ed., ed. Joseph Miller (New York: H. W. Wilson, 2000); and *Sears List of Subject Headings: Canadian Companion*, 5th ed., rev. by Lynne Lighthall (New York: H. W. Wilson, 1995).

7.   More information about the use of specialized subject heading lists for special library collections can be found in Sheila S. Intner and Jean Weihs, *Special Libraries: A Cataloging Guide* (Englewood, CO: Libraries Unlimited, 1997), chap. 18–23.

8.   Catalogers need not wait for a new edition of LCSH to obtain subject heading changes. LC publishes them on an ongoing basis on its website and also in its cataloging periodical *Cataloging Service Bulletin.*

9.   As of late 2005, the H. W. Wilson Company was developing access to changed headings via the Internet.

10.   *Dewey Decimal Classification and Relative Index*, 22nd ed., ed. Joan S. Mitchell et al. (Dublin, OH: OCLC Forest Press, 2003); Library of Congress, Subject Cataloging Division, *Classification* (Washington, DC: Library of Congress, 1901–).

11.   See, for example, Jean Weihs, *The Integrated Library: Encouraging Access to Multimedia Materials*, 2nd ed. (Phoenix, AZ: Oryx Press, 1991).

12.   For a broad range of options for preparing materials in many forms for intershelving, see Karen C. Dreissen and Sheila A. Smyth, *A Manager's Guide to Physical Processing of Nonprint Materials* (Westport, CT: Greenwood Press, 1995).

3

Description and Access: Standards

Describing an item usually is the first activity catalogers perform. This involves recording information from the item that identifies it uniquely and completely, differentiating it from similar items with which it might be confused. Over the years, to formalize the way the many pieces of information needed for such specific identifications are presented, rules developed about what to put into bibliographic descriptions, where to find it, and how to record it. This chapter covers the history and background of the descriptive cataloging rules current at this writing, and current basic models used for bibliographic description and access. Chapter 4 continues explaining and illustrating specific rules for describing all types of materials, including materials published on an ongoing basis and digital materials, which are transmitted electronically. Chapter 5 completes this part of the cataloging process by explaining and illustrating the selection and standard formulation of access points derived from descriptive elements.

Development of Rules for Description and Access

Current at this writing, the standard code of rules for description and access used by North American libraries is titled *Anglo-American Cataloguing Rules*, second edition, 2005 revision (AACR2–2005). AACR2–2005 is used beyond the shores of North America in the United Kingdom, Australia, New Zealand, and other English-speaking countries. It is also used beyond the English-speaking world in a number of authorized translations by catalogers in countries that speak those languages.

Although England and the United States each had its own cataloging code that preceded it, one can trace the origins of the international cataloging code to a 1908 publication titled *Cataloguing Rules, Author and Title Entries*,[1] published in American and British editions by the library associations of the two countries. The rules focused on access—that is, the way headings were formulated for titles and authors—leaving it to each country to provide its own rules for describing materials. *Cataloguing Rules, Author and Title Entries* was used until mid-century, when publication variations had become so numerous and far reaching that the rules failed to provide catalogers with needed guidance in addressing them. Updated rules were sorely needed, but the exigencies of World War II interfered with transatlantic consultations and meetings.

In 1949, a new set of rules for access was developed and published unilaterally by the American Library Association, titled *A.L.A. Cataloging Rules for Author and Title Entries*.[2] Together with rules for description provided by the Library of Congress, titled *Rules for Descriptive Cataloging in the Library of Congress*,[3] they served as the standard for North American practice for almost two decades. During this period, joint efforts to develop a common descriptive cataloging code for the United States, Canada, and the United Kingdom continued, led by their library associations and national libraries.

In 1967, years of painstaking work on both sides of the Atlantic Ocean culminated in the publication of the *Anglo-American Cataloging Rules* (AACR1). This edition appeared in two versions: a "North American Text" using American style spellings; and a "British Text" using British style spellings, including spelling the title word *Cataloguing* differently. Other differences appeared in the two texts, mainly concerning corporate bodies, maps, music, and serials. The rule makers agreed to disagree, preferring to issue two versions than to continue negotiating to resolve the problem areas.

AACR1 succeeded in combining rules for describing materials with rules for creating headings for titles and authors. Its rules were very complicated because they were aimed at creating catalog records suitable for the very large collections of general research libraries (such as the national libraries of the countries involved in its development).[4] The new code was criticized almost immediately for the following:

1. Failing to unite its partners under one set of rules

2. Ignoring the needs of public, school, and college libraries, particularly small and medium-sized libraries that did not want as much information in catalog records as the rules mandated, but that needed many more examples and illustrations than AACR1 provided to help catalogers understand and apply the rules

3. Failing to standardize rules for description and access of materials in all physical formats, separating rules for books and printed serials from those for nonbook formats, resulting in records for various formats that were difficult to file together in one catalog

4. Failing to address matters of concern for computerized cataloging, which was looming on the horizon at that time

Widespread criticism throughout the field in all three countries prompted formation of a committee called the Joint Steering Committee for Revision of AACR (JSC), sponsored by the three publishers. The committee included representatives from each of the library associations and each of the national libraries along with the editors of the publication. These delegates proceeded to revise AACR1 to address these and other criticisms.

At the same time, work was progressing in the international library community to achieve enough uniformity in the cataloging rules used by the world's national libraries that their catalog records could be merged into a kind of super union catalog. The goal was called "Universal Bibliographic Control." The International Federation of Library Associations and Institutions (IFLA) was at the forefront of facilitating global uniformity by surveying the differences among national cataloging codes and mandating a uniform structure for description, called International Standard Bibliographic Description (ISBD), discussed later in this chapter.

Interim updates to AACR1 were issued during the time the JSC was working on AACR1's second edition, incorporating some of IFLA's ISBD recommendations. New punctuation intended to facilitate computer programming was added to Chapter 6, which covered the description of printed books. A few years later, updates to Chapters 12 and 14 were issued also, covering sound recordings and audiovisual aids, respectively.

In 1978, the long-awaited second edition of *Anglo-American Cataloguing Rules* (AACR2) was published.[5] Only one version appeared, and British spellings prevailed throughout the text, including its title, now spelled only with the *u* in *Cataloguing*. Some differences between North American and British practice remained in the text, however, generally presented as options; but in the case of terms to be used to highlight the physical format of materials, two lists were provided, one for North Americans and one for the British.

The Basic Descriptive Model

The basic model underlying the rules of AACR2 is embodied in the ISBD, developed by working committees of IFLA. ISBD mandates four things:

1. Where catalogers should look for the bibliographic information they put into descriptions

2. The elements of the bibliographic description

3. The order in which the elements should appear in catalog records

4. The manner in which each part of each element should be punctuated

The ISBD standard was incorporated into the updates to AACR1 and is an integral part of AACR2.

The first ISBD was developed for printed monographs and issued by IFLA in the late 1960s, followed by ISBDs for printed serials and other material formats. Eventually, experts agreed that one model should govern all material formats, and a generalized ISBD, called ISBD(G), was issued. The individual ISBDs are reviewed on a five-year schedule, ensuring they will be updated as needed to maintain their relevance. The next several paragraphs examine in greater detail how ISBD meets its goals.

Data Sources: Sources for the bibliographic data librarians put in catalog records have been evolving since the beginning of modern publishing, but for books, videorecordings, sound recordings, and most other material formats, they have stabilized into a handful of possible locations. For example, books usually display bibliographic data on their covers, spines, title pages, the backs (versos) of title pages, and final pages (colophons). Similarly, videorecordings usually display bibliographic information on title screens that appear at the start of a recording as well as on the credits screens that follow the end of the main content. ISBD identifies two types of sources for bibliographic information—*chief* and *prescribed sources*—and mandates a set of prescribed sources for each element of description. (The chief source is always the first prescribed source; for the title statement, it is the only source.) Information taken from sources other than the prescribed sources is enclosed in square brackets to show it does not meet the specifications of the standard.

Number and Order of Bibliographic Elements: The number of descriptive elements, called *areas of description*, and their order in catalog records has also evolved over the centuries. ISBD mandates eight areas of description, although all eight are not required for every material format. The ISBD model is as follows:

Area 1: Title and statement(s) of responsibility (also called title statement)

Area 2: Edition statement

Area 3: Material specific details (used for selected material formats)

Area 4: Publication, distribution information

Area 5: Physical description (not used for remote electronic resources)

Area 6: Series statement

Area 7: Notes (optional, with a few exceptions, discussed in Chapter 4)

Area 8: Standard numbers (that is, ISBN or ISSN) and terms of availability

Identifying Punctuation: ISBD punctuation identifies each element and subelement of description in a manner used by early computer programmers. It was developed to facilitate programming as well as to handle bibliographic information in unfamiliar languages and scripts. Although current programming methods probably don't rely on it anymore, ISBD punctuation has persisted and can be helpful to catalogers and/or acquisitions librarians when they retrieve records in languages and scripts they cannot read. With a cut-and-paste or copy-and-paste function, librarians can locate and insert titles, authors, editions, and other needed elements into bibliographies or order records, to name two possibilities.

The ISBD model is the "glue" that knits national or local variations in descriptive cataloging into packages of data consistent enough to be merged and manipulated in commonly held databases.

Future Developments

Since the publication of AACR2–2005, members of the JSC have been working on developing an entirely new descriptive cataloging code, which is to be titled *Resource Description and Access* (RDA). They seek to base RDA on a solid theoretical foundation rather than merely revising AACR2–2005's existing rules and/or adding new rules to make it possible for catalogers to deal with new cataloging issues that have arisen. Experts have developed a theoretical model for cataloging to serve as the basis for the new code, described briefly in the next paragraphs.

Functional Requirements for Bibliographic Resources: In the waning years of the twentieth century, cataloging leaders began to analyze the principles underlying AACR2 and the objectives of the catalog, attempting to build a theoretical model explaining them. The result is "Functional Requirements for Bibliographic Resources" (FRBR, pronounced "Ferber"). According to Wikipedia, "FRBR is a conceptual entity-relationship model developed by the International Federation of Library Associations and Institutions (IFLA) that relates user tasks of retrieval and access in online library catalogues and bibliographic databases from a user's perspective. It represents a more holistic approach to retrieval and access as the relationships between the entities provide links to navigate through the hierarchy of relationships."[6]

The article goes on to explain: "FRBR establishes three groups of entities:

- Group 1 entities are Work, Expression, Manifestation, and Item, and represent the products of intellectual or artistic endeavour.

- Group 2 entities are person and corporate body, responsible for the custodianship of Group 1's intellectual or artistic endeavour.

- Group 3 entities are subjects of Group 1 or Group 2's intellectual endeavour, and include concepts, objects, events, places."[7]

The group 1 entities, on which library cataloging are based, may sound strange, but are, in fact, quite familiar. A work is defined as "a distinct intellectual or artistic creation," in other words, the content of something being cataloged. An expression is "the specific intellectual or artistic form that a work takes each time it is 'realized.'" A manifestation is "the physical embodiment of an expression of a work." An item is "a single exemplar of a manifestation [or, what we call a copy]."[8]

Future of Cataloging Rules, RDA: At this writing, RDA's publication is predicted in 2009. RDA's rules are expected to be simpler, have fewer exceptions, and be written in such a way that catalogers can judge for themselves how to handle variations from the norm without causing problems in local catalogs or bibliographic databases extending beyond the local library. For nearly seventy years, library administrators have been begging for a simple code based on a coherent set of principles that experienced catalogers could apply to the materials on which they work by using their judgment.[9] Their aim has been to speed the cataloging process and make it possible for catalogers to respond to new problems without having to wait for years to obtain instructions on how to resolve them from national libraries and library association committees. RDA is supposed to be this kind of code.

The JSC, as it usually does, has circulated a prospectus and drafts of RDA, and solicited comments from the field.[10] The principal difference between RDA and AACR2–2005 is the organization of its rules, which was according to physical medium in all the editions of AACR (see Chapter 4), but will now be according to areas of description. The proposed table of contents for RDA's "Part A—Description" is as follows:

Introduction to Part A

Chapter 1. General guidelines on resource description

Chapter 2. Identification of the resource

Chapter 3. Carrier description

Chapter 4. Content description

Chapter 5. Acquisition and access information

Chapter 6. Related resources

Chapter 7. Persons, families, and corporate bodies associated with the resource[11]

Other noteworthy changes include making ISBD punctuation optional, altering the way information about physical formats is expressed in catalog records, and eliminating the phrase "main entry" from the text. However, RDA will still have rules for creating primary access points if they are desired and needed to gather materials into bibliographies, create shelf marks, and so on.

It remains to be seen how much of a difference the new rules will make in the contents of records in library catalogs. Experts do not anticipate radical changes because one of RDA's stated aims is minimizing the need to alter preexisting records.

Conclusion

RDA, when it is published, will be the newest step in an evolution that has gone on for well over 100 years. In 1876, Charles A. Cutter published *Rules for a Dictionary Catalog*,[12] the first such rules published in North America; and several decades earlier, British librarian Anthony Panizzi codified practice in his library with a set of rules known as the "91 Rules,"[13] which were the basis for British practice. Since then, to recapitulate briefly, Cutter's (and Panizzi's) rules were superseded in 1908 by the first Anglo-American code; that code was replaced in 1949 by the ALA rules for entry and LC rules for description;[14] the ALA-LC rules were replaced in 1967 by AACR1; and AACR1 was replaced in 1978 by AACR2. Between 1978 and 2005, AACR2 was republished in revised versions four times, in 1988, 1998, 2002, and 2005. At this writing, descriptive cataloging in North America follows the rules of AACR2–2005 and its updates, and will continue to do so until RDA is published.

Chapters 4 and 5 continue explaining AACR2–2005's rules for description and access, respectively, for all types of materials.

Recommended Reading

Association for Library Collections and Technical Services Committee on Cataloging: Description and Access. *The Future of AACR* (April 2003). Available at www.libraries.psu.edu/tas/jca/ccda/future1.html

Anderson, James D., and José Pérez-Carballo. *Information Retrieval Design: Principles and Options for Information Description, Organization, Display, and Access in Information Retrieval Databases, Digital Libraries, Catalogs, and Indexes.* St. Petersburg, FL: Ometeca Institute, 2005.

Borgman, Christine L. *From Gutenberg to the Global Information Infrastructure: Access to Information in the Networked World.* Cambridge, MA: MIT Press, 2000.

Harvey, Ross, and Philip Hider. *Organising Knowledge in a Global Society: Principles and Practice in Libraries and Information Centres.* Wagga Wagga, NSW, Australia: Centre for Information Studies, 2004.

International Conference on AACR 2, Florida State University, 1979. *The Making of a Code: The Issues Underlying AACR 2.* Chicago: American Library Association, 1980.

Intner, Sheila S., et al., eds. *Cataloging Correctly for Kids: An Introduction to the Tools*, 4th ed. Chicago: American Library Association, 2006.

Lubetzky, Seymour. *Cataloging Rules and Principles: A Critique of the A.L.A. Rules for Entry and a Proposed Design for Their Revision.* Washington, DC: Library of Congress, 1953.

Lubetzky, Seymour. *Code of Cataloging Rules, Author and Title Entry: Additions Revisions, and Changes Prepared in Light of Discussions of the March 1960 Draft for Consideration of the Catalog Code Revision Committee.* Chicago: American Library Association, 1961.

RDA: Resource Description and Access. Joint Steering Committee for Revision of AACR. Available at http://collectionscanada.ca/jsc/rda.html

Smiraglia, Richard P. *The Nature of "A Work": Implications for Knowledge Organization.* Lanham, MD: Scarecrow Press, 2001.

Statement of International Cataloguing Principles. Draft approved by the IFLA Meeting of Experts on an International Cataloguing Code. Available at www.loc.gov/loc/ifla/imeicc/ source/Statement-draftsep05-clean.pdf

Strout, Ruth French. "The Development of the Catalog and Cataloging Codes." *Library Quarterly* 26 (October 1956): 254–275.

Taylor, Arlene G. *Introduction to Cataloging and Classification*, 10th ed. Westport, CT: Libraries Unlimited, 2006.

Weihs, Jean, ed. *The Principles and Future of AACR: Proceedings of the International Conference on the Principles and Future Development of AACR.* Chicago: American Library Association, 1998.

Notes

1. *Cataloguing Rules, Author and Title Entries, Compiled by Committees of the American Library Association and the (British) Library Association,* American ed. (Boston, 1908).

2. *A.L.A. Cataloging Rules for Author and Title Entries*, prepared by the Division of Cataloging and Classification of the American Library Association, 2nd ed. edited by Clara Beetle (Chicago: American Library Association, 1949).

3. *Rules for Descriptive Cataloging in the Library of Congress* (Washington, DC: Library of Congress, 1949).

4. "Preface," *Anglo-American Cataloging Rules, North American Text*, ed. Sumner Spaulding (Chicago: American Library Association, 1967).

5. *Anglo-American Cataloguing Rules*, 2nd ed., eds. Paul W. Winkler and Michael Gorman (Ottawa: Canadian Library Association, 1978).

6. "FRBR," *Wikipedia,* available at www.wikipedia.org (Viewed October 25, 2006).

7. Ibid.

8. Ibid.

9. See Andrew D. Osborn, "The Crisis in Cataloging," *The Library Quarterly* 11, no. 4 (October 1941): 393–411.

10. Available at http://collectionscanada.ca/jsc/rdaprospectus.html and http://collections canada.ca/jsc/rda.html, respectively.

11. http://collectionscanada.ca/jsc/rdaprospectus.html (Viewed November 8, 2006).

12. Charles A. Cutter, *Rules for a Dictionary Catalog*, 4th ed. (Washington, DC: Government Printing Office, 1904).

13. Antonio Panizzi, "Rules for the Compilation of the Catalogue," in *The Catalogue of Printed Books in the British Museum* (London: British Museum, 1841).

14.   *A.L.A. Catalog Rules: Author and Title Entries*, prepared by the Catalog Code Revision Committee of the American Library Association with the collaboration of a committee of the (British) Library Association, preliminary American 2nd ed. (Chicago: American Library Association, 1941), states:

> Had not the turn of affairs in England disrupted an exchange of opinions and prevented the possibility of a joint conference in 1939, this edition might have recorded more fully the reactions of the committee. It may be stated, however, that there was substantial agreement in the sections of the tentative rules on which the British had made a definite report.

Thus we conclude that the 1941 book was used until 1949.

4

Descriptive Cataloging

The *Anglo-American Cataloguing Rules*, second edition, 2002 revision, plus its updates issued in 2003, 2004, and 2005 (abbreviated AACR2–2005 in this book), is the current set of cataloging rules used by catalogers to make bibliographic descriptions. AACR2–2005 is available in two formats: online as part of a product called *Cataloger's Desktop*[1] and in print.[2] The printed version is sold as unbound 8.5 × 11 inch pages punched to fit an oversized three-holed binder. (Binders are purchased separately from the publishers: the American Library Association, Canadian Library Association, and Chartered Institute of Library and Information Professionals.)

The online version of AACR2–2005 has a number of advantages over the printed text. It is completely indexed, enabling catalogers to search by any word in the text. Search words can be truncated and/or combined using the Boolean operators AND, OR, and NOT. Chapter numbers and rule numbers are searchable, as are the contents and index. Users of the online version can bookmark and highlight items, copy and paste excerpts, and so on, similar to features commonly encountered in other online documents. Notes can be added to annotate the text, making it easy to document local policy decisions or local variations in the way rules are implemented. Links are available to help users move quickly through the text. Multiple windows can display different pages of text simultaneously. In addition to AACR2–2005, the complete *Cataloger's Desktop* product includes policy decisions made by LC for AACR2's rule options and the like, known as *Library of Congress Rule Interpretations*; three valuable policy manuals covering LC's subject access practices (for subject headings, classification numbers, and shelflisting); the MARC 21 formats; and the latest editions of MARC code lists.

AACR2–2005 is divided into two parts: Part I covering descriptive cataloging; Part II covering access. In addition, five appendixes instruct about proper capitalization, abbreviation, and numerals; furnish a glossary; and list initial articles in multiple languages. A comprehensive index completes the text. In the first part, chapters after the first are organized by physical medium. The first chapter covers general rules applicable to all materials regardless of the physical form in which they appear (or, as FRBR might state, in which they are manifested). The first chapter also contains a few special rules for materials consisting of parts in multiple formats and materials that are not originals, but reproductions of other materials. The rest of the chapters are as follows:

Chapter 2:   Books, Pamphlets, and Printed Sheets

Chapter 3:   Cartographic Materials

Chapter 4:   Manuscripts

Chapter 5:   Music

Chapter 6:   Sound Recordings

Chapter 7:   Motion Pictures and Videorecordings

Chapter 8:   Graphic Materials

Chapter 9:   Electronic Resources

Chapter 10:   Three-dimensional Artefacts and Realia

Chapter 11:   Microforms

Chapter 12:   Continuing Resources

Chapter 13:   Analysis (that is, part[s] of larger works)

All cataloging requires the combined use of at least two chapters of AACR2–2005: Chapter 1 and the relevant chapter covering the physical format of the material being cataloged. Books are cataloged using Chapters 1 and 2; printed music is cataloged using Chapters 1 and 5; but recorded music is cataloged using Chapters 1, 5, and 6, because it requires rules for the musical information, the physical format information relating to the recording, and Chapter 1. Continuing resources and analytics (catalog records for parts of larger works) are not physical formats but types of publication; therefore, materials requiring the use of these chapters have to be combined with Chapter 1 and a format-specific chapter as well. For example, a continuing resource in videorecording format requires the use of Chapter 7 as well as Chapters 1 and 12, and if only a part of that videorecording were being cataloged, Chapter 13 would be added to the others. Catalogers who work with large numbers of continuing resources or who do analytics (now rare in public library or school library media centers) quickly learn how to combine information needed from those chapters of AACR2–2005. In the next section of this chapter, the way the rules are applied to a variety of materials is described.

Applying AACR2–2005 to Materials for Description

First Steps: Rule 0.24 suggests catalogers to begin by determining what type of material is being described in order to select the appropriate chapters of AACR2–2005 to use. The following decision tree can help to decide which chapters to use for an item being cataloged.

1. Is the item made up of one part?
    Yes: Go to step 4.
    No: Go to step 2.

2. Are the parts intended to continue indefinitely?
    Yes: Use Chapter 12; continue with step 4.
    No: Continue with step 3.

3. Are all the parts in the same physical format?
    Yes: Go to step 4.
    No: Go to step 5.

4. In what physical format is the item or its parts?
   Use the relevant chapter in combination with Chapter 1.

5. Is there one predominant part?
   Yes: Catalog the item as that type of material and treat the rest of the parts as accompanying material.
   No: Catalog the item as a multimedia/kit, using rule 1.10.

Once one selects the appropriate chapter(s) of AACR2–2005, these chapters dictate where to look for bibliographic information, much of which is transcribed (copied) directly from the item being cataloged, as well as what information to record and how to record it.

Sources of Information: Each physical format has several information sources, one of which is considered the best, or *chief, source.* For books and other printed materials, including music and printed serials, the chief source is the title page, including its verso. Other places the rules recommend (called *prescribed sources*) include the *preliminaries* (the cover and all the pages up to the title page verso), colophon (last page, if it contains bibliographic information, but not if it is merely the final page of the text, appendix, index, etc.), the rest of the book, and accompanying material issued with the book by the publisher. Several of these sources are illustrated in Figures 4.1, 4.2, and 4.3. In the illustrations, no major differences appear in the way titles, authors, and so forth are presented; but, in some books, titles, names, dates, and other elements are dramatically different, depending on where one looks.

FIGURE 4.1

(chief source of information)

(title page)

Metadata and Its Impact on Libraries

Sheila S. Intner, Susan S. Lazinger,
and Jean Weihs

Library and Information Science Text Series

LIBRARIES
U N L I M I T E D
A Member of the Greenwood Publishing Group

Westport, Connecticut • London

FIGURE 4.2 *(information on verso)*

Library of Congress Cataloging-in-Publication Data

Intner, Sheila S.
   Metadata and its impact on libraries / by Sheila S. Intner, Susan S. Lazinger, and Jean Weihs.
      p. cm. — (Library and information science text series)
     Includes bibliographical references and index.
     ISBN 1-59158-145-1 (alk. paper)
     1. Metadata. 2. Information organization. 3. Cataloging—Standards. 4. Cataloging of electronic
information resources. 5. Cataloging of integrating resources. 6. Information storage and retrieval
systems. 7. Machine-readable bibliographic data formats. 8. Electronic information resources—
Management. 9. Digital preservation. 10. Digital libraries. I. Lazinger, Susan S. (Susan Smernoff)
II. Weihs, Jean Riddle. III. Title. IV. Series.
    Z666.7.I58 2006
    025.3—dc22   2005030803

British Library Cataloguing in Publication Data is available.

Copyright © 2006 by Libraries Unlimited

All rights reserved. No portion of this book may be
reproduced, by any process or technique, without the
express written consent of the publisher.

Library of Congress Catalog Card Number: 2005030803
ISBN: 1-59158-145-1

First published in 2006

Libraries Unlimited, 88 Post Road West, Westport, CT 06881
A Member of the Greenwood Publishing Group, Inc.
www.lu.com

Printed in the United States of America

The paper used in this book complies with the
Permanent Paper Standard issued by the National
Information Standards Organization (Z39.48-1984).

10 9 8 7 6 5 4 3 2 1

FIGURE 4.3 *(information on cover)*

Some types of materials require projectors, viewers, or playback equipment to hear or view. Therefore, two types of sources for bibliographic information are permitted for them: sources that are part of the material itself (such as film and video opening and closing credits) and sources issued by the publisher or distributor along with the material, but external to it (such as jewel cases, slipcases, liner notes, and boxes in which discs, cassettes, and tapes are packaged). Figures 4.4. and 4.5 illustrate some of these sources.

The list of acceptable sources for materials that require playback or projection includes some that can be seen without the equipment. As a matter of principle, sources closest to the content are preferred over external sources, with one exception: recorded sound is not preferred over information appearing on the disc or tape that carries it or on labels pasted directly on the disc or tape, called *integral labels*. If spoken information heard when the item is played differs from what appears on the carrier or on an integral label, the spoken information is not preferred.

Title Statements: The first piece of information in a bibliographic description is the title statement, which, for most materials, consists of three elements for books (see Figure 4.6) and four elements for nonbook materials:

- The main title (called the *title proper*)
- General material designation (if applicable, but not used for books)
- Other title words or phrases (for example, subtitles)[3]
- Statement(s) of responsibility

FIGURE 4.4

(information on cassette)

(information on insert)

FIGURE 4.5

(information on back cover)

(information on insert)

FIGURE 4.6

This example is an illustration of:

- three authors
- series statement
- bibliography and index note
- ISBN qualified
- Library of Congress CIP data
- 2nd level cataloging

Intner, Sheila S.
  Metadata and its impact on libraries / Sheila S. Intner, Susan S. Lazinger, and Jean Weihs. -- Westport, Conn. : Libraries Unlimited, 2006.
  262 p. : ill. ; 26 cm. -- (Library and information science text series)
  Includes bibliographical references and index.
  ISBN 1-59158-145-1 (alk. paper).

The only prescribed source for the title statement is the chief source. If the title is taken from another source, the source must be noted in the catalog record. The words of the title statement are copied from the item being cataloged exactly as they appear there, except for the way they are capitalized and punctuated. Capitalization follows the rules given in AACR2–2005's Appendix A, which usually follow a rule of thumb that says to capitalize the first word of the main title and proper nouns, but no others. The punctuation is altered to avoid the use of colons, semicolons, equal signs, square brackets, slashes, and the like, which could be confused with ISBD punctuation. If any other sources on the item—such as covers, spines, versos, colophons, captions, credits, labels, boxes—bear different titles, they are transcribed also, but not in the title statement. The sources of information for the bibliographic record in Figure 4.6 are found in Figures 4.1, 4.2, and 4.3.

A *general material designation* (gmd) is given for nonbook items in square brackets immediately following the title proper. Two lists of general material designations are found in AACR2 rule 1.1C1—list 1 to be used by British agencies and list 2 by agencies in Australia, Canada, and the United States. The assignment of an appropriate gmd is usually an easy decision, but occasionally a library receives an item that does not fit comfortably into one of the designations. The item in Figure 4.7 is an example of this dilemma. If a library or school uses or promotes the *Magnetic Composition Journal* as a game, the material designation "game" should be applied. However, if this seems an unsuitable designation, a cataloger might consider using another gmd or possibly "graphic" from AACR2 rule 1.1C1, list 1 (although mixing gmds from the two lists is not encouraged).

Decisions also must be made for items containing more than one medium. AACR2–2005 defines *kit* as an item containing two or more categories of materials, no one of which is identifiable as the predominant constituent of an item. In Figure 4.8 on page 36 neither the book nor the sound cassette is predominant, and each can be used separately. Therefore, the item would be designated "kit" according to AACR2–2005 rules. However, in an OLAC listserv message of July 21, 2006, Jay Weitz, Senior Consulting Database Specialist at OCLC, stated that this type of book/sound cassette package can be considered "read-along materials," making the cassette the dominant medium with the book as accompanying material.

Statements of responsibility are given exactly as they appear on the chief source of information. If the statement of responsibility is taken from another source, the statement is enclosed in square brackets (see Figure 4.7). Words such as *editor* or *edited* are not abbreviated in this area. See AACR2 rule 1.1F7 for parts of personal names that are to be omitted.

Edition Statements: If an edition, version, release, or the equivalent is named on the item, it is transcribed exactly as it appears on the item, after the title statement. Words in the edition statement may be abbreviated if they appear that way on the item or if abbreviations for them appear in Appendixes B and C. Thus, if a given title page states, "Third edition," it would be transcribed into the description as "3rd ed." Below is a table of edition statements one might see on selected types of materials and the ways they would be given in the bibliographic descriptions:

MATERIAL FORMAT	WORDS ON ITEM	TRANSCRIPTION
Books	First revised edition	1st rev. ed.
	First edition, revised & enlarged	1st ed., rev. & enl.
Videorecordings	Colorized version	Colorized version
	Letterbox edition	Letterbox ed.
Electronic resources	Release 1.7	Release 1.7
	Macintosh version	Macintosh version
Continuing resources	New England edition	New England ed.
	Édition française	Éd. Française

FIGURE 4.7

```
This example is an illustration of:
    •  nonbook item
    •  responsibility not in chief sources of information
    •  general material designation
    •  probable date (1998 listed in instruction booklet at the
       end of a quotation)
    •  accompanying material given in the physical description
       area (in 2nd level description)
    •  responsibility note (in 2nd level description)
    •  two levels of cataloging
```

2nd level cataloging

```
Kapell, Dave.
  Magnetic composition journal [general material designation] /
[creator Dave Kapell]. -- Minneapolis : Magnetic Poetry, [2000?]
  1 magnetic board, 360 magnetic word pieces : b&w ; in vinyl
envelope 31 x 24 cm. + 1 instruction booklet.

  Responsibility statement from instruction booklet.
```

1st level cataloging

```
Kapell, Dave.
  Magnetic composition journal [general material designation] /
[creator Dave Kapell]. -- Magnetic Poetry, [2000?]
  1 magnetic board, 360 magnetic word pieces + 1 instruction
booklet.
```

Fig. 4.7—Continues

Material Specific Details: Maps, music, and continuing resources use this area of description to provide specific kinds of information useful to patrons. Other material formats do not use it and leave it out. Some aspects of material specific details are transcribed as found on items, but others must be given in a prescribed form according to specific rules.

Maps and other cartographic materials give statements describing the scale, projection, and coordinates and equinox in this area. Scale is given as a representative fraction expressed as a ratio in the form (1:). Sometimes, this means converting dimensions stated in other ways; for example, a map might have a bar scale showing that one inch equals ten miles. Catalogers must convert miles to inches to put it in the proper form: (1:633,600). Statements of projection are given in the description the way they appear on the item; but, as with edition statements, the words can be abbreviated if they appear that way on the item or if the abbreviations for spelled out words are given in Appendixes B and C. Statements of coordinates and equinox are optional. When they are given, they are expressed as follows: westernmost longitude; easternmost longitude; northernmost latitude; southernmost latitude (see Figure 4.9 on page 39).

Printed music employs the material specific details area to provide information about the type of musical presentation; for example, if the item is a miniature score, a score and parts, an orchestra score, or something else. The statement is transcribed as given on the item. However, if a presentation statement is recorded in another area because it is grammatically linked, for example, to the title or edition statements, it is not repeated here.

FIGURE 4.7 *(continued)*

(information on back cover)

www.magneticpoetry.com

404 N. Washington Ave. #101 Minneapolis, MN 55401

magnetic poetry®

(information on cover)

magnetic composition journal

(information in instruction booklet)

Introduction

Magnetic Poetry is just the most clever idea we've seen in a long time...[it's] worth it's weight in gold....

From <u>Teaching K-8 Magazine</u>, April, 1998, pp.78-80

A Note from the Inventor:

Though Magnetic Poetry is sold at retail as a novelty, I originally created it as a serious writing tool, or more specifically, as a device to help me break through my own writer's block. Fiddling around with my "poetry kit" (the very first one was stuck to a cookie sheet stored next to my desk) seemed to free up a brain clogged with intimidation, preconception and cliche, and get the rusty language gears lubed up and grinding to a start. It didn't occur to me that a lot of other folks--especially kids--must have been feeling the same barriers when they sat down to write, and that they too might benefit from this simple little tool that helped me so much.

As I write this, five years and millions of Magnetic Poetry Kits later, I can see that my little tool is helping to satisfy a deep-seated need. It's something that gnaws at our collective soul, a craving for strong, potent language, language that transports us to all kinds of incredible places deep within and far away from ourselves. More significantly, I think that Magnetic Poetry is actually elevating that craving, or to mix metaphors, infecting people with the language bug.

And that's crucial, especially in kids. I think that one of the most important things a teacher can do is to get kids playing with words. Word play can ignite a love of language in general, which is essential in a lifetime of reading, writing, and higher thinking and learning. I'd go as far as saying that word play can save lives.

Here's some words on Magnetic Poetry from teachers who've used it; they will give you a feeling for its strengths and potentialities. Following that are some good directed activities using Magnetic Poetry, though I would encourage you to keep a kit installed in some "public" place, with few or no rules; Magnetic Poetry works wonderfully as a completely open-ended, unsupervised game (and you've got enough stuff to do as it is!).

Good luck, and may the muse of the magnets be with you and your students!

--Dave Kapell

Magnetic Poetry: You'll Wonder How You Ever Taught Without It
by Maggie Knutson, MAEd and Angela Lind, MAEd
Orono, MN and Forest Lake, MN

An elementary and middle school teacher examine the profound impact Magnetic Poetry has had on their students' learning
Magnetic Poetry, though sometimes thought of as a toy, has entered our Language Arts classrooms and has been tearing down walls of intimidation and passivity for hundreds of students. In addition to encouraging reluctant writers, Magnetic Poetry has increased the quality of writing from our more advanced students. We believe the words of our students tell most powerfully how Magnetic Poetry has made writing an empowering and engaging experience:

FIGURE 4.8

This example is an illustration of:
- kit or sound cassette
- general material designation
- publication date not listed; copyright date given
- paging supplied for unpaged book
- accompanying material (in second record)
- responsibility notes
- summary
- two ISBNs qualified
- CIP data (source not stated)
- 2nd level cataloging

2nd level cataloging as a kit

Munsch, Robert.
  Aaron's hair [kit] / Robert Munsch. -- Toronto : Scholastic, c2000.
    1 book ([29] p. : col. ill. ; 26 cm.)
    1 sound cassette (5 min.) : analog.
    In hanging bag 26 x 24 cm.

    Narrated by Robert Munsch.
    Text illustrated by Alan & Lea Daniel.
    Summary: When Aaron hurts his hair's feelings by saying he hates it, his hair runs away and jumps onto other people and into trouble.
    ISBN 0-439-98716-4 (book). -- ISBN 0-439-98759-8 (cassette).

Authors' note: physical description statement may also be given as:
    1 book, 1 sound cassette ; in hanging bag 26 x 24 cm.

2nd level cataloging with the cassette as the predominant item

Munsch, Robert.
  Aaron's hair [sound recording] / by Robert Munsch. -- Toronto : Scholastic, c2000.
    1 sound cassette (5 min.) : analog + 1 book ([29] p. : col. ill. ; 26 cm.)

    Narrated by Robert Munsch.
    Text illustrated by Alan & Lea Daniel.
    Summary: When Aaron hurts his hair's feelings by saying he hates it, his hair runs away and jumps onto other people and into trouble.
    ISBN 0-439-98759-8 (cassette). -- ISBN 0-439-98716-4 (book).

Fig. 4.8—Continues

FIGURE 4.8 *(continued)*

(chief source of information)
(title page)

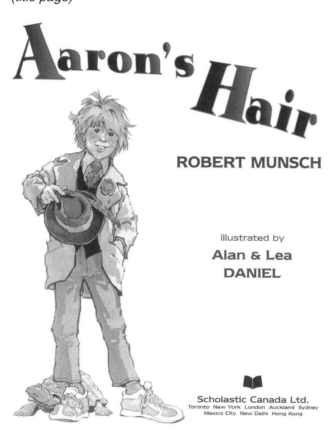

(information on cassette)

Fig. 4.8—Continues

FIGURE 4.8 *(continued)*

(information on verso)

The paintings for this book were created in watercolour on Arches paper.

This book was designed in QuarkXPress, with type set in 18 point Caxton Light.

Munsch, Robert N., 1945-
Aaron's hair

ISBN 0-439-98716-4

I. Daniel, Alan, 1939- . II. Daniel, Lea. III. Title

PS8576.U575A73 2000   JC813'.54   C00-930505-X
                              PZ7.M86Aa 2000

5 4 3 2 1   Printed and bound in Canada   0 / 0 1 2 3 4 /0

FIGURE 4.9

This example is an illustration of:
- map
- main entry under corporate body
- general material designation
- other title information
- joint responsibility
- statement of scale and projection with optional addition of coordinates
- place, publisher, and date not listed on item; decade of publication known
- language note
- contents note
- 2nd level cataloging

Tungavik Federation of Nunavut.
  Inuit owned lands [cartographic material] : Nunavut / prepared by the Tungavik Federation of Nunavut (TFN) and JLC Repro Graphic. -- Scale 1:3,000,000 ; Lambert conformal conic proj., standard parallels at 49°N and 77°N central meridian of origin, longitude 95°W and latitude 77°N. -- [S.l. : s.n., 199-]
  1 map : col. ; 109 x 100 cm.

  Legend in English, Inuktitut (both eastern and western orthography), and French.
  Inset: Sanikiluao.

Fig. 4.9—Continues

Continuing resources that are published serially (that is, in parts intended to continue without end, such as periodicals) employ this area for the dating and numbering information typical to these materials; however, this is not applicable to integrating resources. Figure 4.10 on page 41 shows examples of the use of area 3 in printed and electronic periodicals.

Publication, Distribution Information: This area is applicable to all published materials, regardless of their physical format, and usually consists of three parts: the city and name of the publisher, the distributor, or both, and the date of publication. In the case of serially published titles, such as journals and integrating resources, the opening date or earliest available date is given in this area, followed by a hyphen and blank spaces where an end date can be recorded if the publication is discontinued.[4] It is not used for the cataloging of unpublished materials.

Information given in area 4 is transcribed from the item being cataloged as succinctly as possible, which means giving, usually, only the first place of publication and the publisher's or distributor's name, and the publication year. Catalogers are allowed to abbreviate some location information (states and provinces, for example) and abridge names when it can be done without creating confusion. More than one place of publication and publisher's or distributor's name may be given for specific reasons; for example, when the first place/name is in a country foreign to the cataloging institution but another place/name is located in the home country, or when a place/name other than the first appears more prominently than the first. In both those instances, two places/names are given. Figures 4.11, 4.12, and 4.13 on pages 42–43 and 45 show publication, distribution information for a book, an art

FIGURE 4.9 *(continued)*

(information on the face of the map)

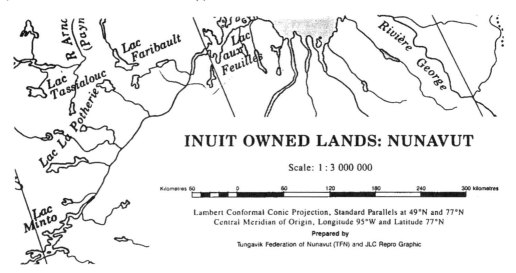

INUIT OWNED LANDS: NUNAVUT

Scale: 1 : 3 000 000

| Kilometres 60 | 0 | 60 | 120 | 180 | 240 | 300 kilometres |

Lambert Conformal Conic Projection, Standard Parallels at 49°N and 77°N
Central Meridian of Origin, Longitude 95°W and Latitude 77°N
Prepared by
Tungavik Federation of Nunavut (TFN) and JLC Repro Graphic

This legend is repeated in Eastern-Orthography Inuktitut, Western-Orthography Inuktitut, and French

NUNAVUT LEGEND

NUNAVUT SETTLEMENT AREA . . . . ▬
    See Article 3 and Schedule 3 1 of the Agreement for full description
HIGH ARCTIC AREA EXEMPT FROM INUIT LAND OWNERSHIP . . . ● ● ● ●
    See Section 19 2 6 and Schedule 19 1 of the Agreement for full description.

INUIT LAND QUANTUM

Regions	Surface only excluding minerals Article 19.2.1b	Surface and Subsurface including minerals Article 19.2.1a
North Balfin	31.026 sq miles	2.372 sq miles
South Balfin	23.941 sq miles	1.771 sq miles
Sanikiluaq	0 sq miles	1.001 sq miles
Keewatin	32.092 sq miles	5.040 sq miles
Kitikmeot East	13.790 sq miles	592 sq miles
Kitikmeot West	21.973 sq miles	3.852 sq miles
Nunavut Totals	122.822 sq miles	14.628 sq miles

1 sq mile – 2 5898 sq kilometers
*(Regional totals above are larger than the negotiated quantum totals listed in Schedule 19 2 to 19 7
of the Agreement and the above are the actual amounts of land Inuit will own).

FORM OF TITLE
    See Article 19 of the Agreement for details, especially see
    Sub-section 19.2.1(a) and 19.2.1(b).
EXISTING MINERAL INTERESTS ON INUIT LAND
    See Section 19.2.2 to 19.2.4 of the Agreement for details.
INUIT OWNED LANDS WITHIN MUNICIPALITIES
    Not shown on this map. The following communities contain Inuit Owned Lands within their
    municipalities:

Iqaluit	Pond Inlet	Coppermine
Cape Dorset	Rankin Inlet	Cambridge Bay
Pangnirtung	Whale Cove	Taloyoak
Lake Harbour	Broughton Island	

    The Hamlet offices of the above communities have copies of maps showing Inuit Owned
    Lands within their municipality.
CROWN (PUBLIC) LANDS
    All other lands are Crown lands. Inuit have the right to hunt, trap, fish and participate in the
    management of all these lands. Please see the Agreement for more details.

TOTAL INUIT OWNED LANDS : 137,450 Square Miles

FIGURE 4.10

This example is an illustration of:
- print serial
- electronic serial
- work emanating from a corporate body entered under title
- other title information
- numeric and/or alphabetic, chronological, or other designation area
- open entry
- same organization responsible for intellectual content and publication
- frequency note
- source of title note
- availability note
- system requirements note
- mode of access note
- ISSN
- 2nd level cataloging

Cataloged as a print journal

ELAN : Ex Libris Association newsletter. -- No. 33 (spring
   2003)-   . -- Toronto : Ex Libris Association, 2003-
      v. ; 28 cm.

   Semi-annual.
   Title from caption.
   Issues no. 1 (1989)-32(spring 2002) have title: Ex Libris news.
   Also available online at
http://exlibris.fis.utoronto.ca/ELAN.html.
   ISSN 0833-4278.

Cataloged as an electronic journal

ELAN [electronic resource] : Ex Libris Association newsletter. --
   No. 33 (spring 2003)-   . -- [Toronto] : Ex Libris
   Association, 2003-

   System requirements: Adobe Acrobat.
   Mode of access: World Wide Web.
   Semi-annual.
   Title from title screen (viewed Nov. 27, 2006).
   Print ed. issues no. 1 (1989)-32(spring 2002) have title: Ex
Libris news.
   http://exlibris.fis.utoronto.ca/ELAN.html.
   ISSN 0833-4278.

*Authors'note: According to AACR2-2005's rule 12.1B2 when a title
is given in full form and as an acronym, the item is entered
under the full form. The item in this figure is only known as
ELAN; "Ex Libris Association newsletter" is the subtitle.*

Fig. 4.10—Continues

FIGURE 4.10 *(continued)*

(information on banner)

(information on back page)

ELAN

Number 33 / Spring 2003
ISSN 0833-4278

Published twice a year by:
Ex Libris Association
c/o The Dean's Office
Faculty of Information Studies
University of Toronto
140 St. George Street
Toronto, ON M5S 3G6
Editor: Lori Knowles
Production:
Ontario Library Association

Newsletter Committee:
Merlyn Beeckmans, Jean Weihs
Murray Sheppard

Contributions and suggestions
should be directed to:
Sherrill Cheda
32 Rosedale Heights Dr
Toronto, ON M4T 1C3
Tel: 416-482-5242
Fax: 416-482-6704
E-mail: scheda@sympatico.ca

Ex Libris News reserves the
right to edit contributions.

FIGURE 4.11

This example is an illustration of:
- only one part of a multipart item is in a library's collection
- edition statement
- distributor noted for U.S. libraries
- publishing date not listed, copyright date given
- index note with unusual placing of the index noted
- 2nd level cataloging

Hessayon, D.G.
  The house plant expert. Book two / D.G. Hessayon. -- 1st ed. --
London : Expert Books ; New York : Sterling [distributor], c2005.
  128 p. : col. ill. ; 24 cm.

  Includes index for Book one and Book two (p. 4-7).
  ISBN 0-903505-61-4.

Fig. 4.11—Continues

FIGURE 4.11 *(continued)*

(chief source of information)

(title page)

The HOUSE PLANT EXPERT Dr. D. G. Hessayon
BOOK TWO

First edition: 100,000 copies

Published by Expert Books
a division of Transworld Publishers

Copyright © Dr.D.G.Hessayon 2005

The right of Dr.D.G.Hessayon to be identified
as author of this work has been asserted in accordance
with sections 77 and 78 of the Copyright Designs and
Patents Act 1988.

A catalogue record for this book is available from the British Library

TRANSWORLD PUBLISHERS
61–63 Uxbridge Road, London W5 5SA
a division of the Random House Group Ltd

Distributed in the United States
by Sterling Publishing Co. Inc.,
387 Park Avenue South,
New York,
NY 10016-8810

EXPERT BOOKS

(information on verso)

Reproduction by Spot On Digital Imaging Ltd, Gomm Road, High Wycombe, Bucks HP13 7DJ
Printed and bound by Mohn Media Mohndruck GmbH

ISBN 0 903505 61 4

reproduction, and an integrating resource. See Figure 5.3 on pages 67–68 for an example of a book published jointly by two organizations with offices in different cities.

For films and videorecordings, "releasing" is the act of publishing or distributing a film or video, not "producing" it. For materials in these formats, production is akin to creation, and producers are considered a kind of creator of the materials they produce.

Dates of publication are so important that catalogers are not permitted to leave them out of catalog records. Under earlier cataloging rules, if catalogers did not find a date, they were allowed to enter "n.d." ("no date") in the record. Since the publication of AACR2 in 1978, however, this practice has been abolished. When no date is given on the item and cannot be found anywhere (order records and reference sources are the best places to look for them), catalogers must give their best guess as to the year the item was published. Depending on the probability that the guess is accurate, catalogers may add question marks to their guessed date ([2006?]), give alternate years ([2001 or 2002]), suggest spans of years ([1999–2001?]), or use question marks in place of digits indicating a decade ([198-?]) or a century ([18—?]). All of the guessed dates are enclosed within square brackets, because they did not come from the prescribed sources.

Unpublished items do not have "publication" dates. Instead, the date of an unpublished item's creation is given in area 4, but no location or name is included (see Figure 4.14).

Only naturally occurring objects are cataloged without an associated date (see Figure 4.15 on page 46).

Physical Description: Information in this area is given for all materials that consist of one or more physical objects, such as books and other printed items, magnetic tape on reels, cassettes, and cartridges, discs containing recordings in various forms, and so on. It is not usually given for remote electronic resources,[5] which are not physical objects; although it is used for the direct access electronic resources that are carried on magnetic tape, optical discs, magnetic disks, and other physical media.

Physical description information consists of four parts: (1) the extent of an item, given in terms of specific material designations and, sometimes, its duration; (2) other physical details; (3) dimensions; and (4) accompanying materials, if any are issued with the material being cataloged. Each material format has its own array of characteristics described here. For example, books are described in terms of pages, leaves (pages printed on only one side), or volumes, as appropriate; other physical details include illustrations, maps, and the like, which are typically found in books; and dimensions are given in terms of the height of the spines. Accompanying materials often found in books include discs, maps, tapes, photographs, or other materials placed in pockets inside the front or back cover, or any other inserts not bound into the book itself. Note that a map reproduced on one of the pages of a book is recorded as other physical details, but a map placed in a pocket inside the cover that can be removed from the book is considered accompanying material.

In the physical description area, the distinction between the intellectual or artistic content of materials and the carrier in or on which the content appears is clear. Books are so familiar that this distinction may be overlooked, but the work of literature, scholarship, or artistry a book contains is distinct from the physical pages, covers, and so forth that "carry" it. The physical description area is where the carriers are described. Direct access electronic resources, sound recordings, and videos are described in terms of their discs (spelled "disks" is some instances), cartridges, cassettes, reels, or other carrier types. Each type has specific characteristics covered in the rules relating to this area given in the relevant chapter. For example, videorecording carriers are covered by rule 7.5, still image carriers are covered by rule 8.5, and so on. The table on page 47 provides examples of physical descriptions for a variety of material formats.

FIGURE 4.12

Information at the bottom of the picture:

PIGGI-BILLA THE PORCUPINE

ROSLYN ANN KEMP. (1950-   )
An artist with a unique style of expressing aboriginal legends on
bark paintings … exhibited at galleries in North Queensland and
at Queensland Aboriginal Creations, Brisbane.

Published by Boolarong Publications in association with
Queensland Aboriginal Creations.

Copyright reserved for the artist.
- -
This example is an illustration of:
- art reproduction
- general material designation
- probable place of publication
- joint publishers
- date of publication unknown
- note relating to the original
- 2nd level cataloging

Kemp, Roslyn Ann.
   Piggi-billa the porcupine [art reproduction] / Roslyn Ann Kemp.
-- [Brisbane?] : Boolarong Publications in association with
Queensland Aboriginal Creations, [19--]
   1 art reproduction : col. ; 33 x 25 cm.

   Reproduction of original bark painting.

FIGURE 4.13

This example is an illustration of:
- integrating resource (loose-leaf format)
- work emanating from a corporate body entered under title
- edition statement
- place of publication not listed, but known
- publication date not listed, copyright date given
- publication date for integrating resource left open
- accompanying material given in note area
- Canadian CIP data
- 2nd level cataloging

Living with kidney disease / Kidney Foundation of Canada. -- 3rd
   ed. -- [Montreal] : Kidney Foundation of Canada, c1999-
   1 v. (loose-leaf) ; 28 cm.

   Five pamphlets and 4 information sheets housed in an envelope
31 x 27 cm. attached to ring binder. Seven of these items are in
English and French.

Fig. 4.13—Continues

FIGURE 4.13 *(continued)*

(chief source of information)
  (title page)

## LIVING WITH KIDNEY DISEASE	*(information on verso)* 	
	
	Copyright © 1999
	The Kidney Foundation of Canada
	
	Canadian Cataloguing in Publication Data
	
	Main entry under title:
	
	   Living with kidney disease
	
	3rd ed.
	Includes index.
	
	   1. Kidneys--Diseases--Popular works. 2. Kidneys--Diseases--Treatment--Popular works. I. The Kidney Foundation of Canada.
	
	RC902.L59 1999 616.6'1 C99-901026-3
	
	Ref. No.: ED-90-001-99

THIRD EDITION

FIGURE 4.14

```
This example is an illustration of:
    • art original
    • title and date of creation taken from author's statement
    • general material designation
    • source of title note
    • accompanying material note
    • 2nd level cataloging


Sandiford, Judith.
  Molecular cloud [art original] / Judith Sandiford. -- 1984.
  1 art original : acrylic on canvas ; 77 x 64 cm.

  Title from artist's statement.
  Artist's statement (3 p.) in vertical file.
```

FIGURE 4.15

```
Five rocks brought from Iceland given to the library and placed
in a transparent container.
```

- -

```
This example is an illustration of:
     •   realia
     •   naturally occurring object
     •   title main entry with supplied title
     •   source of title note
     •   edition and history note
     •   2nd level cataloging
```

```
[Icelandic lava] [realia].
   5 samples ; in container 30 x 30 x 15 cm.

   Title supplied by cataloger.
   From Valnaorder area, Iceland.
```

Physical Description for Various Formats

BOOKS

xii, 298 p. : ill. ; 28 cm.	
2 v. : ill., maps ; 29 cm. + 3 maps	(separate maps in pocket inside back cover)
[132] leaves ; 20 cm.	(all unpaged leaves)
65 p. : all col. ill. ; 32 cm.	(picture book without text)
78 p. : chiefly col. ill. ; 32 cm.	(picture book with text)

NONBOOK MATERIALS

3 maps : col. ; 60 x 80 cm.	
100 leaves : parchment ; 45 cm.	(for a manuscript)
1 score (25 p.) ; 32 cm. + 3 parts	
2 sound discs (117 min.) : digital, stereo ; 4 3/4 in.	
2 videocassettes (60 min. each) : sd., col. ; 1/2 in.	
1 videodisc (49 min.) : sd., col.	(dimensions omitted for standard-sized DVD)
5 art originals : pastel on paper ; 16 x 21 cm.	
1 art print : engraving, col. ; 31 x 42 cm.	
1 computer optical disc : sd., col. ; 12 in. + 1 user's guide	
1 quilt : cotton, red and white ; 120 x 100 cm.	
3 microfiches (120 fr. each) : ill., maps	(dimensions omitted for standard fiche)
v. : ill. ; 28 cm.	(open entry for a periodical)
8 v. : ill. ; 29 cm.	(closed entry for a discontinued periodical)

Series Statement: If material being cataloged belongs to a series, information for the series is given in this area, generally the main title and the number of the title in the series (see Figure 4.16). When needed for identification, statements of responsibility may also be given. Sometimes, International Standard Serial Numbers (ISSNs) are assigned to series titles. They are useful to record in the catalog record, also. Some series titles that appear regularly have both ISSNs and International Standard Book Numbers (ISBNs), making it possible for catalogers to treat them as monographs in series or as serially published continuing resources. A policy should be developed for such materials or a decision made to treat them on a case-by-case basis in the library or media center, depending on the types of materials involved and the likely service benefits for patrons.

Series statements are important and useful for many reasons. For example, an author, asked to contribute a title to a series, wants to see what other titles are listed before agreeing to the invitation; or a teacher finds a title useful to his or her teaching that is part of a series and wants to see whether the series has other titles he or she could use; or a young reader likes one or two titles in a series and decides to read more, if there are any; or a collection development librarian wants to add to the library's collection all the titles in a scholarly series on a subject of interest. Series information does not have to be included in first level bibliographic description and can be omitted if that is the library's policy. However, if a series title would be a useful access point in the catalog, it must be included here as the basis for the heading (series titles are a type of added entry heading, explained further in Chapter 5).

Series statements are recorded in this area of description when they appear on an item on the series title page, title page, or cover. Publishers and distributors of materials sometimes put statements on the versos of title pages that seem to be series statements, but are not. Such statements may even use the word *series*. A rule of thumb for determining whether a title is a genuine series title is to ask whether it appears as part of a full sentence, such as "This book is one of a series of scholarly works emanating from the University College annual lectures." If the answer to the question is "yes," the statement is not a series title, but an explanation of the origin of the contents. A real series title would be worded more like an ordinary title and capitalized accordingly, for example, "University College Annual Lectures."

Notes: The seventh area of description is devoted to information that users of the catalog might find helpful, but did not belong in any of the previous areas. In some instances, the added information in notes is crucial for selecting an edition or version of a title that meets specific user needs, such as having indexes and bibliographies, or determining that it matches a listing in a bibliography, such as the cast of a motion picture including particular actors. Catalog searchers who, for any reason, cannot examine materials directly rely on note information to explain enough about the materials to decide whether obtaining them is worthwhile; therefore, notes should be made with as much attention, care, and accuracy as in the other areas of description. A selection of important notes are described and illustrated in the following paragraphs.

- *Physical description note.* This is the place to include information about the hardware to be used with a particular material. For some collections this would indicate whether an item uses a VHS or Beta videocassette recorder; or Blue Ray or HD-DVD recorders for high-definition videodiscs (see Figure 4.17 on page 51). Information about electronic resources is placed in a formal system requirements note or a mode of access note.

- *Contents note.* Here is the place where the titles of individual works in anthologies are given. It is particularly important if library users are likely to search for the individual

FIGURE 4.16

This example is an illustration of:
- map
- bilingual work
- main entry under corporate body
- general material designation
- edition statement
- statement of scale
- place of publication unknown
- joint publishers
- probable date
- numbered series statement
- contents notes
- 2nd level cataloging

Ontario East Cycling Association.
  Ontario east cycling map [cartographic material] / Ontario East Cycling Association = Carte du cycliste l'est Ontarien / L'est Ontarien association touristique. -- 1st ed. 1999/2000. -- Scale 1:250,000. -- [S.l.] : Ontario Cycling Association and Advermap, [1999?]
  1 map : both sides, col. ; 69 x 100 cm., folded to 24 x 10 cm. -- (Ontario cycling route map series ; map 6 = Serie des cartes des cyclists de l'Ontario ; carte 6)

  Includes lists of cycling loops, tour corridors, hotels, inns, bed & breakfasts, camping sites, attractions.
  Insets: Southwestern region; Ottawa's off-road cycling routes.
  ISBN 0-9685016-0-5.

Authors' note: it is difficult to determine the publisher. "Advermap" is only listed on the cover while the Ontario Cycling Association is mentioned as well elsewhere on the map. The authors have chosen to name both as publishers.

Fig. 4.16—Continues

works than the titles of the anthologies in which they are presented. Few searchers ask for titles such as *Three Plays by Ibsen* or *The Best of Bob Dylan*. They usually are looking for one of the plays or songs, and want to know whether it is in a particular anthology. Added entries for the titles of the individual works cannot be made unless the reason for them appears in the catalog record. This note is where the reason can be found (see Figure 5.10 on page 82).

- *Summary note.* In the past, when catalog users were local patrons who could go to the shelves to examine items directly and decide on the spot whether they wanted them, summary notes were considered unnecessary for many materials. Materials that could not be browsed, such as films and other nonbook items lacking projectors or playback equipment or held in closed stacks, and children's materials being searched by parents or teachers, were most likely to be given summary notes, but not the rest of collections. In

FIGURE 4.16 *(continued)*

(information on cover)

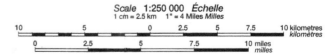

FIGURE 4.17

This example is an illustration of:
- serial
- remote access electronic resource
- work emanating from a corporate body entered under title
- title with acronym
- numeric and/or chronological, or other designation area
- open entry
- mode of access note
- frequency note
- source of title note
- basis for description note
- ISSN
- 2nd level cataloging

Canadian online library and archives journal [electronic
   resource] : COLAJ. -- Vol. 1, no. 1 (2005)-   . -- Kingston,
   ON. : Queen's University Librarians and Archivists, 2005-

   Mode of access: World Wide Web, www.queensu.ca/law/COLAJ.htm.
   Semi-annual.
   Title from title screen.
   Description based on contents viewed October 2, 2006.
   ISSN 1715-1526.

*Authors' note: AACR2-2005 contains no rules for a URL. Many
libraries add this to the mode of access note.*

Sources of information will be found at the URL listed in the
mode of access note.

---

the twenty-first century, however, people living or working far from holding libraries can search catalogs on the World Wide Web and ask for materials to be sent to them via interlibrary loan or electronic transmission. For these remote users as well as for local users who search online, summary notes have become an important addition to catalog records for all materials, and catalogers should make them whenever possible. Summary notes should be brief and objective but thorough in covering the content of the materials (see Figure 4.18)

- *Details of the library's copy note.* This is the appropriate place to describe unique characteristics of the holding library's copy that do not appear in any other copies issued by the publisher or distributor, such as special markings, torn or missing pages, autographs, and margin notes (see Figure 4.18).

- *Numbers on the item note.* Although the final area of description is the proper place to include the ISBN or ISSN of an item, other important numbers may appear on materials

FIGURE 4.18

```
This example is an illustration of:
     •  joint responsibility
     •  other title information
     •  subsidiary responsibility
     •  detailed pagination
     •  series statement
     •  contents (bibliography and index) note
     •  summary
     •  library's copy note
     •  Library of Congress CIP
     •  2nd level cataloging
```

```
Smith, Sharron.
   Canadian fiction : a guide to reading interests / Sharron Smith
and Maureen O'Connor ; foreword by Catherine Sheldrick Ross. --
Westport, Conn. : Libraries Unlimited, 2005.
   xxii, 423 p. ; 26 cm. -- (Genreflecting advisory series)

   Includes bibliographical reference and indexes.
   Summary: Guide to more than 650 books published between 1990
and 2004, sorted into setting, story, character, language, and
genre fiction.
   Blank p. 189 replaced by errata sheet.
   ISBN 1-59258-166-4.
```

Fig. 4.18—Continues

that should be given in the catalog record. This note is where all but the ISBN or ISSN can be given, including Library of Congress Control Numbers (LCCNs), product code numbers, publishers' catalog numbers, and so on. Some of the numbers are encoded in specially designated fields when catalog records are entered into computer databases, such as the LCCN and product code numbers; others appear only in the note area.

Standard Numbers and Terms of Availability: The eighth and final area of description is where ISBNs, ISSNs, and *key titles* (title codes unique to each published serial) are entered along with information about bindings and paper, purchase or rental prices, and the like. Because ISBNs and ISSNs can be searched as access points in computerized databases, it is important to enter them into catalog records. Part of the information relating to a specific ISBN, for example, is binding and paper quality of the material it represents, so catalogers usually add that after the ISBN, in parentheses (see Figure 4.19 on page 54). In contrast, price information is optional and many libraries choose not to include it, because prices change over time. The amount given in a catalog record prepared at the time an item is published may not remain accurate for long. If a patron loses material and the library's policy is to charge a replacement fee that is higher than the price stated on the catalog record for the material, it can create unnecessary contention. Should the policy of a library or media center be to record prices in catalog records despite the limits on their accuracy, the price

FIGURE 4.18 *(continued)*

(chief source of information)

(title page)

Canadian Fiction

A Guide to Reading Interests

Sharron Smith
and Maureen O'Connor

Foreword by Catherine Sheldrick Ross

Genreflecting Advisory Series

Diana Tixier Herald, Series Editor

LIBRARIES
U N L I M I T E D
A Member of the Greenwood Publishing Group

Westport, Connecticut • London

(information on verso)

Library of Congress Cataloging-in-Publication Data

Smith, Sharron.
    Canadian fiction : a guide to reading interests / Sharron Smith and Maureen O'Connor ; foreword by Catherine Sheldrick Ross.
        p. cm. — (Genreflecting advisory series)
    Includes bibliographical references and index.
    ISBN 1-59158-166-4 (alk. paper)
        1. Canadian fiction—Bibliography—Handbooks, manuals, etc. 2. Books and reading—English-speaking countries—Handbooks, manuals, etc. 3. Books and reading—Canada—Handbooks, manuals, etc. I. O'Connor, Maureen, 1947- II. Title. III. Series.
    Z1377.F4S65   2005
    [PR9192.2]
    016.813—dc22   2005016100

British Library Cataloguing in Publication Data is available.

Library of Congress Catalog Card Number: 2005016100
ISBN: 1-59158-166-4

First published in 2005

Libraries Unlimited, 88 Post Road West, Westport, CT 06881
A Member of the Greenwood Publishing Group, Inc.
www.lu.com

Printed in the United States of America

The paper used in this book complies with the Permanent Paper Standard issued by the National Information Standards Organization (Z39.48–1984).

10 9 8 7 6 5 4 3 2 1

given should be the publisher's recommended list price, not the price actually paid for the item, which is likely to have been discounted by the seller.

Punctuating Bibliographic Descriptions

ISBD punctuation is mandated by AACR2–2005, although this is likely to change in the future. This section explains the basic punctuation rules in use at this writing.

Areas of Description: ISBD requires that a full stop (period), a space, a long dash, and another space follow the end of each area of description to separate it from the beginning of the next area, unless the next area begins in a new paragraph. In North American tradition, card-style catalog records placed areas 1 through 4 together, in one paragraph; areas 5 and 6 in the next paragraph; each note in a new paragraph; and area 8 in its own paragraph. As a result, the full stop–space–dash–space was used to separate areas 1 and 2, 2 and 3 if it were used, and 3 and 4. If area 3 were not used, the punctuation would appear between areas 1 and 2, and 2 and 4.

Parts of the Areas of Description: Although individual parts within an area of description each have their own punctuation rules, when parts commonly given in the area are all

FIGURE 4.19

```
This example is an illustration of:
     •  named conference
     •  entry under corporate body
     •  two other title information statements
     •  joint editors
     •  relationship to other publications note
     •  contents (bibliography and index) note
     •  two ISBNs qualified
     •  2nd level cataloging


North American Serials Interest Group (17th : 2002 :
     College of William and Mary)
   Transforming serials : the revolution continues : proceedings
of the North American Serials Interest Group, Inc. 17th Annual
Conference, June 20-23, 2002, the College of William and Mary,
Williamsburg, Virginia / Susan L. Scheiberg, Shelley Neville,
editors. -- New York : Haworth Information Press, 2003.
   365 p. ; 21 cm.

   Co-published simultaneously as The serials librarian, v. 44,
nos. 1/2 and 3/4 2003.
   Includes bibliographical references and index.
   ISBN 0-7890-2281-8 (alk. paper). -- ISBN 0-7890-2282-6 (pbk. :
alk. paper).
```

Fig. 4.19—Continues

that appear in areas 1, 4, and 5, colons are used to separate the first part from the second. The table that follows gives examples for a book and a sound recording on compact disc. (Commas used within these parts do not have special ISBD significance, but are used in their ordinary grammatical functions to separate the components of serial listings.)

Area 1 Punctuating Title Proper and Other Title Information

Access to media : a guide to integrating and computerizing catalogs

High, bright, light and clear : the glory of baroque brass

Area 4 Punctuating Place and Name of Publisher or Distributor

New York : Neal Schuman Publishers

New York : RCA Records

Area 5 Punctuating Extent and Other Physical Details

viii, 301 p. : ill.

1 sound disc : digital, stereo.

List continues on page 56

FIGURE 4.19 *(continued)*

(chief source of information)

(title page)

TRANSFORMING SERIALS: THE REVOLUTION CONTINUES

Proceedings of the
NORTH AMERICAN SERIALS
INTEREST GROUP, Inc.

17th Annual Conference
June 20-23, 2002
The College of William and Mary
Williamsburg, Virginia

Susan L. Scheiberg
Shelley Neville
Editors

(information on verso)

Transforming Serials: The Revolution Continues has been co-published simultaneously as *The Serials Librarian*, Volume 44, Numbers 1/2 and 3/4 2003.

The development, preparation, and publication of this work has been undertaken with great care. However, the publisher, employees, editors, and agents of The Haworth Press and all imprints of The Haworth Press, Inc., including The Haworth Medical Press® and Pharmaceutical Products Press®, are not responsible for any errors contained herein or for consequences that may ensue from use of materials or information contained in this work. Opinions expressed by the author(s) are not necessarily those of The Haworth Press, Inc.

Cover design by Thomas J. Mayshock Jr.

Library of Congress Cataloging-in-Publication Data

North American Serials Interest Group. Conference (17th : 2002 : College of William and Mary)
   Transforming serials : the revolution continues : proceedings of the North American Serials Interest Group, Inc. 17th Annual Conference, June 20-23, 2002, the College of William and Mary, Williamsburg, Virginia / Susan L. Scheiberg, Shelley Neville, editors.
      p. cm.
"Co-published simultaneously as The serials librarian, v. 44, nos. 1/2 and 3/4 2003."
Includes bibliographical references and index.
      ISBN 0-7890-2281-8 (alk. paper) – ISBN 0-7890-2282-6 (pbk : alk. paper)
1. Serials librarianship–Congresses. 2. Libraries–Special collections–Electronic journals–Congresses. 3. Electronic journals–Congresses. I. Scheiberg, Susan L. II. Neville, Shelley. III. Serials librarian. IV. Title.
      Z692.S5N67 2002
      025.17'32–dc21   2003005542

The Haworth Information Press
An Imprint of
The Haworth Press, Inc.
New York • London • Oxford

In area 1, other title information is separated from statement(s) of responsibility by means of a space, a slash, and another space; for example, continuing the first two examples above:

Access to media : a guide to integrating and computerizing catalogs / Sheila S. Intner

High, bright, light, and clear : the glory of baroque brass / The Canadian Brass.

In area 4, an ordinary-looking comma separates the second part from the third; for example, continuing the examples above:

New York : Neal Schuman Publishers, c1984.

New York : RCA Records, p1983.

In area 5, a space, a semicolon, and another space separate the second from the third part of the area; for example, continuing the examples given above:

viii, 301 p. : ill. ; 23 cm.

1 sound disc : digital, stereo. ; 4 3/4 in.

When one of the elements is missing, the punctuation *preceding* it is omitted, never the punctuation following it. Thus, if the book and sound recording examples above had no subtitles and no other physical details, the data would be punctuated as follows:

Book, Area 1:	Access to media / Sheila S. Intner
CD, Area 1:	High, bright, light, and clear / The Canadian Brass
Book, Area 5:	viii, 301 p. ; 23 cm.
CD, Area 5:	1 sound disc ; 4 3/4 in.

Because these examples have neither edition statements nor musical presentation statements, combining title and publication, distribution data from the above examples into one paragraph would require the following punctuation:

Access to media : a guide to integrating and computerizing catalogs / Sheila S. Intner. — New York : Neal Schuman Publishers, c1984.

High, bright, light and clear : the glory of baroque brass / The Canadian Brass. — New York : RCA Records, p1983.

AACR2–2005 contains punctuation rules for every area of description and, within each area, every part it might possibly contain. Among the reasons it is difficult to absorb the rules is that ISBD punctuation frequently includes spaces both before and after the marks and because punctuation marks related to an area or part of an area that precede them, which is not where readers of text expect to find punctuation marks such as colons, slashes, and semicolons. In fact, the only "normal" looking punctuation mark in the ISBD punctuation scheme is the comma immediately following publisher or distributor names. All the other marks are preceded and followed by spaces.

Two marks of punctuation that have not yet been described are the equal sign and the plus sign. The former is used when an area or part of an area is given in two languages or scripts (see Figure 4.16); the latter is used when accompanying material is included in the physical description statement, after dimensions (for example, see Figure 4.7 on page 34). Both of these marks have spaces before and after them, but despite the less-than-usual spacing, both mean much the same thing as when they are used without the ISBD spacing in an ordinary grammatical context.

Series statements (area 6) are enclosed in parentheses. Within the parentheses, the series title proper is separated from the ISBN or ISSN that applies to the series by a comma (no space before it) and a space after it. The standard number or a title proper for a series that does not have a standard number is separated from the number of the material within the series by a space, a semicolon, and another space. Generally, even when the data are present, other title information and statement(s) of responsibility are not given for series, unless they are important for identification purposes.

Each note in a catalog record appears in its own paragraph, so many of them do not require any special ISBD punctuation. Some notes, such as the contents note, do have special punctuation mandated, and certain notes are required to be formatted in a particular way, such as the dissertation note. AACR2–2005 gives examples of how these notes are to appear.

The final area of description, standard number and terms of availability, is both formatted in a particular way and punctuated with ISBD punctuation. If the area contains a standard number and a price (or other term of availability), these elements will be separated by a space, a colon, and another space. If a serially published item has both an ISSN and a key title, these will be separated by a space, an equal sign, and another space. If a term of availability follows the key title, it will be preceded by a space, a colon, and another space, exactly as it would be if the key title were not given.

The only area for which punctuation has not been discussed is area 3. Because this area varies with the type of material to which it applies, punctuation used for data given here varies also.

Summary of Areas of Description

To recapitulate, constructing standard bibliographic descriptions for catalog records involves finding and giving the following information when it is available from the prescribed sources in or on the materials being cataloged:

Area 1, Title and Statement of Responsibility: First level description includes title proper, general material designation, if used, and statements of responsibility, provided they do not repeat the information contained in the main entry (see Chapter 5). Second level description includes title proper, general material designation, if used, other title information, and statement(s) of responsibility are given for second level description.

Area 2, Edition Statement: First level description includes solely the edition statement transcribed as it appears on the material. Second level description includes the edition statement and a statement of responsibility for this edition, if applicable.

Area 3, Material Specific Details: Used in both first and second level description for maps, music, and serial continuing resources, these details vary according to the type of material. Some elements are omitted from first level description.

Area 4, Publication, Distribution, etc., Information: First level description includes the name of the first publisher or distributor and the date of publication or distribution. Second level description includes the first place of publication or distribution, name of the publisher or distributor, and date of publication or distribution, and, if appropriate, additional places, names, and dates of publication or distribution.

Area 5, Physical Description: First level description includes the number and specific material designation and, for some material formats, the duration of the physical items comprising the item being cataloged. Second level description includes the number and specific material designations of the physical items, the duration, if applicable, other physical details, dimensions unless they are standard for the material format, and accompanying materials, if any.

Area 6, Series Statement: First level description omits this area. Second level description includes series titles proper, standard numbers associated with the series if applicable, and the number of the item within the series. If necessary for identification, a statement of responsibility for the series may be added.

Area 7, Notes: Notes are optional, with a few exceptions, such as a source of title note for electronic resources, which is always made regardless of the bibliographic level followed. If a note is mandated or if the omission of a note would affect the use of the material, it should be included in the catalog record.

Area 8, Standard Numbers and Terms of Availability: This information is required in both first and second level description. It includes the ISBN or the ISSN and key title. Some agencies add binding data (hardcover or paperback) and the use of alkaline paper, in parentheses, after the ISBN. Terms of availability are optional.

These eight areas complete the bibliographic description. The next chapter explores adding access points derived from the description to the catalog record.

Recommended Reading

Maxwell, Robert L. *Maxwell's Handbook for AACR2: Explaining and Illustrating the Anglo-American Cataloguing Rules Through the 2003 Update.* Chicago: American Library Association, 2004.

Reynolds, Regina Romano. "ISSN: Dumb Number, Smart Solution." In Sheila S. Intner et al., eds. *Electronic Cataloging: AACR2 and Metadata for Serials and Monographs.* New York: Haworth Information Press, 2003.

Roe, Sandra K., ed. *The Audiovisual Cataloging Current.* New York: Haworth Information Press, 2001. [See, especially, pp. 1–188.]

Taylor, Arlene G. *Introduction to Cataloging and Classification*, 10th ed. Westport, CT: Libraries Unlimited, 2006.

Notes

1. *Cataloger's Desktop,* (Washington, DC: Library of Congress, Cataloging Distribution Service). Available at http://desktop.loc.gov/

2. *Anglo-American Cataloguing Rules*, 2nd ed., 2002 revision, prepared under the direction of the Joint Steering Committee for Revision of AACR (Ottawa: Canadian Library Association; London: Chartered Institute of Library and Information Professionals; Chicago: American Library Association, 2002–); plus updates issued in 2003, 2004, and 2005.

3. With a few exceptions, all title words appearing between the end of the main title and the beginning of the statement of responsibility are considered *other title information.* The principal exceptions are *parallel titles*, which are the main titles translated into other lan-

guages or scripts, and *alternative titles*, which are titles preceded by the word *or* that follow the main titles; for example, *Trial by Jury, or, The Lass Who Loved a Sailor*. Parallel titles are separate from the main title, but always precede other title information; alternative titles are considered integral parts of the main titles.

4.   Discontinued serial titles sometimes revive and begin to be published again. In such cases, the dates in area 3 must be updated to reflect the situation and notes added to explain the sequences.

5.   An option is available in AACR2–2005 to give this information if a library wishes to do so.

5

Access Points

Part II of AACR2–2005 contains rules that instruct catalogers how to choose headings to add to the bibliographic descriptions they have created and, also, how to put the headings into proper form. Following an unnumbered introduction, six chapters make up Part II, numbered consecutively beginning with Chapter 21,[1] as follows:

Chapter 21   Choice of Access Points

Chapter 22   Headings for Persons

Chapter 23   Geographic Names

Chapter 24   Headings for Corporate Bodies

Chapter 25   Uniform Titles

Chapter 26   References

Two types of headings are derived from descriptive information: names and titles. Names are associated with the people responsible for creating works, that is, the intellectual or artistic content of materials being described. Simply put, they are the "authors" and other parties responsible for content, such as composers, arrangers, programmers, editors, illustrators, artists, and photographers. The names may be personal names or the names of groups of people acting together, known as *corporate bodies*. Some corporate body names involve geographic locations; for example, governments such as the province of "Ontario" or the state of "Maryland," or musical groups such as the New York Philharmonic Orchestra or The Beatles. Corporate bodies include a wide range of entities, whose names can present complex problems for catalogers.

Titles, which are, in fact, the "names" of the works comprising content, include the titles of the materials being cataloged, or parts of those materials (analytic titles), or larger material groups to which the materials being cataloged belong (series titles). Uniform titles are specially constructed titles designed to bring together catalog records for a work when it is published under different titles; for example, a book in one language that is translated into another language and, thus, bears a translated title, or a film that is released in different places under different titles. Classic stories and scholarly works, and sacred scriptures are two kinds of works published many times, often with different titles; for example, *The Holy*

Bible and *The Anchor Bible* or *Alice in Wonderland* and *Alice's Adventures in Wonderland*. This chapter is devoted to explanations of AACR2–2005's rules for choosing name and title access points and formulating them in standard forms.

Choosing the Headings/Access Points

Headings may be designated either main or added entries.[2] *Main entries* are the first and most important access points chosen; *added entries* are all others considered appropriate for material being cataloged. If a catalog record had only one access point, which was not unusual in the past, it was the main entry. Computerized catalogs index all access points alike and respond to search inquiries the same way whether a search term is a main or added entry heading, but librarians retained the concept for other reasons. Today, the most important use of main entries is in creating cutter numbers that form part of shelf addresses assigned to materials to indicate their position on library shelves, explained in greater detail in Chapter 9.

The Anglo-American tradition since the nineteenth century is based on the assumption that the name of a work's creator is the work's most important identifying feature. For this reason, in AACR2–2005, main entry usually is assigned to the creator (or principal creator) of a work, though there are some exceptions, described below. In general, once the main entry is selected, added entry headings are made for other people or corporate bodies also responsible for the existence of the work as well as for its title and any other titles associated with it. In other words, *access points* are made for all names and titles that people might use in trying to find the work in the catalog.

Choosing the Main Entry: Only one person, one corporate body, or one title can be chosen as the main entry. There are no "joint" main entries, even when two people or two corporate bodies share equal responsibility. The fundamental rule is that the creator of a work is its most important identifying element and is selected as its main entry unless the work is the product of a corporate body, known as an *emanation* of the body. When a work emanates from a corporate body, it must first be determined whether the work qualifies for a corporate body main entry. If it does, the corporate body is chosen as its main entry; if it does not, the decision goes back to the fundamental principle of attributing main entry to its creator. Thus, the choice of main entry begins by eliminating the possibility of corporate body main entry, even before seeking one or more creators of the material. The following decision tree illustrates the process:

1. Does the material emanate from a corporate body?
   Yes: Consult rule 21.1B2.
   No: Go to step 6.

2. Is the item one of the six types of material eligible[3] for corporate body main entry?
   Yes: Go to step 3.
   No: Go to step 6.

3. Does the item emanate from one corporate body?
   Yes: Choose that body as the main entry.
   No: Go to step 4.

4. Is there one corporate body that predominates?
   Yes: Choose that body as the main entry.
   No: Go to step 5.

5. Are there two or three corporate bodies responsible for the work?
    Yes: Choose the first named body as the main entry.
    No: Choose the title as the main entry.

6. Is one person primarily responsible for the work?
    Yes: Choose the person as the main entry.
    No: Go to step 7.

7. Is the person or persons responsible for the item unknown?
    Yes: Choose the title as the main entry.
    No: Go to step 8.

8. Do all persons responsible for the work share the same responsibility?
    Yes: Go to step 9.
    No: Consult rules 21.8 through 21.28 to find relevant instructions.

9. Are there two or three persons involved?
    Yes: Choose the first named person as the main entry.
    No: Choose the title as the main entry.

Figures 5.1 through 5.6 illustrate applications of the choices outlined above.

Choosing Added Entries: In a number of instances, rules for choosing main entries when two or more persons or bodies are involved include instructions to make one or more added entries for some or all of the names not chosen. For example, if two persons share equal responsibility for a work (two authors of a book or two composers of a piece of music), the first named is chosen main entry. The rule goes on to instruct catalogers to make an added entry for the other. If three persons share equal responsibility, added entries are made for both names that were not chosen main entry (see Figure 5.5 on pages 71–72). However, if more than three people share equal responsibility, the title is chosen as the main entry, and the rule goes on to instruct catalogers to make an added entry solely for the first named person. This instruction assumes that if searchers remember any of the names, they are most likely to remember the first (see Figure 5.6 on page 73).

Other added entries usually made for all types of works include their titles (that is, titles proper), title variations found in materials (cover titles, spine titles, etc.), and series titles when series information is given in the record. One frequently encountered variation that should be considered a matter of policy is making added entries containing spelled out versions of title words that appear on chief sources as digits, ampersands, or other symbols. If this is not done, searchers entering the title with spelled out words, thinking that librarians do not use digits and symbols in the catalog, could fail to find the material even though it is part of the collection.

Analytic titles appearing in contents notes may or may not be made headings, often depending on whether there are only a few such titles likely to be searched individually by patrons (for example, three novellas presented together in one volume) or a great many (for example, a musical recording containing twenty short pieces, each by a different composer), and whether doing so requires more additional work than catalogers believe is useful. Series titles are not always traced (that is, made searchable headings), depending on local policy. Some libraries and media centers trace only scholarly series; some trace selected series, deciding on a case-by-case basis; some trace all series. Local policy decisions about series headings should be based on the needs of most catalog users. These and other policy deci-

FIGURE 5.1

```
This example is an illustration of:
    • atlas
    • entry under corporate body
    • bibliographic form of name taken from CIP
    • general material designation
    • edition statement inferred from verso and the fact that
      previous editions have been published
    • statement of scale (mathematical data area)
    • no place of publication listed
    • variations in title note
    • contents (index) note
    • alternate title added entry
    • Library of Congress CIP incorrect (title, edition, and
      title added entry)
    • 2nd level cataloging


Hammond World Atlas Corporation.
  Ambassador world atlas [cartographic material]. -- [2000 ed.].
-- Scales vary. -- [S.l] : Hammond, c2000.
  1 atlas (xxxii, 328 p.) : col. ill., maps ; 28 cm.

  At head of title: Hammond.
  Includes indexes.
  ISBN 0-8437-1382-8.

  I. Title. II. Title: World atlas.
```

Fig. 5.1—Continues

sions should be carefully recorded so new catalogers can consult the documentation to find out what to do.

In the eighteenth and nineteenth centuries, it was not unusual for an author to conceal his or her identity by publishing material anonymously, under pseudonyms, or using initials or appellations; but in recent years, the practice is rare. When a novel about a U.S. presidential election titled *Primary Colors* was published anonymously in 1996, a great effort was made to find the author. Years later, after protesting that he did not write it, journalist Joe Klein admitted being the author. The book appears with "Anonymous" on the title page, although other books by Klein advertise him as the "author of *Primary Colors.*" At the author's request, LC's catalog record maintains a title main entry, although an autographed copy is part of the collections. (See Figure 12.1 on pages 208–209 for an example of an anonymous author whose name has never been revealed.)

Establishing Proper Forms for Headings/Access Points

The process of establishing a proper form for each name and title heading in the catalog is known as *authority control.* The assumption underlying authority control is that it is desirable to limit the way name and title headings appear in the catalog in order to bring together

FIGURE 5.1 *(continued)*

(chief source of information)

(title page)

HAMMOND

Ambassador World Atlas

HAMMOND World Atlas **L**
Part of the Langenscheidt Publishing Group

(information on verso)

Hammond Publications Advisory Board

JOHN P. AUGELLI
*Professor and Chairman,
Department of Geography - Meteorology,
University of Kansas*

KINGSLEY DAVIS
*Distinguished Professor of Sociology,
University of Southern California
and
Senior Research Fellow,
The Hoover Institution,
Stanford University*

ALICE C. HUDSON
*Chief, Map Division,
The New York Public Library*

P. P. KARAN
*Professor, Department of Geography,
University of Kentucky*

VINCENT H. MALMSTROM
*Professor, Department of Geography,
Dartmouth College*

TOM L. McKNIGHT
*Professor, Department of Geography,
University of California, Los Angeles*

CHRISTOPHER L. SALTER
*Professor and Chairman, Department of Geography,
University of Missouri*

WHITNEY SMITH
*Executive Director,
The Flag Research Center,
Winchester, Massachusetts*

NORMAN J. W. THROWER
*Professor, Department of Geography,
University of California, Los Angeles*

PRINTED IN THE UNITED STATES OF AMERICA

Library of Congress Cataloging-in-Publication Data
Hammond World Atlas Corporation.
   Citation world atlas. -- Rev.
      p.   cm.
   At head of title: Hammond
   Includes indexes.
   ISBN 0-8437-1295-3 (softcover)
   ISBN 0-8437-1382-8 (hardcover)
   1. Atlases. I. Title. II. Title: Hammond citiation world atlas.
G1021. H2446   1998   <G&M>
912--DC21   98-12358
                                               CIP
                                               MAP

FIGURE 5.2

This example is an illustration of:
- item emanating from a corporate body entered under author
- two authors
- other title information
- subsidiary responsibility
- numbered series statement
- contents (bibliography) note
- ISBN qualified
- added entry for joint author
- added entry for editor
- added entry for corporate body
- added entry for title
- added entry for series
- 2nd level cataloging

Brancolini, Kristine R.
  Video collections and multimedia in ARL libraries : changing
tachnologies / Kristine R. Brancolini, Rick E. Provine ; edited by
Laura A. Rounds. -- Washington, D.C. : Association of Research
Libraries Office of Management Services, 1997.
  53 p. ; 28 cm. -- (OMS occasional paper ; no. 19)

  References: p. 39-40.
  ISBN 0-918006-79-1 (pbk.).

  I. Provine, Rick E. II. Rounds, Laura. III. Association of Research
Libraries. Office of Management Services. IV. Title. V. Series:
Occasional paper (Association of Research Libraries. Office of
Management Services) ; 19.

(chief source of information)

(title page)

VIDEO COLLECTIONS AND MULTIMEDIA IN ARL LIBRARIES:
CHANGING TECHNOLOGIES

OMS Occasional Paper #19

April 1997

Kristine R. Brancolini, Indiana University
  <brancoli@indiana.edu>

Rick E. Provine, University of Virginia
  <provine@virginia.edu>

Edited by Laura A. Rounds, Association of Research Libraries

The authors would like to acknowledge the assistance of Yung-Rang Cheng
and Laura M. Hecht in the statistical data analysis for this paper.

ASSOCIATION OF RESEARCH LIBRARIES
OFFICE OF MANAGEMENT SERVICES
Washington, DC

(information on verso)

ISBN# 0-918006-79-1

Cataloging in Publication data is available.

Price: ARL Members $18, plus shipping
      Nonmembers $25, plus shipping

OMS Occasional Papers are published by the

ASSOCIATION OF RESEARCH LIBRARIES
OFFICE OF MANAGEMENT SERVICES
21 Dupont Circle Washington, DC 20036
(202) 296-8656   (202) 872-0884 fax
<pubs@cni.org>   <http://arl.cni.org>

Copyright © 1997

This volume is copyrighted by the Association of Research Libraries. ARL grants permission to reproduce and
distribute copies of this work for nonprofit educational or library purposes, provided that copies are distributed at or
below cost, and that the author, source, and copyright notice are included on each copy. This permission is in addition
to rights of reproduction granted under Sections 107, 108, and other provisions of the U.S. Copyright Act.

♾ *The paper used in this publication meets the minimum requirements of American
National Standard for Information Sciences—Performance of Paper for Printed
Library Materials, ANSI Z39.48-1992.*

Printed in the United States of America

FIGURE 5.3

This example is an illustration of:
- work emanating from a corporate body entered under title
- subsidiary responsibility
- two publishers
- ISBN qualified
- added entry for editor
- optional addition of designation to editor's name
- added entry for corporate body
- Library of Congress CIP data
- 2nd level cataloging

AMIA compendium of moving image cataloging practice / edited by
  Abigail Leab Martin ; written and complied by AMIA Cataloging
  and Documentation Committee's Subcommittee for the Compendium
  of Cataloging Practice. -- Beverly Hills, Calif. : Association
  of Moving Image Archivists ; Chicago : Society of American
  Archivists, 2001.
  vii, 272 p. ; 28 cm.

  ISBN 0-931828-23-6 (alk. paper).

  I. Martin, Abigail Leab, ed.   II. Association of Moving Image
Archivists. Subcommittee for the Compendium of Cataloging
Practice.

Fig. 5.3—Continues

under an authorized heading all the works by an individual or a corporate body, and all manifestations of a work, no matter how many different names or titles appear in the publications. For example, the name of W. S. Gilbert, author of the words of the famous Gilbert and Sullivan operettas, can appear on published material with the initials W. S. or with his name spelled out, as can the names of poets e. e. cummings and T. S. Eliot, novelist D. H. Lawrence, and many other well-known authors. Similarly, uniform titles are constructed to bring together all versions of a work known by many titles, as in the examples of the Bible and Lewis Carroll's story of Alice mentioned at the beginning of this chapter.

The principle used to determine which name form to choose for any person or group is simple: catalogers are directed to select the most commonly known form.[4] The rationale for the rule is equally simple: this name is what people are most likely to search in the catalog. Two conditions may require a different formulation, however: (1) if a person's name changes and the change is likely to persist (for example, a woman who adopts and uses her husband's name); and (2) if a person makes known that he or she prefers a different formulation. In that event, the person's preference will supersede the rules.

Authority control practice has three phases: (1) researching all name forms appearing in all the published works of the person or body in question and counting the number of times each form appears; (2) selecting the name form that appears most often as the authorized access point and designating other forms cross-references; and (3) documenting the decision and the source(s) of the information.

FIGURE 5.3 *(continued)*

(chief source of information)

(title page)   *(information on verso)*

AMIA Compendium of
Moving Image Cataloging Practice

THE SOCIETY OF AMERICAN ARCHIVISTS
527 S. Wells Street, 5th Floor
Chicago, IL 60607-3992 USA
312/922-0140 • Fax 312/347-1452
info@archivists.org • www.archivists.org

ASSOCIATION OF MOVING IMAGE ARCHIVISTS
8949 Wilshire Boulevard
Beverly Hills, CA 90211
310/550-1300 • Fax 310/550-1363
amia@amianet.org • www.amianet.org

edited by

Abigail Leab Martin

written and compiled by

AMIA CATALOGING AND DOCUMENTATION COMMITTEE'S
SUBCOMMITTEE FOR THE COMPENDIUM OF CATALOGING PRACTICE

First printed in 2001
Printed in the United States of America

Abigail Leab Martin (chair)
Linda Elkins
Jane D. Johnson
Christine Lee
Amy Wood
Linda Tadic (former chair)

ISBN 0-931828-23-6

Library of Congress Cataloging-in-Publication Data

AMIA compendium of moving image cataloging practice / edited by Abigail Leab
Martin ; written and compiled by AMIA Cataloging and Documentation Committee's
Subcommittee for the Compendium of Cataloging Practice.
        p. cm.
    ISBN 0-931828-23-6 (alk. paper)
    1. Cataloging of motion pictures. 2. Cataloging of video recordings. 3. Library surveys.
I. Martin, Abigail Leab. II. Association of Moving Image Archivists. Subcommittee for
the Compendium of Cataloging Practice.

Z695.64 .A45 2001
025.3'473--dc21
                                                                    2001033816

AMIA
ASSOCIATION OF MOVING IMAGE ARCHIVISTS
Beverly Hills, Calif.

THE SOCIETY of
AMERICAN ARCHIVISTS
Chicago

About the Cover: Robert F. Kennedy speaks to newsreel cameramen before sailing with his
family to meet his father, U.S. Ambassador Joseph P. Kennedy, in England. From the newsreel
story "U.S. Ambassador has John Bull all excited!" in *News of the Day, Vol. 9, no. 250*
(released March 9, 1938). *Photo courtesy of the UCLA Film and Television Archive.*

Many personal authors publish only one work. For those individuals, the authority control process involves determining that no other published works exist in which their names are given differently than they appear in the material being cataloged. That done, the name is established as it appears in the material, provided it does not conflict with a previously established name. If it does conflict, efforts are made to avert confusion by differentiating the name in some way (see the next section). Personal authors who publish more than one work and corporate body authors (whose names are likely to appear in multiple publications) require more work. Copies of all their published material have to be examined to see how the name appears, different forms are noted, the number of times each form appears is counted, and the form with the most appearances is authorized. The research by which a name form is established can take time and must be done by a knowledgeable person, making it a costly process.

Once the authority control process is completed, the documentation is stored in a file known as an *authority file*, generally a computerized database, which can be consulted whenever necessary by the library or media center. This describes a local authority file. If the process and the resulting data meet the requirements of the library's or media center's network, it can be uploaded to a network file and shared by network partners. The largest and most widely used authority file in North America is the Library and Archives Canada–Library of Congress–Program for Cooperative Cataloging Name Authority File (NAF), available from LAC, LC, OCLC, and other sources. Although *NAF* implies the file is limited to

FIGURE 5.4

This example is an illustration of:
- work by one author entered under that author
- other title information
- more than one place of publication
- detailed pagination statement
- descriptive illustration statement
- contents (bibliography and index) note
- added entry for title
- 2nd level cataloging

Winchester, Simon.
  The meaning of everything : the story of the Oxford English
dictionary / Simon Winchester. -- New York : Oxford University
Press, 2003.
  xxv, 260 p. : ill., facsims., ports. ; 22 cm.

  Includes bibliographical references (p. 251-253) and index.
  ISBN 0-19-860702-4.

  I. Title.

*Authors' note: If cataloged in Canada, the publication statement
would read:* New York ; Toronto : Oxford University Press, 2003.

Fig. 5.4—Continues

names, authorized forms of uniform titles and series titles are included in it as well as personal and corporate body names.

Form of Personal Names

AACR2–2005 authorizes the name form most likely to be known to users of the catalog: that is, the form that appears most frequently in the person's works or by which he or she is most commonly known. Applying this test to the creators of *Tom Sawyer* and *Hannah and Her Sisters*, catalogers select Mark Twain and Woody Allen, respectively, not Samuel Clemens or Allen Stewart Konigsberg, as the authorized headings. Two exceptions are made to the rules that authorize multiple headings for a single individual: (1) a person uses different names on works in different genres (for example, Carolyn Heilbrun published nonfiction under her real name, but adopted a pseudonym, Amanda Cross, for her mystery novels); and (2) a contemporary person deliberately wishes to create "separate bibliographic identities" (for example, British writer Eleanor Hibbert, who used numerous pseudonyms, including Jean Plaidy, the name used for her *authority record* in LC's NAF, shown in Figure 5.7 on page 74). In such instances, the name that appears on the material being cataloged is used as the authorized heading.

FIGURE 5.4 *(continued)*

(chief source of information)

(title page)

The Meaning
of Everything

The Story of the

Oxford English Dictionary

Simon Winchester

OXFORD
UNIVERSITY PRESS

(information on verso)

OXFORD
UNIVERSITY PRESS
Great Clarendon Street, Oxford OX2 6DP

Oxford University Press is a department of the University of Oxford.
It furthers the University's objective of excellence in research, scholarship,
and education by publishing worldwide in

Oxford New York

Auckland Bangkok Buenos Aires Cape Town Chennai
Dar es Salaam Delhi Hong Kong Istanbul Karachi Kolkata
Kuala Lumpur Madrid Melbourne Mexico City Mumbai Nairobi
São Paulo Shanghai Taipei Tokyo Toronto

Oxford is a registered trade mark of Oxford University Press
in the UK and in certain other countries

Published in the United States
by Oxford University Press Inc., New York

© Simon Winchester 2003

Database right Oxford University Press (maker)

First published by Oxford University Press 2003

All rights reserved. No part of this publication may be reproduced,
stored in a retrieval system, or transmitted, in any form or by any means,
without the prior permission in writing of Oxford University Press,
or as expressly permitted by law, or under terms agreed with the appropriate
reprographics rights organizations. Enquiries concerning reproduction
outside the scope of the above should be sent to the Rights Department,
Oxford University Press, at the address above

You must not circulate this book in any other binding or cover
and you must impose this same condition on any acquirer

British Library Cataloguing in Publication Data
Data available

Library of Congress Cataloging in Publication Data
Data available

ISBN 0-19-860702-4

1 3 5 7 9 10 8 6 4 2

Typeset in Pondicherry, India, by
Alliance Interactive Technology
Printed in the United States of America
on acid-free paper

AACR2–2005 has rules for establishing name forms in many languages in addition to English. They are formulated as they would be listed in authoritative alphabetical listings in their home countries. For English-language names, the rule of thumb is to enter a name that contains a surname under the surname, followed by a comma and the forename(s) in direct order (for example, Jones, Mary Anne). Surnames may consist of a single element (John Doe), two elements connected by a hyphen (Joan Smith-Green), or multiple elements without hyphens (Elizabeth St. James; Joseph de la Fontaine). When English-language names are hyphenated, the surname is filed under the first element; for example, Joan Smith-Green is filed in the S's as "Smith-Green, Joan," *not* in the G's as Green, Joan Smith-. English-language names with compound surnames are usually entered under the first element, for example, St. James, Elizabeth and Van Buren, Martin.

Name authority files may give the fullest form of personal names because large collections are likely to contain similar names. These fuller forms are most useful for smaller libraries when an author's name given on a title page is the same as that of another author

FIGURE 5.5

This example is an illustration of:
- work by three authors with first named as main entry
- edition statement
- detailed pagination
- descriptive illustration statement
- contents (index) note
- personal name added entries for joint authors
- corporate body added entry
- additional title added entry
- sources of information in colophon
- 2nd level cataloging

Bedford, Neal.
  Czech & Slovak republics / Neal Bedford, Jane Rawson, Matt
Warren. -- 4th ed. -- Footscray, Victoria : Lonely Planet, 2004.
  488 p., [8] p. of plates : ill. (some col.), maps ; 20 cm.

  Includes index.
  ISBN 1-74104-046-9.

  I. Rawson, Jane. II. Warren, Matt. III. Lonely Planet
Publications (Firm). I. Title. II. Title: Czech and Slovak
republics.

*Authors' note: Added entries are not usually made for publishers
when their function is simply publishing. In this instance,
first, there is some doubt as to the publisher's contribution to
content and, secondly, the public might look for these guides
under the name of this particular publisher.*

Fig. 5.5—Continues

listed in the catalog so that the works of the authors can be distinguished. For example, the bibliographic name of two authors called C. E. Smith might be Smith, C. E. (Charles Edward) and Smith, C. E. (Carolyn Elizabeth). Birth and death dates can also be added to distinguish authors with similar names.

Special rules cover names that include titles of nobility, names that do not include surnames but contain patronymics, names of kings and queens, and other special cases.

Form of Corporate Body Names

The same principle that guides the formulation of personal names—the most frequently encountered form—guides the formulation of corporate body names as well. Sources consulted by catalogers include publications and other things bearing its name that the body issues, such as letterhead and official documents, whether or not they are published. Sometimes, a corporate body will announce its intention to change its name, either because it has actually changed in some way (for example, the change from Forest Press to OCLC Forest

FIGURE 5.5 *(continued)*

(chief source of information)

(title page)

Czech & Slovak Republics

Neal Bedford, Jane Rawson, Matt Warren

(information on colophon)

LONELY PLANET OFFICES

Australia
Head Office
Locked Bag 1, Footscray, Victoria 3011
☎ 03 8379 8000, fax 03 8379 8111
talk2us@lonelyplanet.com.au

USA
150 Linden St, Oakland, CA 94607
☎ 510 893 8555, toll free 800 275 8555
fax 510 893 8572, info@lonelyplanet.com

UK
72–82 Rosebery Ave,
Clerkenwell, London EC1R 4RW
☎ 020 7841 9000, fax 020 7841 9001
go@lonelyplanet.co.uk

France
1 rue du Dahomey, 75011 Paris
☎ 01 55 25 33 00, fax 01 55 25 33 01
bip@lonelyplanet.fr, www.lonelyplanet.fr

Published by Lonely Planet Publications Pty Ltd
ABN 36 005 607 983

© Lonely Planet 2004

© photographers as indicated 2004

Cover photographs by Lonely Planet Images: Bojnice Chateau, reconstructed in the early 20th century, Richard Nebeský (front); sunlight streams through the window into Hostinec Pub, Prague, Richard Nebeský (back). Many of the images in this guide are available for licensing from Lonely Planet Images: www.lonelyplanetimages.com.

All rights reserved. No part of this publication may be copied, stored in a retrieval system, or transmitted in any form by any means, electronic, mechanical, recording or otherwise, except brief extracts for the purpose of review, and no part of this publication may be sold or hired, without the written permission of the publisher.

Printed through SNP SPrint Singapore Pte Ltd at
KHL Printing Co Sdn Bhd Malaysia

Lonely Planet and the Lonely Planet logo are trademarks of Lonely Planet and are registered in the US Patent and Trademark Office and in other countries.

Lonely Planet does not allow its name or logo to be appropriated by commercial establishments, such as retailers, restaurants or hotels. Please let us know of any misuses: www.lonelyplanet.com/ip.

Although the authors and Lonely Planet have taken all reasonable care in preparing this book, we make no warranty about the accuracy or completeness of its content and, to the maximum extent permitted, disclaim all liability arising from its use.

(information on bar code)

ISBN 1 - 74104 - 046 - 9

USA $21.99
UK   £14.99

Published April 2004
4th Edition
First Published February 1995

FIGURE 5.6

This example is an illustration of:
- item with more than three authors entered under title
- other title information
- marks of omission
- edition statement
- detailed pagination statement
- contents (index) note
- ISBN qualified
- added entry for first author
- Library and Archives Canada CIP
- 2nd level cataloging

The book of lists : the original compendium of curious
   information / by David Wallechinsky ... [et al.]. -- 1st
   Canadian ed. -- Toronto : Knopf, 2005.
   x, 518 p. : ill. ; 23 cm.

   Includes index.
   ISBN 0-676-97720-0 (pbk).

   I. Wallechinsky, David.

(chief source of information)

(title page)

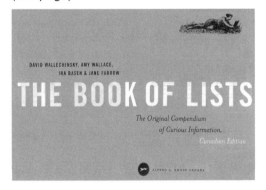

DAVID WALLECHINSKY, AMY WALLACE,
IRA BASEN & JANE FARROW

THE BOOK OF LISTS

*The Original Compendium
of Curious Information,
Canadian Edition*

ALFRED A. KNOPF CANADA

(information from verso)

PUBLISHED BY ALFRED A. KNOPF CANADA

Original edition copyright © 1977, 1980, 1983, 2004 David Wallechinsky and Amy Wallace
Canadian edition copyright © 2005 Ira Basen and Jane Farrow
Published by agreement with Canongate Books Ltd., Edinburgh, Scotland

Published in 2005 by Alfred A. Knopf Canada, a division of
Random House of Canada Limited. Distributed by Random House of Canada Limited, Toronto.

LIBRARY AND ARCHIVES CANADA CATALOGUING IN PUBLICATION

The book of lists / David Wallechinsky ... [et al.]. — Canadian ed.

Includes index.
ISBN 0-676-97720-0

1. Handbooks, vade-mecums, etc. 2. Curiosities and wonders.
3. Curiosities and wonders—Canada. I. Wallechinsky, David, 1948– .

AG106.B66 2005   031.02   C2005-901023-1

First Canadian Edition

FIGURE 5.7   LC Authority Record for Jean Plaidy

LC Control Number: n 79060552

HEADING: Plaidy, Jean, 1906-1993

000 01514cz a2200325n 450
001 4217203
005 20060629161917.0
008 790731n| acannaabn |a aaa
010 __ |a n 79060552
035 __ |a (OCoLC)oca00293580
040 __ |a DLC |b eng |c DLC |d DLC |d GU |d OCl |d OCoLC |d DLC
053 _0 |a PR6015.I3
100 1_ |a Plaidy, Jean, |d 1906-1993
400 1_ |a Pleĭdi, Dzhin, |d 1906-1993
400 1_ |a Hibbert, Eleanor, |d 1906-1993
400 1_ |w nnaa |a Hibbert, Eleanor, |d 1906-
400 1_ |a Burford, Eleanor, |d 1906-1993
500 1_ |w nnnc |a Ford, Elbur, |d 1906-1993
500 1_ |w nnnc |a Kellow, Kathleen, |d 1906-1993
500 1_ |w nnnc |a Tate, Ellalice, |d 1906-1993
500 1_ |w nnnc |a Holt, Victoria, |d 1906-1993
500 1_ |w nnnc |a Carr, Philippa, |d 1906-1993
663 __ |a For works of this author entered under other names, search also under |b Carr, Philippa, 1906-1993, |b Ford, Elbur, 1906-1993, |b Holt, Victoria, 1906-1993, |b Kellow, Kathleen, 1906-1993, |b Tate, Ellalice, 1906-1993
670 __ |a Her Beyond the Blue Mountains, 1947.
670 __ |a Holt, V. The silk vendetta, 1988, c1987: |b CIP t.p. (Victoria Holt)
670 __ |a Contemp. auth., c1976, |b v. 17-20 (Hibbert, Eleanor Burford, 1906- ; Eleanor Burford; pseuds.: Philippa Carr, Elbur Ford, Victoria Holt, Kathleen Kellow, Jean Plaidy, Ellalice Tate)
670 __ |a New York times, Jan. 21, 1993: |b p. C21 (Eleanor Hibbert d. Jan. 18, 1993)
670 __ |a Li☐u☐bimit☐s☐y korolevy, 1997: |b t.p. (Dzhin Pleĭdi)
952 __ |a RETRO
953 __ |a xx00 |b vl09

Press) or because it has elected to do so for its own reasons (for example, the change from State University of New York at Albany to University at Albany, State University of New York).

The principal complication in determining the proper form of corporate body names is that some bodies that issue publications are part of larger entities. This raises the problem of whether to enter such bodies under their own names or under the names of the parent bodies (called *subordinate* entry). The Association for Library Collections & Technical Services (ALCTS), the division of the American Library Association responsible for cataloging and classification, provides a good example of how the rules guide the decisions. Even though it is a division of a larger body, ALCTS's name does not imply that subordination and it is entered under its own name. Before 1990, however, ALCTS's name was Resources and Technical Services Division (RTSD). Because this former name implied subordination, RTSD was entered indirectly under the name of the larger association: *American Library Association. Resources and Technical Services Division.*

AACR2–2005 instructs catalogers to formulate corporate body names subordinately, under the name of a larger or parent body, for six types of names:

1. The name contains a term that implies it is part of another, such as *Division, Department*, and the like. The heading for RTSD, above, is an example.

2. The name contains a word normally associated with administrative subordination, such as *Committee, Commission*, and so on. For example:

    Association for Library Collections & Technical Services. Nominating Committee.

3. The name is general in nature, indicating only a geographic, chronological, numbered, or lettered subdivision, such as "Class of 2006." For example:

    Simmons College. Class of 2006.

4. The name does not convey the idea of a corporate body, such as "Public Relations." For example:

    Exxon-Mobil. Public Relations. (Note: This is a fictitious example)

5. The name is a university faculty, school, college, and so forth, such as "School of Information" (of the University of Michigan). For example:

    University of Michigan. School of Information.

6. The name includes the entire name of the parent body, such as "Harvard University Libraries." For example:

    Harvard University. Libraries.

Still more complicated are bodies that include many layers of hierarchy, such as the Committee on Cataloging: Description and Access (CC:DA), the committee concerned with descriptive cataloging rules. It is a committee of a section of a division of an association, as follows:

American Library Association (parent body)

Association for Library Collections & Technical Services (division)

Cataloging and Classification Section (section of the division)

Committee on Cataloging: Description and Access (committee of the section)

In the case of multiple layers, the body is entered under the name of the lowest unit of hierarchy that can stand alone, provided it is a unique identification. For CC:DA, the heading form would be under ALCTS, which is the lowest body that can stand alone, and the intervening section, Cataloging and Classification Section, would not be included because there is no other committee by the same name in any other section of ALCTS:

Association for Library Collections & Technical Services. Committee on Cataloging: Description and Access.

(Note that an ampersand is used in the name of the Association, but not in the name of the section or the committee.)

If, however, catalogers wished to establish that a heading is for the Nominating Committee of the Cataloging and Classification Section, it would differ from the one for CC:DA. The intervening section would have to be named, because ALCTS has a nominating committee, as does each of its sections:

> *Association for Library Collections & Technical Services. Cataloging and Classification Section. Nominating Committee.*

Two important rules of thumb to remember when formulating corporate body headings is that initial articles are omitted unless they are the filing element, and names that do not sound like corporate bodies may be given an explanatory qualifier. An example of both rules of thumb is the example:

> *Los Angeles Symphony (Orchestra).*

Although "Los" is an initial article, we file it as part of the geographic location known as "Los Angeles," and because "Los Angeles Symphony" does not sound like a typical corporate body, the qualifier "(Orchestra)" is added to clarify it.

Special rules in AACR2–2005, Chapter 24, cover heading forms for governments, government bodies, and government officials; religions, religious bodies, and religious officials; conferences and similar events; and so on. Whenever a corporate body name does not appear in the name authority files used by a library or media center, the rules in Chapter 24 should be consulted before trying to establish a heading for the body.

Forms of Geographic Names

Geographic names appear in catalogs as descriptive headings, generally as the first part of the name of a governmental body or official. The rules in AACR2–2005 for formulating geographic names are, perhaps, the simplest of all. Rule 23.2A1 states: "Use the English form of the name of a place if there is one in general use . . . ,"[5] but it adds that in case of doubt about the existence of an English form in general use, the form used by the people in that place (vernacular form) is preferred. Examples of this rule include using Sweden, not Sverige, and Florence, not Firenze. However, AACR2–2005 gives the example of Livorno, the vernacular form for that Italian city, which is preferred over Leghorn, the English-language form, explaining that Leghorn is no longer in general use.[6]

Two problems occur with geographic names: multiple names for one location and multiple locations that share one name. Although it is confusing for a place to be entered in the catalog in more than one way, this happens for a good reason: because the names of places as well as the places themselves change in response to changes in the political environment. Whereas for decades following World War II there were two separate nations known colloquially as East and West Germany, they were reunited into one nation generally known in English simply as "Germany." Headings for the former separate nations are Germany (Democratic Republic) and Germany (Federal Republic). Official changes to the names of cities and towns as well as entire countries occur all the time, and the catalog must represent the publications of each one under the heading appropriate to it.

The second problem, multiple locations that share the same name, is solved by adding elements to the basic name that create unique headings for each location. Two kinds of elements may be added, depending on the type of location. If it is smaller than a country, the name of the country is added; or, for localities in Australia, Canada, the United States, and several other countries, the name of a state, province, or part of the British Isles is added to it. Examples are Miami (Ohio) and Miami (Florida), or Bangor (Wales) and Bangor (Northern Ireland), and, of course, Bangor (Maine). If the places are countries, then dates or other terms may be added to indicate each one at a particular point in time or under a particular government, such as Vichy France during World War II, known as France (Territory under German occupation, 1940–1944).

One drawback to AACR2–2005's rules for geographic names is that they are biased toward English-language names, rather than using vernacular names for places that might be more recognizable in nations that do not speak English. However, given that this is an "Anglo-American" code, it is not surprising. Efforts to create a universal authority file must deal with these issues and have generally done so by creating parallel authorities in each of the relevant languages. Thus, an English-German authority file might use Germany for the English speakers and Deutschland for German speakers. Alternatively, the rules could agree to use one language for all places or use only vernacular names.

Forms of Titles

Titles Proper: Titles proper are entered the way they appear on the materials being cataloged and, with some exceptions, are traced. Computer indexing can be coded to ignore the initial articles and file on the first significant word, so a title such as *The Long Gray Line* files as if it were *Long Gray Line*. The Library of Congress once followed a policy of not making title proper headings if they included words such as "Fundamentals of the . . . ," "A History of the . . . ," or "An Introduction to the . . . ," because they were difficult to search successfully in card files. Computerized searching, both using title keywords and entering whole titles, has made such titles readily accessible. Most catalogers now make title proper headings routinely.

Uniform Titles: Uniform titles serve two quite different functions: (1) they bring together versions of one work that bear different titles proper; and (2) they differentiate two different works that bear the same title proper. Scores and recordings of classical music are a good example of the first function of uniform titles. They are released over and over by publishers in many countries because language is not a barrier to listening to or reading music, and publishers also design titles to differentiate one edition from another or to highlight well-known performers or particular features. Assigning one "uniform" title to all versions of the same piece of music enables them to be filed in the same place in the catalog (see Figure 5.8). Rules for uniform titles enable each version or edition to be identified appropriately. Title added entries are not usually made for uniform titles that begin with generic words, such as *Symphony*, *Concerto*, and the like.

Periodical titles, which often consist of one or a few similar words, are examples of the second function of uniform titles. Multiple organizations, associations, clubs, and other groups publish periodicals they call *Newsletter* or *Bulletin*. Adding a uniform title to their titles enables them to be differentiated and identified by library or media center patrons who wish to read one, but not the others (see Figure 5.9 on page 80). It is not unusual for a film to be remade starring a new cast of actors. Here, too, the differentiating uniform title helps to identify them.

Analytic Titles: When a material being cataloged contains a number of smaller works together in one volume, recording, or software package, catalogers can note the existence of these analytic titles in a contents note. Whenever a contents note is present in a catalog record, catalogers should ask whether tracing the titles of the parts is likely to be helpful to patrons. Policies on when to trace analytic titles and when to include them in the biblio-

FIGURE 5.8

This example is an illustration of:
- sound recording (compact disc)
- item without a collective title
- uniform title
- general material designation
- bibliographic forms of name different than those listed on item
- program date
- specific material designation has optional term in common use
- publisher's number given in optional placement as first note (in item cataloged as a unit)
- performer note
- accompanying materials listed in note area
- with note for item cataloged as separate units
- added entries for performers
- added entry for second piece on item with a uniform title (in item cataloged as a unit)
- 2nd level cataloging showing alternate methods of description

Item cataloged as one unit

Prokofiev, Sergey.
  [Concertos, violin, orchestra, no. 2, op. 63, G minor]
  Violin concerto no. 2 in G minor, op. 63 [sound recording] / Sergei Prokofiev. Violin concerto no. 2 in C sharp minor, op. 129 / Dmitri Shostakovich. -- Hamburg : Teldec Classics, p1997.
  1 compact disc (62 min., 18 sec.) : digital ; 4 3/4 in.

  Teldec: 0630-13150-2.
  Maxim Vengerov, violin; London Symphony Orchestra, Mstislav Rostropovich, conductor.
  Program notes in English, German, and French, by Christiane Kuhnt.

  I. Vengerov, Maksim. II. Rostropovich, Mstislav.
III. Shostakovich, Dmitrii Dmitrievich. Concertos, violin, orchestra, no. 2, op. 129, C# minor. IV. London Symphony Orchestra.

Item cataloged as separate units

Prokofiev, Sergey.
  [Concertos, violin, orchestra, no. 2, op. 63, G minor]
  Violin concerto no. 2 in G minor, op. 63 [sound recording] / Sergei Prokofiev. -- Hamburg : Teldec Classics, p1997.
  Part of 1 compact disc : digital ; 4 3/4 in.

  Maxim Vengerov, violin; London Symphony Orchestra, Mstislav Rostropovich, conductor.

Fig. 5.8—Continues

FIGURE 5.8 *(continued)*

Program notes in English, German, and French, by Christiane
Kuhnt.
  Teldec: 0630-13150-2.
  With: Concertos, violin, orchestra, no. 2, op. 129, C# minor, /
Dmitri Shostakovich.

  I. Vengerov, Maksim. II. Rostropovich, Mstislav. III. London
Symphony Orchestra.

Shostakovich, Dmitrii Dmitrievich.
  [Concertos, violin, orchestra, no. 2, op. 129, C# minor]
  Violin concerto no. 2 in C sharp minor, op. 129 [sound
recording] / Dmitri Shostakovich. -- Hamburg : Teldec Classics,
p1997.
  Part of 1 compact disc : digital ; 4 3/4 in.

  Maxim Vengerov, violin; London Symphony Orchestra, Mstislav
Rostropovich, conductor.
  Program notes in English, German, and French, by Christiane
Kuhnt.
  Teldec: 0630-13150-2.
  With: Concertos, violin, orchestra, no. 2, op. 63, G minor /
Sergei Prokofiev.

  I. Vengerov, Maksim. II. Rostropovich, Mstislav. III. London
Symphony Orchestra.

(chief source of information)

(information on CD)   *(information on jacket)*

FIGURE 5.9

This example is an illustration of:
- serial that has ceased publication
- electronic resource
- uniform title main entry for a title that has the same title as other serials
- general material designation
- numeric and/or alphabetic, chronological, or other designation area
- closed entry
- mode of access note
- frequency note
- source of title note
- publication, distribution, etc., note
- edition and history notes
- corporate body added entry
- variant title added entries
- ISSN
- 2nd level cataloging

Bulletin (National Library of Canada). English.
  Bulletin [electronic resource] / National Library of Canada. --
Vol. 27, no. 6 (June 1995)-vol. 36, no. 2 (Mar./Apr. 2004). --
Ottawa : National Library of Canada, 2002-2004.

  Mode .of access: World Wide Web,
www.collectionscanada.ca/bulletin/index-e.html.
  Bi-monthly.
  Title from contents page (viewed Jan. 1, 2007).
  Issues from 1995 to May 2000 have title: National Library News.
  Ceased publication.
  Also issued in print ed. previous to 2003.
  Also issued in French-language ed.
  ISSN 1492-4676.

  I. National Library of Canada. II. National Library of Canada
bulletin. III. National Library news.

*Authors' note: This publication was discontinued when the
National Library of Canada and the National Archives of Canada
were merged into the Library and Archives of Canada (LAC).
Therefore, LAC was not responsible for this publication. If a
library believes that the publication should also be accessed
through LAC, a note can be made that this publication is housed
on the LAC Web site and an added entry provided; or "see also"
references could be made from one to the other.*

*The sources of information for this figure can be found at the
URL given in the first note.*

graphic description but not trace them should be made and documented to guide local practice. Headings for analytic titles may be made as name-title headings, that is, headings that begin with the name of the creator (in authorized form) followed by the title proper of the work, as shown in Figure 5.10.

Series Titles: Series statements in bibliographic descriptions are recorded exactly as they appear on the material being cataloged, following rules almost identical to those for recording titles proper. However, the headings created for the series title headings do not have to be identical to the titles given in the description. Decisions about how to formulate series title headings depend on several factors, described in the following decision tree:

1. Is this title the first in the series?
   Yes: Establish the series heading exactly as it appears on the item.
   No: Go to step 2.

2. Search the catalog to see whether a heading for the series already appears there.
   Yes: Use the established heading for the access point, whether or not it matches the wording on the material.
   No: Go to step 3.

3. Search the *Name Authority File* to see whether a series title heading has been established for the series.
   Yes: Use the established heading, whether or not it matches the wording on the material.
   No: Establish the series title heading exactly as it appears on the material.

In 2006, the Library of Congress announced it would discontinue its practice of establishing new series headings, although other members of the Program for Cooperative Cataloging's Name Authority Cooperative (NACO) could continue to do so. Some groups in the North American cataloging community expressed opposition to the decision and asked LC to reconsider it, while other groups supported the policy change as a means of speeding up the cataloging process and saving money. Supporters believe that, because catalogs can be searched by word strings, the need for authority control for series titles may have dwindled in importance to the point where the benefits do not outweigh the cost.

Cross-References

AACR2–2005's Chapter 26 covers how cross-references are to be made. For personal names, rules cover how to formulate headings for three kinds of see references: different names for the same person, different forms of a name, and different entry elements. Examples of see references include "Dodgson, Charles Lutwidge, *see* Carroll, Lewis" (different names for the same person); "Intner, Sheila, *see* Intner, Sheila S." (different forms of a name); and "Mare, Walter de la, *see* De la Mare, Walter" (different entry elements). A see reference leads a searcher from unauthorized names and name forms to the authorized name form.

More rules for personal name cross-references discuss three important types: name-title references (headings that include a name plus a title); see also references; and explanatory references. Name-title references are useful for linking two records for which titles alone would not be sufficiently revealing; for example, an opera written by one composer based on a play by another author, as in "Verdi, Giuseppe, Otello, *see also* Shakespeare, William, 1564–1616. Othello." See also references link two related authorized headings; for example,

FIGURE 5.10

This example is an illustration of:
- videorecording
- collective title
- title main entry
- item emanating from a corporate body
- general material designation
- place of publication not stated but known
- probable publication date
- accompanying material
- cast note
- edition and history notes
- contents note
- personal name added entries
- corporate body added entry
- name/title added entries
- additional title added entries
- 2nd level cataloging

The casebook of Sherlock Holmes [videorecording] / Granada
   Television. -- [Orland Park, Ill.] : MPI Home Video, [2004?].
   3 videodiscs (ca. 6 hr., 30 min.) : sd., b&w ; 4 3/4 in. + 1
descriptive pamphlet.

   Cast: Jeremy Brett (Sherlock Holmes); Edward Hardwick (Dr.
Watson).
   Originally broadcast on television in 1991.
   Based on the novels by Sir Arthur Conan Doyle.
   Contents: disc 1. The disappearance of Lady Frances Carfax. The
problem of Thor bridge. Commentary track with director John
Madden -- disc 2. Shoscombe old place. The Boscombe Valley
mystery -- disc 3. The illustrious client. The creeping man.
Daytime live : an interview with Jeremy Brett and Edward
Hardwicke. Sherlock Museum short. Production notes.

   I. Brett, Jeremy. II. Hardwicke, Edward. III. Madden, John.
IV. Granada Television. V. Doyle, Arthur Conan, Sir. The
disappearance of Lady Frances Carfax. VI. Doyle, Arthur Conan,
Sir. The problem of Thor bridge. VII. Doyle, Arthur Conan, Sir.
Shoscombe old place. VIII. Doyle, Arthur Conan, Sir. The
Boscombe Valley mystery. IX. Doyle, Arthur Conan, Sir. The
illustrious client. X. Doyle, Arthur Conan, Sir. XI. Doyle,
Arthur Conan, Sir. The creeping man. XII. Title: The
disappearance of Lady Frances Carfax. XII. Title: The problem of
Thor bridge. XII. Title: Shoscombe old place. XIV. Title: The
Boscombe Valley mystery. XV. Title: The illustrious client.
XVI. Title: The creeping man.

Fig. 5.10—Continues

FIGURE 5.10 *(continued)*

(information on cover)

(information on CD)

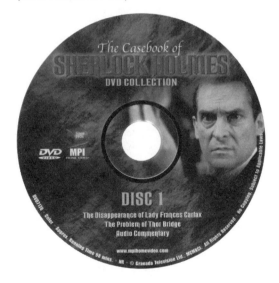

a searcher looking for Carolyn Heilbrun might also be interested in the works she wrote under her pseudonym, Amanda Cross. The see also heading is "Heilbrun, Carolyn, *see also* Cross, Amanda." A reciprocal heading is also made from Cross to Heilbrun. Explanatory references are exactly what their name implies: references that explain a particular name issue, such as the way in which the file for a series of rulers bearing the same name is organized. AACR2–2005's example is:

> Gustaf Adolf, King of Sweden
>   Kings of Sweden with this name are entered in a single sequence of all the kings of Sweden with the first name Gustaf, e.g.,
>
> Gustaf I Vasa, King of Sweden
>
> Gustaf II Adolf, King of Sweden (etc.)[7]

Rules for geographic name references and corporate body references are merged. They include links via see references to resolve the following problems:

- Differing name forms for the same place (for example, Venezia, *see* Venice)
- General and specific names of conferences
- Differences in name forms caused by languages, acronyms, spellings, and so on

See also and explanatory references are established for geographic and corporate body names exactly as they are made for personal names. See also references link two or more authorized heading forms for the same place or body; and explanatory references give guidance to searchers on the way headings are formulated, filed, and/or displayed.

Conclusion

Access is the process of selecting names and titles—the most important descriptive elements—to use as headings in the catalog, and formulating them consistently, so that searchers can find them expeditiously. Although it may not be necessary to select one heading for each title being cataloged as the main entry, AACR2–2005 still requires this be done. Chapter 21's rules for choosing main entry tend to favor persons over corporate body creators, and both of these over titles. All other headings for a single material, which may include additional creators, titles proper, and varying forms of title, are called added entries.

Three chapters of AACR2–2005—Chapters 22, 23, and 24—contain rules instructing catalogers how to formulate headings for personal names, geographic names, and corporate body names, respectively. When a title entry is made, it is understood to be the title proper of a material; however, some works are published many times with different titles proper. In that event, they require a constructed title called a uniform title to bring them together in the catalog. Rules for when and how to create uniform titles are in Chapter 25.

AACR2–2005's final chapter, Chapter 26, covers cross-references. Cross-references are established to lead searchers who use an unauthorized form of a name or title to the correct heading, to lead them to related headings in which they might also be interested, or to explain a matter complicating the way that a heading is displayed in the catalog. The guidance of explanatory references can save time and trouble, and, thus, these are worth including in order to make the catalog more user-friendly.

Readers may wish to try applying the practices described in Chapter 4 and this chapter by constructing bibliographic descriptions from typical sources. Figures 5.11 through 5.20, on this page and the following pages, show examples of the chief sources of information for a variety of materials that might be purchased by a typical public library or school library media center. Try cataloging them according to the first or second level of description, using the bibliographic level appropriate to your agency. (Note that AACR2–2005 requires edition statements to be given for both first and second level descriptions. However, in practice "1st ed." is not given in first level descriptions.) Completed descriptions are given in Appendix B.

FIGURE 5.11

(chief source of information)

(title page)

William Walton

CONCERTO

FOR VIOLA

AND ORCHESTRA

I Andante comodo

II Vivo, con molto preciso

III Allegro moderato

OXFORD UNIVERSITY PRESS

MUSIC DEPARTMENT · 37 DOVER STREET · LONDON W1X 4AH

Additional information:
on front cover: full score
on back cover: ISBN 0 19 36846 1 6
on first page of music: c1964
on internal contents: 23 min.

FIGURE 5.12

(chief source of information)

(title page)

THE QUESTING KNIGHTS OF THE FÆRIE QUEEN

Retold by

GERALDINE MCCAUGHREAN

FROM THE WORKS OF EDMUND SPENSER

Illustrated by JASON COCKCROFT

h
Hodder
Children's
Books

A division of Hodder Headline Limited

(information on verso)

THE QUESTING KNIGHTS OF THE FAERIE QUEEN
retold by Geraldine McCaughrean and illustrated by Jason Cockcroft
British Library Cataloguing in Publication Data
A catalogue record of this book is available from
the British Library.
ISBN 0340 86621 7 (HB)

Text copyright © Geraldine McCaughrean 2004
Illustration copyright © Jason Cockcroft 2004

The right of Geraldine McCaughrean to be identified as
the author and Jason Cockcroft as the illustrator of this Work
has been asserted by them in accordance with
the Copyright, Designs and Patents Act 1988.

First edition published 2004
10 9 8 7 6 5 4 3 2 1

Published by Hodder Children's Books
a division of Hodder Headline Limited
338 Euston Road London NW1 3BH

Printed in China
All rights reserved

Visit Geraldine's website at www.geraldinemccaughrean.co.uk

FIGURE 5.13

(information on cassette)

(information on liner)

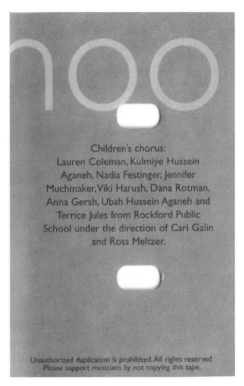

(information on liner)

FIGURE 5.14

(chief source of information)

(title page)

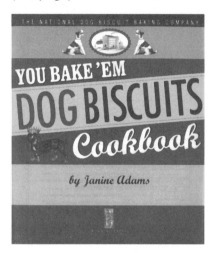

(information on verso)

© 2005 by Running Press
All rights reserved under the Pan-American and International Copyright Conventions

Printed in the United States

This book may not be reproduced in whole or in part, in any form or by any means, electronic or mechanical, including photocopying, recording, or by any information storage and retrieval system now known or hereafter invented, without written permission from the publisher.

9 8 7 6 5 4 3 2 1

Digit on the right indicates the number of this printing

Library of Congress Control Number: 2004116801

ISBN 0-7624-2336-6

Book design and collage illustrations by Corinda Cook
Edited by Sarah O'Brien and Diana von Glahn

Typography: Caslon, Clarendon, Script, Trade Gothic, Bodega, and Willow

This book may be ordered by mail from the publisher. Please include $2.50 for postage and handling.
But try your bookstore first!

Running Press Book Publishers
125 South Twenty-second Street
Philadelphia, Pennsylvania 19103-4399

Visit us on the web!
www.runningpress.com

FIGURE 5.15

(information on CD)

(information from verso of liner)

```
3 volume set -- 23 minutes each -- Grades K-4
Teacher's Guides Included and Available Online

ISBN 1 57225 904 3

DVD Features:
Spanish Language Track
Closed-captioned
```

FIGURE 5.16

(chief source of information)

(title page)

V. S. PRITCHETT

Mr. Beluncle

A Novel

(information on verso)

2005 Modern Library Paperback Edition

ISBN 0-8129-7379-8

This edition is published by arrangement with PFD on
behalf of the Estate of Dorothy Ridge Pritchett.

Modern Library website address:
www. modernlibrary.com

Printed in the United States of America

2 4 6 8 9 7 5 3 1

Introduction by Darin Strauss

THE MODERN LIBRARY

NEW YORK

FIGURE 5.17

(chief source of information)

(title page)

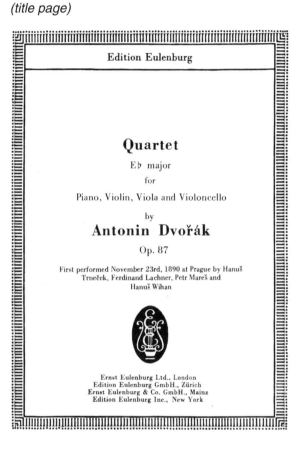

Edition Eulenburg

Quartet

Eb major

for

Piano, Violin, Viola and Violoncello

by

Antonín Dvořák

Op. 87

First performed November 23rd, 1890 at Prague by Hanuš
Trneček, Ferdinand Lachner, Petr Mareš and
Hanuš Wihan

Ernst Eulenburg Ltd., London
Edition Eulenburg GmbH., Zürich
Ernst Eulenburg & Co. GmbH., Mainz
Edition Eulenburg Inc., New York

FIGURE 5.18

(chief source of information)

(title page)

(information on verso)

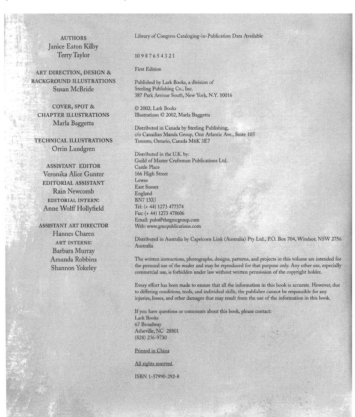

FIGURE 5.19

This item consists of twelve small colored penguins resting on pegs and a set of 42 cards in a plastic container. The lid of the container is the game board.

    Wording on the cardboard box that holds the container: "Cool Moves!" on four sides; "Made in China, Distributed by Discovery Toys, Inc., Livermore, CA."; "It's a way-cool strategy game that helps develop thinking and fine motor skills"; "from 8 years"

    Instruction cards have date c2000.

FIGURE 5.20

(chief source of information)

(title page)

(information from verso)

Native Americans

Arctic Peoples

Mir Tamim Ansary

Heinemann Library
Des Plaines, Illinois

© 2000 Reed Educational & Professional Publishing
Published by Heinemann Library,
an imprint of Reed Educational & Professional Publishing,
1350 East Touhy Avenue, Suite 240 West
Des Plaines, IL 60018

Library of Congress Cataloging-in-Publication Data
Ansary, Mir Tamim.
    Arctic peoples / Mir Tamim Ansary.
      p. cm. – (Native Americans)
    Includes bibliographical references and index.
    Summary: Describes various elements of the traditional life of Arctic people including their homes, clothing, games, crafts, and beliefs as well as changes brought about by the arrival of Europeans.
    ISBN 1-57572-920-2 (lib. bdg.)
      1. Eskimos Juvenile literature. 2. Inuit Juvenile literature. 3. Aleuts Juvenile literature. [1. Eskimos. 2. Inuit. 3. Aleuts.] I. Title. II. Series: Ansary, Mir Tamim. Native Americans.
E99.E7A68 1999
979.8'004971—dc21

99-17407
CIP

Recommended Reading

Anderson, James D., and José Pérez-Carballo. *Information Retrieval Design: Principles and Options for Information Description, Organization, Display, and Access in Information Retrieval Databases, Digital Libraries, Catalogs, and Indexes.* St. Petersburg, FL: Ometeca Institute, 2005.

Borgman, Christine L. *From Gutenberg to the Global Information Infrastructure: Access to Information in the Networked World.* Cambridge, MA: MIT Press, 2000.

Getty Thesaurus of Geographic Names. Los Angeles, CA: J. Paul Getty Trust, Vocabulary Program. Available at www.getty.edu/research/conducting_research/vocabularies/tgn/

Maxwell, Robert L. *Maxwell's Guide to Authority Work*, 2nd ed. Chicago: American Library Association, 2006.

"NACO Program for Cooperative Cataloging." Available at www.loc.gov/catdir/pcc?naco/naco.html (Viewed December 12, 2006).

Taylor, Arlene G., and Barbara B. Tillett, eds. *Authority Control in Organizing and Accessing Information: Definition and International Experience.* New York: Haworth Information Press, 2004.

Notes

1.   The assumption underlying the chapter numbers, which skip from 13, the last chapter in Part I, to 21, the first chapter in Part II, was that new chapters could be added to Part I to accommodate new media groups in description without requiring changes in the chapter numbers in Part II. Between 1978 and 2006, however, no new chapters were added.

2.   In the future, under the rules of RDA, this distinction will have greatly reduced emphasis.

3.   The six types are (1) an internal document of the corporate body, such as a library's catalog or an association's membership directory; (2) an administrative document of the corporate body, such as an annual report of a company; (3) a document representing the collective thought of the body, such as minutes of a meeting or a report of a committee; (4) a document representing the collective effort of a voyage, expedition, or conference; (5) a document that is a sound recording, film, or video and the responsible corporate body does more than perform it; (6) a cartographic document emanating from a corporate body that does more than publish it.

4.   AACR2–2005, pp. 22–3 and 24–3.

5.   AACR2–2005, p. 23–2.

6.   Ibid.

7.   AACR2–2005, p. 26–9.

6

Subject Authorities

Introduction

The three preceding chapters have explained descriptive cataloging, which identifies and describes items being cataloged, and enables them to be searched via the names of their creators and their titles. It is half the job of cataloging. Descriptive cataloging treats items as the books, videorecordings, electronic resources, or whatever material types they are. The rest of the job is identifying and describing their contents. In a process called *subject analysis*, catalogers determine what items are about; ascertain whether any special approaches to the topics covered, genres, or styles, need to be highlighted; and, then, give that information in the catalog records.

In library cataloging, contents are represented by subject headings and call numbers. Subject headings, also called subject authorities, subject descriptors, and index terms, are access points listed alphabetically in the catalog along with the descriptive headings. Call numbers, which are also given in catalog records, reflect subject matter because they are based on classification numbers, but they serve simultaneously as shelf addresses for arranging the materials within the library. For materials having physical existence, such as books and videorecordings, call numbers identify the locations where these items can be found. For materials lacking physical form, such as the resources in a digital library, call numbers provide subject-oriented virtual "locations" for individual items within a repository.

Subject-Related Standards

Unlike descriptive cataloging, for which AACR2 is the only standard set of rules, subject headings have several standard tools, and libraries can choose to adopt those best suited to their purposes. Three standard subject heading tools are discussed here, in general, and in the next two chapters in greater detail: keywords; *Sears List of Subject Headings* (Sears); and *Library of Congress Subject Headings* (LCSH). Two standard classification systems, which are also subject-oriented tools, albeit using symbols in place of verbal terms, *Dewey Decimal Classification* and *Library of Congress Classification*, are covered in Chapters 10 and 11.

Keywords: Subject keywords are words taken from titles, tables of contents, menus, and other subject-rich elements of items being cataloged. These elements contain the words of their authors. No one in the library community controls the words used; therefore, subject keywords are a kind of *uncontrolled* vocabulary. An advantage of keywords is that they employ authors' own terminology and, thus, enable searchers who recall it to retrieve the materials. Key Word In Context (KWIC) and Key Word Out of Context (KWOC) catalogs, once popular types of publication lists, use title keywords to create their lists (see Figure 6.1). Computerized library catalogs usually are programmed to search title keywords, which are automatically indexed. Despite the fact that they are not controlled, keywords enrich the catalog's subject vocabulary considerably.

Controlled Vocabularies: Sears and LCSH are lists of words and phrases that their compilers, the editors working for the H. W. Wilson Company and subject specialists at the Library of Congress, respectively, authorize for use as subject headings, along with other words and phrases designated as cross-references. Because these lists are limited to prese-lected groups of words and phrases, they are known as *controlled vocabularies.*

Sears and LCSH are not the sole controlled vocabularies available to subject catalogers. Others are published and maintained by recognized organizations, such as the Getty Art History Information Project's *Art & Architecture Thesaurus* or the (U.S.) National Library of Medicine's *Medical Subject Headings.* Some alternative controlled vocabularies are not distributed outside a local institution or are distributed informally to small numbers of librar-

FIGURE 6.1   KWIC and KWOC Lists

KWIC LIST

Multimedia materials: shelving for library	ACCESS	
Facts about	CANADA,	its provinces and territories
Civilization and	CAPITALISM	in the fifteenth century
	CIVILIZATION	and capitalism in the fifteenth century
Civilization and capitalism in the	FIFTEENTH CENTURY	
Multimedia materials: shelving for	LIBRARY	access
	MULTIMEDIA MATERIALS: shelving for access	
Facts about Canada, its	PROVINCES	and territories
Multimedia materials:	SHELVING	for access
Facts about Canada, its provinces and	TERRITORIES	

KWOC LIST

ACCESS,   Multimedia materials: shelving for
CANADA,   its provinces and territories, Facts about
CAPITALISM   in the fifteenth century, Civilization and
CIVILIZATION and capitalism in the fifteenth century
FIFTEENTH CENTURY, Civilization and capitalism in the
LIBRARY   access, Multimedia materials: shelving for
MULTIMEDIA MATERIALS: shelving for access
PROVINCES   and territories, Facts about Canada, its
TERRITORIES, Facts about Canada, its provinces and

ies that know about them and choose to use them, such as the subject heading list formerly sponsored by Hennepin County Library.[1]

Controlled vocabularies may either list authorized headings and cross-references without displaying the relationships among them fully, or be organized to show the relationships of each term to other terms in its subject hierarchy. Sears and LCSH are examples of the former type of controlled vocabulary; the *Art & Architecture Thesaurus* and *Medical Subject Headings* are examples of the latter.

Application Options: For most of the twentieth century, librarians believed a library had to choose one standard subject heading tool and follow it exclusively. In the latter part of the century, however, subject specialists realized that the use of multiple subject heading tools in a library's catalog could produce positive results for patrons, and began doing so.[2] However, adopting multiple subject heading tools requires catalogers to be alert to potential conflicts among the headings and to be ready to resolve any conflicts that arise.

Employing both keywords and controlled subject headings in a catalog maximizes the possibility that searchers can find desired materials on a subject. Computer programming designed to index significant words from titles and other parts of the catalog record containing content-related information (such as summary notes and contents notes) can index the keywords automatically, thus enabling them to be searched as if they were subject headings. Library catalogers still must supply the controlled subject headings, because automated indexing systems have not been able to achieve the same level of accuracy and specificity as human beings in doing so.

Principles of Subject Cataloging

1. *Summary-level indexing.* Subject cataloging provides summary-level access to the content of items being cataloged. Contrast this with back-of-the-book indexing, in which all identifiable concepts covered in an item are given. These differing types of indexing are at opposite ends of a continuum defining the bibliographic unit appropriate to consider for an index term. In library subject cataloging, the entire content is the bibliographic unit. Each of these units is likely to have between one and, perhaps, five or a few more than five subject headings assigned to it. In back-of-the-book indexing, mention in a sentence or a paragraph is enough to warrant assignment of an index term, although often the coverage of a topic is far longer than that. The total number of index terms assigned to an item may be in the hundreds, or even in the thousands, depending on the publisher's desired level of detail.

   Between these extremes, the periodical indexes and anthologies in book form seem to represent a middle ground. When individual articles in periodical issues, chapters in books, reviews, and pieces of similar length are the bibliographic units to be indexed, the number of index terms may be larger than mere mention of a concept, but smaller than the entire content of a book or a periodical run. The number of subject headings in a periodical index assigned to a periodical issue or an anthology in book form typically exceeds that for subject cataloging of either the issue or the book, but is smaller than a back-of-the-book-style index.

   At one time, when card catalogs were the rule and cards had to be filed by hand, minimizing the number of subject headings to cut down on the amount of filing work was a priority. A rule of thumb called the "Rule of Three" prevailed that mandated no more than three subject headings be assigned to a book. If a book covered four distinct subjects, a broader subject heading was to be assigned that included all of them. (Applying the Rule of Three still is recommended practice for users of *Sears List of Subject*

Headings.) Later, the Library of Congress expanded subject heading assignments to a new rule of thumb called the "20% Rule," which mandated a subject heading for a subject if it comprised at least 20 percent of a book's content. Currently, the 20% Rule has been relaxed and subject catalogers are encouraged to assign as many subject headings as they believe will prove useful to searchers. (An example of multiple subject headings is found in Figure 8.4 on page 141.)

2. *Identification and collocation.* Charles Cutter's objectives of the catalog, to show what the library has and to collocate related items, apply to subjects as well as to names, titles, and editions. The subject catalog aims to present to catalog users the contents of its collections as well as to bring together items that cover the same subjects. As described earlier in connection with descriptive cataloging, the objectives conflict, making it difficult to achieve ideal subject catalogs. However, when a catalog employs both keywords and controlled vocabularies, both are served. Keywords, which use authors' own language, facilitate showing what the library has to searchers using the same language as the works themselves. Controlled vocabularies, which gather all material on a subject by means of one authorized term no matter what language authors use, collocate works on the same subjects and facilitate searchers selecting what they want from among the displayed items.

3. *Elimination of synonyms.* Synonyms are not used simultaneously as headings in a catalog. One of the objectives of controlled vocabularies is the elimination of synonyms as subject headings, in order to promote the collocation feature of the catalog.

    When a term is chosen from among two or more synonymous terms to express a subject, the alternatives usually are added to the catalog as references, called "cross" references or "see" references, that lead the searcher from the unused term(s) to the one chosen to be used. In addition, other cross-references known as "see also" references lead searchers from one approved term to related approved terms in which they might also be interested. A debate has gone on for decades about the efficacy of including cross-references that lead to approved terms under which no actual materials are listed. Such references that lead to dead ends are called *blind references.* Librarians who support blind references claim the references teach searchers about the nature of the subject area and its terminology. Librarians who oppose it, which include the authors of this book, do so because these references frustrate and, often, anger searchers interested in finding usable material.

4. *Unambiguous terminology.* Words or phrases used as subject headings should have one clear and precise meaning. In the event this is not possible, additional definitions in the form of parenthetic qualifiers or scope notes are added to guide the interpretation of the terms. Ambiguous words or phrases are generally avoided for use as subject headings.

5. *Coextensive terminology.* Terms should be *coextensive* with the topics they represent. *Coextensive* means having an exact match in specificity. For example, if the topic to be represented is "trees," the subject heading chosen to represent it should be neither broader ("plants") nor narrower ("maple trees"), but exactly match the breadth of the topic ("trees").

6. *Overlapping meanings are avoided.* Subject headings should not overlap in meaning, but have discrete boundaries, especially at the same levels of specificity. For example, the topic "cakes" can be successfully subdivided into "frosted" and "unfrosted," because

these are discrete categories with no overlaps. All cake recipes can be assigned to one heading or the other, depending on whether they do or do not call for the cakes to be frosted. But if a third heading, "decorated" cakes, at the same level as "frosted" and "unfrosted" were allowed, its meaning would overlap with "frosted" cakes. By offering three possibilities with overlapping meanings (frosted, unfrosted, decorated), a cataloger would be hard pressed to decide how to assign headings for frosted cakes, which are decorated, and cakes sprinkled with powdered sugar or cocoa powder, which are unfrosted but decorated.

7. *Terminology is "user-friendly."* The vocabulary used for subject headings should aim to match that of the people who will use the headings in searching for material. In addition, words and phrases in common usage among the people who use the catalog should be preferred. David Judson Haykin, the well-known and highly respected head of LC's subject division in the mid-twentieth century, included these points among his five-point interpretation of Cutter's objects for subject headings and called them "the reader as focus" and "usage," respectively.[3] When a choice is made among multiple possibilities for a topic, the words or phrases not authorized as subject headings are usually made cross-references. This enhances the likelihood that searchers will get a response for the words they enter, even if it is merely a reference sending them to the authorized heading.

8. *Arrangement of subject headings.* Subject catalogs can be arranged in classified or alphabetical order. In the classified arrangement, headings are organized according to their places in subject hierarchies. Classification systems do this, substituting symbolic representations for the subject words and arranging the file in symbolic order. In the alphabetical arrangement, headings are organized by alphabetizing the words and phrases chosen to represent the subjects. Insofar as there is no need to figure out where each subject belongs within a subject schema, alphabetizing is the simpler way to arrange a subject file. Still, some problems of alphabetizing that must be resolved are discussed below.

Cutter suggested a third option that combines elements of both: the *alphabetico-classified catalog.* This type of subject catalog arranges the main classes in classified order, but uses alphabetical arrangements within the subdivisions. The differences in these arrangements are demonstrated below. Figure 6.2 on the next page shows the alphabetico-classified arrangement again with indentations that highlight the hierarchical relationships.

A word is in order here about the way subject headings are alphabetized. It sounds easy to do, but problems occur when headings include digits, initials, abbreviations, punctuation, and/or additional elements such as qualifiers and subdivisions. When card catalogs were the norm, a method of alphabetizing developed that treated digits and abbreviations as if they were the spelled out words. The abbreviation *Dr.* was filed as if it were the whole word *Doctor,* and digits such as *10* were filed as if they were the word *ten.* Another of these rules was to treat all forms of the prefix *Mc* in names as if they were spelled *Mac.* For example, McBride, Macfarland, McFarland, and Mackenzie would have filed as follows:

McBride, John
McFarland, Lawrence
Macfarland, Susan
Mackenzie, Patricia

Since the advent of computerized catalogs, however, two different methods of alphabetizing subject headings developed and are used for the subject cataloging tools de-

FIGURE 6.2

ALPHABETICO-CLASSIFIED CATALOG

```
HUMANITIES
  ART
  LITERATURE
  MUSIC
    RHYTHM
      DYNAMICS (MUSIC)
      TEMPO
NATURAL SCIENCES
  ASTRONOMY
    COMETS
    PLANETS
    STARS
  PHYSICS
    MECHANICS
    OPTICS
    THERMODYNAMICS
```

scribed in this book and the catalogs that employ them. The first, titled *ALA Filing Rules*, is sponsored by the American Library Association and used to arrange the headings in *Sears List of Subject Headings.*[4] The second, titled *Library of Congress Filing Rules*,[5] is sponsored by the Library of Congress and used to arrange headings in LCSH. Both sets of rules mandate treating digits as digits, preceding the alphabetic characters and arranged in numeric value order: 1.2, 11, 1031, 1334, and so on. Both sets of rules accept abbreviations "as is" and file them the way they appear; for example, Doctor, Donation, Dr., Duration. The principal difference between ALA and LC filing rules is the way they accommodate different kinds of punctuation and the way they handle subdivisions. The ALA rules ignore all punctuation, filing the entire string of words in a subject heading word by word regardless of the punctuation that separates them, including the long dashes that indicate subdivision. In contrast, the LC rules mandate recognizing punctuation within headings and filing headings with commas differently than headings with parentheses, and the like, and filing subdivisions of different types in order: chronological subdivisions first, topical subdivisions second, geographic subdivisions last. Figures 6.3 and 6.4 illustrate the differences.

The arrangement of index terms offers a choice in the way subject headings are displayed to searchers, but the principles described in points 1 through 8 above apply to the choice of terms used as subject headings and their assignment.

Using Controlled Vocabularies

The closest thing to a book of rules for subject headings (similar to AACR2 for description) is a manual giving guidelines for assigning subject headings. LC issues the most extensive guidelines, developed for its own subject catalogers, titled *Subject Cataloging Manual: Subject Headings*, available in multiple loose-leaf volumes or online, as part of *Cataloger's*

FIGURE 6.3

HEADINGS FILED USING ALA FILING RULES (1980)

Anti-Aircraft School (South Africa)
Antimalarials
Anti-Masonic Herald
Antiques for fun and profit
Anti-slavery International
The antislavery origins of British policy

Children, Adopted see Adopted children
Children as inventors
Children – Diseases
Children (International law)
The children of the North Sea
Children – Surgery

Desktop.[6] Application policies in the form of memoranda are issued as needed. From time to time (twice annually in 2005 and 2006), they are cumulated and issued as updated pages to be integrated into the rest of the manual. (This makes *Subject Cataloging Manual: Subject Headings* a good example of the integrating type of continuing resource.)

The American Library Association has also issued guidelines in selected areas. Its publications, although useful and designed with patron service in mind, do not carry the same weight as AACR2. Its recommendations, which are optional, are less likely to be adopted as universally as LC's policies on LCSH, because LCSH users feel bound to conform to what LC deems standard practice for its own catalogs. ALA's subject heading guidelines are generated by the Subject Analysis Committee, an arm of the Cataloging and Classification Section

FIGURE 6.4

HEADINGS FILED USING LC FILING RULES (1980)

Anti-Aircraft School (South Africa)
Anti-Masonic Herald
Anti-slavery International
Antimalarials
Antiques for fun and profit
The antislavery origins of British policy

Children – Diseases
Children – Surgery
Children, Adopted see Adopted children
Children (International law)
Children as inventors
The children of the North Sea

of the Association for Library Collections & Technical Services. An example is the Committee's *Guidelines on Subject Access to Individual Works of Fiction, Drama, Etc.,*[7] which LC encourages catalogers to apply, although it does not do so for the majority of its own cataloging.

Application of controlled vocabularies to a library catalog can be expected to produce positive results. In evaluating the performance of a catalog, the following criteria generally are applied.

1. *"Good" recall.* Recall refers to the number of hits a searcher gets, on average, for the subject headings he or she enters as search terms. When the subject vocabulary matches the searchers' own vocabularies and the amount of collocation achieved is "good," the number of total failures is minimized and the average number of responses is thought to be neither too large nor too small. (The terms *large* and *small* are imprecise, but the attempt to define them specifically for varied patron populations is difficult. Each searcher has a subjective idea of what an ideal number of responses is, and the numbers of responses are a function of the collections represented, not just the headings used. In answer to the authors' informal queries, students reply that averaging zero or one hit per heading is too small a response, and averaging more than fifty hits per heading is too large. Presumably, the ideal number of hits lies somewhere between these extremes.)

2. *Relevance.* It is never enough to retrieve materials; the materials must be relevant to the searcher's quest. It is an accepted rule that the larger the number of retrieved documents, the smaller the proportion that are relevant. Thus, searching with a subject heading that is broader than necessary will retrieve many irrelevant items. For example, if one were interested only in poodles, searching under the subject heading "Dogs" would retrieve many items having little or nothing to do with poodles. Either many would be too general, dealing with dogs of all breeds, or they might deal with breeds other than poodles. Substituting the subject heading "Poodles" would likely return fewer responses, but all could be expected to deal with that breed. If, however, one searched under "Poodles" and retrieved too little material, broadening the search by using "Dogs" could retrieve items that included poodles among other breeds covered.

3. *Precision.* Precision is the ability of the subject headings to specify exactly what the searcher wants. In the previous example, "Dogs" is not sufficiently precise if searchers want materials that deal with only one type of dog, such as "Retrievers."

    Precision varies with the specificity of terms as well as with the way terms are defined and applied. It is greatly affected by the presence of overlapping and ambiguous terms, as well as by the addition of subdivisions or other modifications. If searchers are interested solely in Indian rugs or Chinese cuisine, the terms "Rugs" and "Cookery," respectively, are not sufficiently precise. However, if the terms were defined further by adding geographic subdivisions (Rugs—India; Cookery—China), precision would improve. The modified terms might still not be perfectly precise, because all rugs in India may not be Indian in design, nor all cookery in China prepared in Chinese style. One can imagine a film about Chinese rugs in India meriting the heading "Rugs—India" or a book about Indian cookery in China being given the heading "Cookery—China." But, they are more precise than unmodified terms (or, perhaps, it is more accurate to say they are less imprecise!).

4. *Exhaustivity.* This quality refers to the depth or breadth of indexing that subject catalogers adopt. Generally, library cataloging aims for summary-level subject representation,

far less exhaustive than that of back-of-the-book indexing, which assigns subject head-ings to every idea that might be of interest to a reader. In recent years, subject cataloging for library catalogs has gone deeper, coming closer to what is done for periodicals—less exhaustive than back-of-the-book indexes but more exhaustive than library subject cata-logs.

5. *Easy to use.* A good subject catalog should be easy to use for three different groups of people: the library's public, library staff members who prepare the cataloging, and library staff who use the subject catalog as a reference tool. Satisfying all three groups with a single controlled vocabulary is not an easy task, but requires sensitivity to the needs of beginners while not "dumbing down" the terminology to the point where it is useless to more advanced searchers. Experts generally prefer more specialized and technical terms, which makes the use of multiple subject vocabularies a valid response.

6. *Easy to maintain.* In addition to ease of use, easy maintenance is important to the staff members charged with this responsibility. Maintenance problems occur when terminol-ogy in the subject tool changes frequently, requiring large amounts of updating and numerous changes to cross-references. Adding more or fewer cross-references than the subject tool specifies involves creating local lists of changes that, themselves, must be maintained. Adding new or different terms locally that do not appear in the subject tool also creates an ongoing maintenance problem that librarians and media specialists should undertake cautiously, and only if they can be certain that the potential benefits outweigh the work involved.

7. *Cost.* All work related to subject cataloging —such as buying or gaining access to the subject tools, assigning the subject headings, maintaining the subject catalog—takes the time and effort of library staff members. The total cost depends on how many person-hours it takes to do the work multiplied by the cost of the people who do it. However, saving money on subject cataloging by doing a cheaper job (less work or using lower-paid staff) may have poor results if the service provided by the catalog declines. In that event, the cost of reference assistance may rise if people need to ask for help more often, or searchers may give up and leave the library empty handed (or, if they are remote users, not request materials electronically) when searches fail to retrieve useful material. An acceptable balance between cost and service must be struck that maximizes the ser-vice provided by a level of subject cataloging that the library or media center can afford.

To sum up, these evaluative criteria indicate there is give-and-take in producing and using subject catalogs. One criterion cannot be used by itself to measure the worth of a catalog, and all must be put into a reasonable balance to achieve good service at bearable cost. There are no magic formulas to decide how deeply to index or how many cross-references to make. Glaring faults should be obvious to a concerned practitioner who is paying attention, and problems can be understood more clearly when considered in light of this list of features.

Subject Headings for Literary Works

Until the latter part of the twentieth century, North American subject cataloging practice was to omit subject headings for individual literary works, including novels, plays, poetry, and so forth. In part, the decision may have been philosophical, because works of imagina-tion, as they are called, are not "true" and, therefore, do not merit subject headings even when they treat real people, places, and events. In part, it may have been a practical way of cutting down the huge job of original subject cataloging for increasing numbers of new materials. In part, it may be attributable to the assumption that members of the public search literary works by author and/or title, and would be disappointed to retrieve a fictional work in response to a subject query. Whatever the reasons underlying the practice, it has changed in the last several decades.

The first to call for subject headings for fiction were children's librarians, who said, rightly, that children were likely to seek information from stories as well as from nonfiction materials. In the 1960s, LC responded by developing the Annotated Card Program, in which subject headings and summaries of the contents of a title were added to catalog records prepared by LC's staff for children's fiction. (See Chapter 8 for details.) Later, catalogers of adult materials began lobbying for subject headings for novels, films, and other kinds of literary materials. They also believed patrons accepted such materials in response to subject searches and, sometimes, they were the preferred form of "information." If a young patron wants to learn something about spiders, *Charlotte's Web* might be a good choice, especially if reading a difficult nonfiction book without pictures is the sole alternative. More mature readers can learn something about British colonial rule in India by reading Kipling; Dickens reveals much about social conditions in nineteenth-century England, even though they are works of fiction. At first, the "no subject headings for fiction" policy was modified to assign them to biographical and historical fiction. Later, the American Library Association's Subject Analysis Committee issued guidelines and terminology for assigning them more broadly.[8] Toward the end of the twentieth century, LC experimented with subject headings for adult fiction and found them useful, but time consuming to assign. LC recommended that catalogers outside LC assign them if they wished, but continued the policy of not doing so within LC. Figure 6.5 is an example of the use of fiction subject headings for adult fiction. There are many nonfiction books about autism and about those that suffer from the savant syndrome; the title of this novel does not indicate that it might be of interest to people concerned about these subjects.

FIGURE 6.5

```
This example is an illustration of:
    • place of publication unknown
    • publishing date not listed, copyright date given
    • Library of Congress fiction subject headings
    • Library and Archives Canada CIP
    • 2nd level cataloging
```

```
Haddon, Mark.
  The curious incident of the dog in the night-time / Mark
Haddon. -- [S.l.] : Doubleday Canada, c2002.
  226 p. : ill. ; 22 cm.

  ISBN 0-38565979-2.

  1. Autism -- Fiction.  2. Savants (Savant syndrome) -- Fiction.
3. England -- Fiction.  I. Title.
```

Fig. 6.5—Continues

FIGURE 6.5 *(continued)*

(chief source of information)

(title page)

THE CURIOUS INCIDENT OF THE DOG IN THE NIGHT-TIME

MARK HADDON

Doubleday Canada

(information on verso)

National Library of Canada Cataloguing in Publication

Haddon, Mark
        The curious incident of the dog in the night-time / Mark Haddon.

ISBN 0-385-65979-2

        1. Autism—Fiction. 2. Savants (Savant syndrome)—Fiction.
3. England—Fiction. I. Title.

PZ7.H1165Cu 2003a   823'.914   C2003-900425-2

This book is a work of fiction. Names, characters, businesses, organizations, places, events, and incidents either are the product of the author's imagination or are used fictitiously. Any resemblance to actual persons, living or dead, events, or locales is entirely coincidental.

Underground logos, fabric designs, and line diagrams are reproduced with the kind permission of Transport for London. Kuoni advertisement reproduced with the kind permission of Kuoni Travel Ltd. A-level maths question reproduced with the kind permission of Oxford Cambridge and RSA Examinations (OCR). Every effort has been made to trace other copyright holders, and the publishers will be happy to correct mistakes or omissions in future editions.

Book design by Maria Carella
Printed and bound in the USA

Published in Canada by
Doubleday Canada, a division of
Random House of Canada Limited
Visit Random House of Canada Limited's website: www.randomhouse.ca

10   9   8   7   6   5   4   3   2   1

Why Use a Subject Authority?

Librarians and media specialists working with very small collections may be tempted to dispense with standard subject tools and assignment practices. They may feel it is easier, simpler, and more patron friendly to make up their own subject headings, thereby avoiding the trouble of buying a subject heading authority containing numerous terms and cross-references they will never need. Why should they invest time and money in Sears or LCSH, and be bound by the policies of the people who prepare those lists? The following considerations offer compelling reasons why it makes sense to adopt standard subject authorities:

1. Patrons of very small libraries are very likely to use larger libraries at some point in their lives, and familiarity with standard practices equips them to use those libraries more knowledgeably.

2. If a local librarian does not have a published list of terms that controls the subject headings used in the catalog, he or she will have to spend time creating a list of the headings that are used, and keep it up-to-date as terms are added, dropped, or changed.

3. When local librarians make up their own subject headings, they cannot copy the ones assigned by libraries that use the standard tools or buy subject cataloging from vendors or cooperative cataloging centers that follow standard practices. The use of local headings means having to do original subject cataloging for every item purchased.

4. If the local librarian who has chosen to make up local subject headings retires or takes a job in a different library, it is difficult to ensure the same practices will continue, because the successor might not want to do it or might be unable to do so. The catalog will suffer as a result, and it will be more difficult for patrons to find what they need.

5. Small collections may grow large enough that a simple local list of headings does not provide the kind of intellectual access to the materials that patrons need. When the time comes to convert the whole catalog to a different, standardized subject heading system, the job will be far more costly and time consuming than if the standardized system was used from the beginning.

In conclusion, the use of a standard subject heading tool gives local catalogers many options. They can choose to share cataloging with other librarians and media specialists within their school district or local network, copy the assignments that appear in cataloging-in-publication, or buy their catalog records from a commercial source or a nonprofit center. In some libraries, all these options are exercised to expedite the job of providing patrons with access to the contents of their collections.

The next two chapters explore the use of the two most popular subject heading tools used in North American libraries and media centers: *Sears List of Subject Headings* and *Library of Congress Subject Headings*.

Recommended Reading

Broughton, Vanda. *Essential Thesaurus Construction.* London: Facet Publishing, 2006. [See chap. 3–7.]

Chan, Lois Mai, et al., eds. *Theory of Subject Analysis: A Sourcebook.* Littleton, CO: Libraries Unlimited, 1985.

Lancaster, F. Wilfrid. *Indexing and Abstracting in Theory and Practice.* Champaign, IL: University of Illinois, 2003.

Roe, Sandra K., ed. *The Audiovisual Cataloging Current.* New York: Haworth Information Press, 2001. [See pp. 189–295.]

Sauperl, Alenka. *Subject Determination during the Cataloging Process.* Lanham, MD: Scarecrow Press, 2002.

Scott, Mona L. *Conversion Tables: LC-Dewey; Dewey-LC; Subject Headings—LC and Dewey,* 3rd ed. Westport, CT: Libraries Unlimited, 2005.

Notes

1. Creation and maintenance of the Hennepin County Library (HCL) subject heading list was a project led by its former principal cataloger, Sanford Berman. New and changed headings were distributed via newsletter. On joining the OCLC bibliographic network, HCL's administration chose to conform to national standards, discontinuing its local list and the use of nonstandard headings in its catalog records.

2. See, for example, Carol A. Mandel, *Multiple Thesauri in Online Library Bibliographic Systems: A Report Prepared for Library of Congress Processing Services* (Washington, DC: Cataloging Distribution Service, Library of Congress, 1987); Marilyn J. Smith and Pauline Atherton Cochrane, "Creating Better Subject Access with Multiple Vocabularies: Upgrading the Subject Heading List for the Alzheimer's Association," *Library Resources & Technical Services* 43, no. 1 (January 1999): 53–58; and "Just MeSHing Around! MeSH and LCSH in Rowland Medical Library's Catalog," *Mississippi Libraries* 67, no. 4 (Winter 2003): 116–119.

3. David Judson Haykin, *Subject Headings: A Practical Guide* (Washington, DC: Government Printing Office, 1951), p. 7–9. Haykin's other points were "unity," "English vs. foreign terms," and "specificity." Unity refers to collocation; English-language terms were preferred with some exceptions; and specificity refers to coextensivity.

4. *ALA Filing Rules* (Chicago: American Library Association, 1980).

5. John C. Rather, *Library of Congress Filing Rules* (Washington, DC: Library of Congress, 1980).

6. At this writing, the current version of this tool is Library of Congress, Subject Cataloging Division, *Subject Cataloging Manual: Subject Headings,* 5th ed., 2004 cumulation (Washington, DC: Library of Congress, 1996–2004), plus updates issued in 2005 and 2006. *Cataloger's Desktop* is available by subscription from LC's Cataloging Distribution Service, http://desktop.loc.gov/.

7. Association for Library Collections & Technical Services, Subject Analysis Committee, *Guidelines on Subject Access to Individual Works of Fiction, Drama, Etc.,* 2nd ed. (Chicago: American Library Association, 2000).

8. The most recent publication of the guidelines is the edition cited above.

7

Sears List of Subject Headings

Introduction

The original title of *Sears List of Subject Headings* (Sears) gives broad hints about its origins: *List of Subject Headings for Small Libraries: Compiled from Lists Used in Nine Representative Small Libraries.* Minnie Earl Sears compiled it in the early 1920s as an alternative to the then-current subject heading lists of the American Library Association and the Library of Congress. Sears was first published in 1923 by H. W. Wilson, which continues to manage and publish it today.[1] Ms. Sears's subject heading project was also part of the work she did as a student in Melvil Dewey's School of Library Service at Columbia University.

Ms. Sears edited two editions after the first, enhancing the original format by adding "*See also*" references (the first edition had only "*See*" and "Refer from" references) and a user manual, titled "Practical Suggestions for the Beginner in Subject Heading Work." Isabel Stevenson Monro succeeded Ms. Sears as editor of the next two editions. Dewey Decimal Classification numbers from H. W. Wilson's reference tool *Standard Catalog for Public Libraries* appeared in these editions and the original subtitle was dropped. In the 1950s, Bertha M. Frick succeeded Ms. Monro as editor of the next three editions, and the title was changed to its current wording. Barbara M. Westby became editor of the ninth edition, in 1965, and continued through the twelfth. Under her leadership, the user manual was renamed "Principles of the Sears List of Subject Headings."

Many changes took place in the 1980s as computers were introduced into both libraries and the publishing industry. With the thirteenth edition, Carmen Rovira and Caroline Reyes succeeded Ms. Westby as co-editors and, in the fourteenth, they were succeeded by Martha T. Mooney. H. W. Wilson began computerizing the production process and introduced simplifications to accommodate new online catalogs; for example, limiting the number of compound headings and subdivisions, and reversing inverted headings to their natural language forms (that is, headings such as "Catalogs, Library" changed to "Library catalogs"). During this period Sears incorporated a selection of Library of Congress Annotated Card (AC) subject headings into its list and, when LCSH AC and adult headings conflicted, chose to include only one of them.

Joseph Miller succeeded Ms. Mooney as editor of the fifteenth edition in 1994 and leads the editorial team at this writing. Over the years, Sears has been responsive to changes in subject heading theory, standards, and practice. Although it has increased in size from edition to edition, it continues to provide fewer, broader headings than *Library of Congress Subject Headings* (LCSH), and uses current terminology and orthography.

Principles of the Sears List

Included in the opening pages of Sears is a section titled "Principles of the Sears List of Subject Headings." In reality, this section does much more than explain the principles on which Sears is based, developing a theoretical context for subject access in general and explaining different approaches to subject representation. The section also describes the basis for Sears heading development, from which the following principles can be derived.

FIGURE 7.1

```
This example is an illustration of:
    • picture
    • general material designation
    • two statements of subsidiary responsibility
    • publishing date not listed, copyright date given
    • accompanying materials given in note area
    • intended audience note
    • editor added entry with optional designation of function
    • illustrator added entry with optional designation of
      function
    • title added entry
    • Library of Congress and Sears subject heading the same
    • 2nd level cataloging
```

```
Moore, Jo Ellen.
  The human body [picture] / author Jo Ellen Moore ; editor
Marilyn Evans ; illustraror Jo Larsen. -- Monterey, CA : Evan-
Moore, c1998.
  24 pictures : col. ; 22 x 28 cm.

  Teacher information on cover verso.
  Intended audience: Grades K-3.
  ISBN 1-55799-692-X.

  1. Human body.  I. Evans, Marilyn, ed.  II. Larsen, Jo, ill.
III. Title.
```

Authors' note: Contradictory audience levels on item (K-2; Gr 1-3) have been amalgamated.

Fig. 7.1—Continues

FIGURE 7.1 *(continued)*

(information on cover)   *(information on verso)*

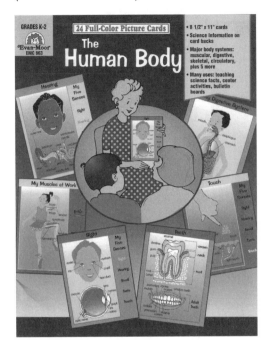

1. *Adoption of the LCSH model.* From its inception, Ms. Sears recognized the value of maintaining a uniform structure between LCSH and her list, making it possible for catalogers to coordinate terms from both lists. If a small library grew beyond the size for which Sears headings provided effective access, it could "graduate" to LCSH without much trouble. It was also attractive to librarians familiar with LCSH, who could apply it without having to learn a new structure. Adopting this model also means Sears is not a true thesaurus, which aims to reflect subject hierarchies as well as provide an authorized vocabulary. Instead, Sears is solely a subject heading list, like LCSH.

There are headings in Sears that are the same as those in LCSH (see Figure 7.1) and some that differ considerably (see Figure 7.2).

2. *Precoordination.* Like LCSH, subdivided subject headings are given in Sears in their authorized forms. This means they are *precoordinated*, or put together in advance for the cataloger. The one exception to this rule is the small number of headings that have specific instructions to use the term also as a subdivision. Otherwise, authorized subject headings may be used as main headings and nothing more. Catalogers are not permitted to take two main subject headings and put them together in heading-subheading combinations.

FIGURE 7.2

```
This example is an illustration of:
    • digital sound disc
    • general material designation
    • phonogram date
    • performer note
    • quoted note
    • summary
    • comparison of Library of Congress subject headings and
      Sears subject headings
    • fiction subject headings
    • title added entry
    • 2nd level cataloging


Coville, Bruce.
  Juliet Dove, queen of love [sound recording] / Bruce Coville.
-- Syracuse, N.Y. : Full Cast Audio, p2004.
  4 sound discs (4 hr., 30 min.) : digital, stereo. ; 4¾ in.

  Read by Bruce Colville and the Full Cast Family.
  "A magic shop book."
  Summary: A shy twelve-year-old girl must solve a puzzle
involving characters from Greek mythology to free herself from a
spell which makes her irresistible to boys.
  ISBN 1-932076-50-6.


The tracing with Library of Congress subject headings

  1. Magic -- Juvenile literature.  2. Bashfulness -- Juvenile
fiction.  3. Mythology, Greek -- Juvenile fiction.  I. Title.


The tracing with Sears subject headings

  1. Magic -- Fiction.  2. Shyness -- Fiction.  3. Greek
mythology -- Fiction.  I. Title.
```

Fig. 7.2—Continues

FIGURE 7.2 *(continued)*

(information on liner)

3. *Literary warrant.* This principle states that subject headings are created after material exists that requires their use. Headings that might be needed in the future are not established before the materials appear. The material (or literature) justifies (or warrants) the creation of the subject heading; ergo, *literary warrant* prompts the establishment of headings.

4. *Specific and direct entry.* Sears states: "According to that rule [i.e., for specific and direct entry] a work is entered in the catalog directly under the most specific subject heading that accurately represents its content. This term should be neither broader nor narrower but coextensive in scope with the subject of the work cataloged."[2] In theory, this means a video about training poodles but not other dog breeds would be given the subject heading "Poodles—Training," not **Dogs—Training**.[3] In small libraries that own very few items about training dogs, however, this might be undesirable. Sears gives catalogers two options. "Poodles" is not a subject heading, but an instruction at **Dogs** allows the cataloger to establish the names of specific breeds if they are needed. Thus, catalogers using Sears have the choice of using **Dogs—Training** for all the relevant materials or establishing "Poodles—Training" as a separate heading for some of them, depending on how much material needs to be categorized. If the library had dozens of videos depicting the training of specific breeds of dogs as well as several more covering multiple breeds,

establishing the narrower heading (and, by extension, all the subdivisions authorized for **Dogs** as well) would be more desirable than putting everything under one heading.

In addition to these basic principles, Sears exhibits the following preferences.

1. *Preference for current usage and orthography.* Over the years, Sears has been quick to adopt current terminology for concepts and alter spellings to conform to current practice. For example, Sears used **Motion pictures** instead of "Moving pictures" and updated the spelling of headings for airplanes from "Aer . . ." to "Air . . ." long before LCSH did so. Sears has also stopped hyphenating words such as *audiovisual*, which LCSH continues to hyphenate. Perhaps this is due to the close contact it maintains with librarians in the field through its advisory group as well as the customer service approach typical of a commercial organization.

2. *Preference for simple terminology.* An important difference between Sears and LCSH vocabularies is that Sears employs terminology that tends to be broad in meaning, non-technical, and understandable to nonspecialists. Sears often has one term for a topical area while LCSH uses more than one, distinguishing finer differences within the area. For example, Sears uses **Aquatic animals**, while LCSH uses "Aquatic animals," "Aquatic mammals," "Aquatic insects," "Aquatic invertebrates," "Aquatic organisms," "Aquatic pests," and "Aquatic warblers." Another example: Sears uses **Cooking**, while LCSH uses "Cookery" and has many more headings beginning with the word "*Cookery.*" A third example: Sears uses **Conferences**, while LCSH uses four different terms for this concept: "Clergy conferences," "Congresses and conventions," "Forums (Discussion and debate)," and "Meetings."

3. *Openness to the addition by local librarians of new headings.* Sears encourages the addition of needed headings by catalogers by providing a list of resources to which they can turn for terms[4] as well as instructions at selected terms within the list to add narrower terms at will. In early editions of Sears, only half of each page was printed. The rest of the page was left blank so catalogers could use the space to write notes about specific headings or, when a needed heading was not available in Sears, record the addition of a term from LCSH or another source. Catalogers still add terms to Sears today, even though print covers the entire page and local authority control must be supplied in other ways.

4. *Minimal subdivision.* At the beginning of the volume, Sears provides a list of about 500 topical subdivisions used within the list, which it states is "every subdivision for which there is a specific provision in the Sears List."[5] Although many more geographical and chronological subdivisions are included in Sears as well, the difference in the level of subdivision use between Sears and LCSH is both clear and logical. A collection indexed using Sears, being very small, is unlikely to need or want many subdivisions to express the contents of its materials. If many narrowly defined headings were used, individual headings could apply to so few items that very little collocation would occur and searching by subject under such a system would retrieve only one or two items. While the relevance might be high in whatever hits the searcher obtained, the recall would be exceptionally limited and unsatisfying.

Format of the List

Sears headings are listed in one volume totaling just over 800 pages. The volume begins with a user guide and other information about subject cataloging in general as well as guidelines on how to apply Sears headings to specific subject areas, which is especially helpful for librarians new to subject cataloging. The headings are arranged alphabetically[6] and appear in two columns per page. Approximately 15,000 to 16,000 terms appear in Sears, although all of them are not authorized for use. A good many of the terms listed are similar in meaning to authorized headings and are intended to be used solely as cross-references to those authorized headings.

Authorized headings in Sears are always printed in boldface type wherever they appear. Roman print is used for cross-references that are not authorized for use. It is easy to distinguish between authorized terms and unauthorized cross-references because of this practice. Subdivided headings that are authorized for use, such as **Plants—Collection and preservation**, appear entirely in boldface type. Individual subdivisions, such as "In literature," authorized solely as subdivisions, are also given entries in Sears, but are listed in Roman print. A few terms are authorized as both main headings and subdivisions; for example, the word "Collectibles." A "see also" (SA) instruction provides the authorization to use **—Collectibles** as a subdivision.[7] As already mentioned, an alphabetical list of topical subdivisions appears in the prefatory material, making it easy to see whether a particular word or phrase is authorized as a subdivision. If it is, one looks the phrase up in the main heading list to obtain instructions on its use.

The list of canceled and replacement headings in the eighteenth edition[8] is very short, consisting of only thirteen terms. Seven of the terms express the change from "—Description" to "—Description and travel" as a subdivision for place names. Two reflect a change from "Computer software" to "Computer programs" when the phrase is used as a modifier or a subdivision; nevertheless, **Computer software** remains the authorized main heading. A second list of revisions titled "Revisions of Specifically Canadian Interest" is also included, giving fourteen changes to subdivisions for various locations in Canada, mostly in Newfoundland.

Entries for authorized subject headings (see Figure 7.3) begin with the heading itself, in bold print, followed by the instruction that the heading may be subdivided geographically, if appropriate, and a Dewey number from the fourteenth abridged edition.[9] In the next paragraph, an instruction about using the heading appears, if one is given, and in subsequent paragraphs, cross-references appear in the following order: Use For (UF), See Also (SA), Broader Term (BT), Narrower Term (NT), and Related Term (RT). Subdivided headings follow, with the entry for each authorized subdivided heading following the same pattern. When one of the elements listed above is not applicable to a particular heading—for example, a heading has no instructions about its application or no Broader Term cross-references—that element is omitted. In some instances, more than one Dewey number might be applicable to materials given a particular subject heading and two headings appear, as in the example in Figure 7.3. Classifiers are alerted to the fact that 342 is used when the emphasis is on civil service legislation, 351 when the emphasis is on public administration, and 352.6 when the emphasis is on personnel administration.

All potential authorized headings are not given in Sears; instead, as has already been mentioned in connection with dog training, catalogers are instructed at some headings to add more specific terms if they need them. They need not wait for Sears to establish the more specific terms and, indeed, Sears will not do so, leaving it up to individual catalogers to make and implement these decisions locally. This puts an added responsibility on the individ-

FIGURE 7.3

(information on Sears List of Subject Headings, page 147)

Civil government
　USE　**Political science**
Civil law suits
　USE　**Litigation**
Civil liberty
　USE　**Freedom**
Civil procedure (May subdiv. geog.)
　　347
　　BT　**Courts**
　　NT　**Probate law and practice**
　　RT　**Litigation**
Civil rights (May subdiv. geog.)　**323;**
　　342
　　Use for materials on citizens' rights as established by law or protected by a constitution. Materials on the rights of persons regardless of their legal, socioeconomic, or cultural status and as recognized by the international community are entered under **Human rights.**
　　UF　Basic rights
　　　　Constitutional rights
　　　　Fundamental rights
　　SA　ethnic groups and classes of persons with the subdivision *Civil rights* [to be added as needed]
　　BT　**Constitutional law**
　　　　Human rights
　　　　Political science
　　NT　**African Americans—Civil rights**
　　　　Anti-apartheid movement
　　　　Blacks—Civil rights
　　　　Children—Civil rights
　　　　Due process of law
　　　　Employee rights
　　　　Fair trial
　　　　Freedom of assembly
　　　　Freedom of association
　　　　Freedom of information
　　　　Freedom of movement
　　　　Freedom of religion
　　　　Freedom of speech
　　　　Freedom of the press
　　　　Right of privacy
　　　　Right of property
　　　　Women's rights
　　RT　**Civil rights demonstrations**
　　　　Discrimination
　　　　Freedom

Civil rights demonstrations (May subdiv. geog.)　**322.4**
　　UF　Demonstrations for civil rights
　　　　Freedom marches for civil rights
　　　　Marches for civil rights
　　　　Sit-ins for civil rights
　　BT　**Demonstrations**
　　RT　**Civil rights**
Civil rights (International law)
　USE　**Human rights**
Civil servants
　USE　**Civil service**
Civil service (May subdiv. geog.)　**342;**
　　351; 352.6
　　Use for general materials on career government service and the laws governing it. Materials on civil service employees are entered under the name of the country, state, city, corporate body, or government agency with the subdivision *Officials and employees.*
　　UF　Administration
　　　　Civil servants
　　　　Employees and officials
　　　　Government employees
　　　　Government service
　　　　Officials and employees
　　　　Tenure of office
　　SA　names of countries, states, cities, etc., and corporate bodies with the subdivision *Officials and employees,* e.g. **United States—Officials and employees; Ohio—Officials and employees; Chicago (Ill.)—Officials and employees; United Nations—Officials and employees;** etc. [to be added as needed]
　　BT　**Administrative law**
　　　　Political science
　　　　Public administration
　　NT　**Municipal officials and employees**
　　RT　**Bureaucracy**
　　　　Public officers
Civil service—Examinations　**351.076**
　　BT　**Examinations**
Civil service—United States　**351.73**
　　UF　United States—Civil service
　　RT　**United States—Officials and employees**

147

ual cataloger to keep track of the headings he or she has established locally and to manage them appropriately. For example, if materials about avian flu, a deadly new strain of influenza, are purchased for a library's collection and the cataloger establishes "Avian flu" for the local catalog following the instruction to do so at **Diseases**, this should be recorded in a local authority file. Then, should the time come when the last item under that heading is weeded, the local heading is deleted from both the catalog and the local authority file.

In addition to instructions at selected entries to add terms for specific diseases, dog breeds, flowers, and so on, which appear within the list, Sears names fifteen kinds of headings to be added by the cataloger as needed, including common things such as foods, sports, plants and animals, chemicals and minerals, enterprises and industries, diseases, organs and regions of the body, languages, ethnic groups and nationalities, wars and battles, and the names of people, places, corporate bodies, and uniform titles.[10] Moreover, authorized subdivisions for seven types of subject headings are given under just one example of each type that serves as a template or key heading. In the prefatory material, Sears gives a general instruction to use these as models for all other headings of the same types.[11] The seven key headings are authors (**Shakespeare, William, 1564–1616**); ethnic groups (**Native Americans**); languages (**English language**); literature (**English literature**); places (**United States**, **Ohio**, **Chicago (Ill.)**); public figures (**Presidents—United States**); and wars (**World War, 1939–1945**).

Types of Headings

Sears subject headings tend to have simple syntax. Many are single nouns such as **Abbreviations** and **Riddles**. Charles Cutter believed single unambiguous nouns were ideal subject headings. Some one-word headings are verbs; for example, **Cycling** and **Dating**. These represent activities rather than things. A good many subject headings are two-word phrases, always given in direct order, such as **Reading readiness** and **Foreign investments**. These are usually modified nouns, but they can be modified verbs, such as **Data processing** and **Collective bargaining**. Years ago, selected phrase headings were inverted to bring the more significant word (that is, the word being modified) to the filing position, but this practice was dropped and all such existing combinations returned to direct or natural order. This change is a benefit of OPAC (Online Public Access Catalog) searching, which makes it possible to search any word in a multiword subject heading as a keyword, not just the first word in the string as was the case with card catalogs. As a result, the order of the words no longer matters.

Less often, a modified noun or verb will consist of three or more words, such as **Creole folk songs** or **Machine readable bibliographic data**. Some multiword headings consist of two nouns, a noun and a verb, or two verbs connected by *and*, such as **Manners and customs**, **Boats and boating**, and **Gliding and soaring**, respectively. A few multiword headings are really just lists of related terms; for example, **Comic books, strips, etc.** A good many multiword headings consist of two concepts connected by a preposition, such as **Theory of knowledge**, **Violence in mass media**, **Life on other planets**, **Grandparents as parents**, **Cooking for the sick**, and the like.

Some subject heading words and phrases might be misinterpreted without more explanation. In many instances, parenthetic qualifiers are added to provide the clarification. Examples are **Depression (Psychology)**, **Democratic Party (U.S.)**, and **Utilities (Computer software)**. The qualifier is part of the subject heading and is filed as if no punctuation separated the words. The previous examples would file as if they were "Depression Psychology," "Democratic Party U.S.," and "Utilities Computer Software." Sometimes qualifiers are not added to provide the explanation; instead, scope notes do the job. An example of this practice is the note under **Human capital**, which states: "Use for materials on investments of capital in training and educating employees to improve their productivity. Materials on the strength of a country in terms of available personnel . . . are entered under **Manpower**."[12] Instructions state explicitly what materials should be given the subject heading and, sometimes, what materials should not be given the heading and what to do with them.

Name headings used as subjects include all the qualifiers, dates, and other extensions that appear in the authority records, for example, **Eliot, T. S. (Thomas Stearns), 1888–1965** and **Chicago (Ill.)**. Catalogers are expected to obtain name authorities from a source other than Sears, such as their bibliographic network's authority file or the Library of Congress online catalog.

Cross-References

The six types of cross-references listed in Sears—USE, UF, BT, NT, RT, and SA—are explained in this section. Some references are reciprocal; that is, if a cataloger makes one of a reciprocal pair, he or she must also make the other. The first, the USE reference, leads someone from an unauthorized term to the authorized heading. For example, the unauthorized phrase "Western States" is followed by a USE reference that says, "USE **West (U.S.)**." The value of USE references is obvious. The second type of cross-reference is the reciprocal of the USE heading and is known as a "Use For" reference, abbreviated UF. An example is the UF reference at **West (U.S.)** that tells the cataloger to use this term in place of "Western States." Every USE reference generates a reciprocal UF reference under the authorized heading. The point in listing unauthorized terms with their USE references is to prompt catalogers to add these words and references to the catalog at the time the authorized terms are established, because searchers are likely to use them in seeking materials. If the references are made, anyone searching the unauthorized terms gets the message to look instead under the authorized terms; if not, he or she gets no answer, no reason for it, and no assistance about what to do next.

Two types of cross-references, Broader Term (BT) and Narrower Term (NT) references, indicate subject relationships at different levels of specificity. As with USE and UF references, BT references always generate NT reciprocals in Sears and vice versa. These references mean exactly what they say: BTs listed under a subject heading will give headings at the next broader level of subject specificity, whereas NTs listed under a subject heading will give headings at the next narrower level. Entire subject hierarchies are not shown in Sears, but BTs and NTs reveal three levels at once. For example, the subject heading **Offenses against property** lists **Crime** as one of its BTs and **Theft** as one of its NTs, showing the subject hierarchy as follows: **Crime** (broadest level); **Offenses against property** (next-narrower level); **Theft** (narrowest level).[13] If one wanted to see whether there were terms even broader than **Crime** or narrower than **Theft**, one could turn to them to see whether they have their own BTs and NTs. Doing so reveals that **Crime** has a BT for **Social problems** whereas **Theft** has several NTs, including **Bank robberies**. **Bank robberies** has no NTs, so one can conclude it is the narrowest level of its hierarchy, but **Social problems** has two BTs: **Social conditions** and **Sociology**. Following both, one discovers that **Sociology** is the top of the hierarchy, because it is listed as a BT of **Social conditions**. The entire subject hierarchy would be:

> **Sociology**
>> **Social conditions**
>> **Social problems**

Crime

Theft

Bank robberies

When no BTs appear under a heading, one can assume it is the broadest level in the subject hierarchy; when no NTs appear, one can assume it is the narrowest. Standard practice has long been that catalogers should make all associated NTs as "see also" references in the catalog when a subject heading is established, but none of the BTs. The rationale for this practice assumes a person searching a term is aware of the broader levels of the subject area, but not necessarily of the more specific levels. BTs are listed merely for educational purposes, to help a cataloger looking for possible subject headings or a library patron seeking potential search terms find something broader than the term he or she is examining.

RT (Related Term) references also indicate subject relationships, but at more or less equivalent levels of specificity. RTs always generate RT reciprocals with the terms they reference. Sometimes, RTs are similar to one another in meaning and other times they are opposites. For example, the RTs **Freedom of speech** and **Freedom of information** mean similar things; whereas the RTs **Free trade** and **Protectionism** have opposite but related meanings. One can assume that a searcher interested in material found using one heading of either of these pairs might be interested in material found using its RT. Subject cataloging practice is to make all RT references as "see also" references.

The final type of cross-reference is the See Also (SA) reference. SAs are references to groups of headings, not individual headings. SA instructions may tell catalogers to establish new headings of a certain kind, to use the heading word or phrase in a particular pattern, or to use it as a subdivision under selected types of main headings. For example, the SA on page 490 in Sears does all of these: first suggesting the option of using more specific types of motion pictures in place of the generic term; then suggesting using the term in several patterns, that is, "Motion pictures and [group of persons], "Motion pictures in [industries or fields of endeavor], [Subjects and groups of people] in motion pictures, and/or [Groups of persons] in the motion picture industry"; and, finally, suggesting establishing new headings for the names of individual motion pictures.

Cross-references expand the vocabulary of the subject catalog and make it possible for searchers to find materials even when they are unaware of the authorized subject headings being used. This contributes to the user-friendliness of the catalog and adds desirable flexibility without losing the gathering function of a controlled vocabulary. Cross-references enable the catalog to add new terminology without requiring immediate changes in established headings. This capability allows time to see whether new terminology does, indeed, completely replace the old, which would warrant a change in the authorized heading, or if the new terminology is, itself, replaced by something else.

Subdivisions

Subdivided headings are present in Sears, although not to the extent they are found in LCSH. As mentioned earlier in the chapter, subdivided terms authorized for use appear in the list in boldface type, whereas subdivided terms unauthorized for use but appropriate as cross-references are listed in roman print. Because Sears uses the ALA rules for alphabetizing, subdivided terms cannot always be expected to follow the term they modify immediately. When several multiword terms intervene, a quick scan might lead one to think subdivisions are absent. For example, **Animals—Training** is two pages beyond **Animals**, and eight different multiword headings intervene along with numerous other subdivided headings starting with the word "Animals." It is always best to do a careful search beyond a term until all variations on that term are examined before coming to the conclusion that a desired subdivision is not available.

Other practices enable subject catalogers to create their own subdivided headings. The first and most obvious method is to follow the parenthetic instruction at the heading in question to subdivide it geographically. Sears's prefatory explanation of geographic subdivision includes advice to catalogers in small libraries to use geographic subdivision solely to distinguish materials that deal with foreign countries, because most of their materials probably focus on the home country.[14] Catalogers are also invited to add geographic subdivisions they desire even if the instruction to do so is not given in the list, as well as to add, if needed, subdivided headings in addition to geographically focused headings authorized by Sears; for example, establishing "Art—France" as well as **French art** or "Italian art—Great Britain" as well as **Italian art**.[15] This flexibility enables a small library holding large numbers of art materials to treat them more specifically than the average Sears user might do. Catalogers are instructed to add place names smaller than a country (or, for the United States and Canada, smaller than a state or province) directly, without putting the country name first. Though this is a simpler method of adding place names, it scatters materials having geographic, but not alphabetic, relationships. Figure 7.4 shows two identical lists of hypothetical subject headings, one subdivided according to Sears instruction to do so directly, the other subdivided indirectly.

Other instructions given at selected headings may authorize the headings to be used as subdivisions with other terms, to be subdivided in a particular manner, or to apply appropriate key headings to them or headings like them. In each instance, this permits additional subdivi-

FIGURE 7.4

DIRECT AND INDIRECT GEOGRAPHIC SUBDIVISION

SUBDIVIDED DIRECTLY	SUBDIVIDED INDIRECTLY
Economics—Canada	Economics—Canada
Economics—Chicago	Economics—Canada—Manitoba
Economics—Denver	Economics—Germany
Economics—Germany	Economics—Japan—Tokyo
Economics—Manitoba	Economics—United States—Colorado—Denver
Economics—New York (State)	Economics—United States—Illinois—Chicago
Economics—Tokyo	Economics—United States—New York (State)
Economics—Wisconsin	Economics—United States—Ohio—Youngstown (Ohio)
Economics—Youngstown (Ohio)	Economics—United States—Wisconsin

sion to be done even though the combinations may not appear in the list. The following examples illustrate these possibilities:

- At **Indexes**, the SA reference says: "SA subjects with the subdivision *Indexes*, e.g. **Newspapers—Indexes** . . . [to be added as needed]."[16]
- At "Homes," which is a cross-reference, the scope note says: "USE **Houses** and ethnic groups, classes of persons, and names . . . with the subdivision *Homes*, e.g. **English authors—Homes**."[17]
- At **Shakespeare, William, 1564–1616**, the scope note says: "When applicable, the subdivisions provided with this heading may be used for other voluminous authors, e.g. **Dante**; **Goethe**; etc."[18]

Yet another method of subdividing is to follow instructions at a term authorized solely as a subdivision to use it with a main heading of the kind the cataloger wishes to subdivide. The example of "In literature" is explained elsewhere in this chapter.

Subdivisions enable catalogers to make broad headings more specific and, as a result, better able to meet the ideal of assigning headings coextensive with the subject matter being represented. They are also useful in dividing a long list of entries into smaller groupings. Both of these elements improve the relevance of materials retrieved by searchers. However, because the libraries using Sears tend to have small collections, subdivision is unlikely to play the major role it does with large collections. Subdivision narrows topics and causes fewer works to collocate under individual headings; therefore, it tends to be appropriate mainly for topics that are collected heavily, such as United States or Canadian history, but not for most other topics.

Applying Sears

In general, the rules for applying Sears are as follows:

1. Determine the subject(s) of the item being cataloged by examining its subject-rich elements (title, table of contents or menu, preface, summary, index), considering these from a user's viewpoint.
2. Write the subject(s) down in your own words.
3. Match each subject listed with the headings in the Sears list, assigning the heading authorized for use that most closely represents it.
4. Assign up to three subject headings per item. If an item covers more than three subjects, assign a broader heading that includes them. If a video covers the cultivation of lemons, bananas, and avocados, assign three headings: **Lemons**; **Bananas**; **Avocados**. If it covers the cultivation of lemons, bananas, avocados, and olives, assign **Fruit culture**.

In addition, consider the following in selecting subject headings:

1. Choose the most specific heading available, not a broader heading.
2. Give the most specific heading available directly, not as a subdivision of a broader heading.

3. Consider items already in the collection relating to the subject of the item being cataloged and try to collocate it with existing holdings on the same subject.

4. Treat items first by topic, then by geographical focus or by form, unless Sears's scope notes instruct doing otherwise.

5. Be "format-blind" in subject cataloging. Treat materials other than books in the same way books are treated.

6. Consult Sears's prefatory pages[19] for specific subject cataloging treatment of biographies, nationalities, literature, and wars and events.

Sears Canadian Companion

As mentioned previously, Sears 18 provides a one-page list of "Revisions of Specifically Canadian Interest"[20] that were found in the sixth edition of *Sears List of Subject Headings: Canadian Companion* (CC6).[21] This page has been added because a new edition of the *Canadian Companion* had not been planned when Sears 18 was published. Lynne Lighthall, the companion's editor, believed that there was not enough new material to warrant publication.

Libraries with significant collections of Canadian materials should continue to use CC6 as well as Sears 18 because some of the subject headings in Sears 18 have a U.S. orientation not suited to Canadian materials. Sears 18 uses the term **Native Americans--Canada** with a USE reference from "First Nations," the term Canadian Indians have chosen for their name. Those libraries that wish to be politically correct should assign **Native Americans--Canada** only to works that deal with both the First Nations and Inuit peoples and assign the subject heading **First Nations** and the qualifier **First Nations people**, for example, **Haida (First Nations people),** to works that used to be listed under the discarded heading "Indians of North America--Canada."

Examples of other differences that reflect Canadian usage are **French-speaking Canadians** (CC6) rather than "French Canadians" (Sears 18) and **Quebec (Province)--Separatist movements** (CC6) rather than "Quebec (Province)--History--Autonomy and independence movements" (Sears 18). Sears 18 reflects the cross-border difference in attitude toward the War of 1812, which each side claims that it won. The Sears 18's UF and BT references ignore Canada's role in the war despite the fact that there were battles on Canadian soil. Libraries with collections of Canadian materials should establish Canadian-oriented UFs and BTs. A different Dewey number (971.03) should be assigned in Canadian libraries and to those works about the War of 1812 written from a Canadian perspective rather than the one in Sears 18 that applies to U.S. history (973.5).

Why Use Sears?

The simplest and most direct answer to the question, "Why use Sears?" is that using its authorized vocabulary brings together a desirable number of materials under individual subject headings—on average, enough "hits" to satisfy users most of the time without overwhelming or disappointing them. Experiments using a larger list such as LCSH could be expected to result in retrieving too few titles and disappointing searchers most of the time. Experiments using fewer, more generic terms such as those used in bookstores, could be expected to result in retrieving an overwhelmingly large number of titles, many of which are not relevant to the searcher's needs. In addition, Sears's terminology is simpler and less sophisticated than LCSH's, which enables young searchers and novice searchers in a subject area, regardless of age, to understand them better.

Some small public libraries and school library media centers adopt Sears because peer libraries, media centers, consortia, or school districts use it and they wish to conform. This is a valid reason to choose Sears. It is easier to use the same tools as one's peers because one can rely on them for assistance and expertise as well as sharing the burden of original subject cataloging. A library or media center might choose Sears if it buys catalog records from a supplier that provides it or that charges more for choosing a different subject authority. This is a good choice so long as the library collection does not grow beyond the size for which Sears is appropriate.

Some catalogers use Sears because it is a simpler tool to learn to understand and use than LCSH. Because both the subject heading list and the manual are contained in one volume, the library does not need to buy auxiliary tools to do original subject cataloging. Sears also furnishes guidance for assigning Dewey classification numbers, which can be of great help for classifying materials in unfamiliar subject areas. Although the Dewey numbers in Sears are taken from the abridged edition (and should never be assigned without first examining the classification directly), they point to appropriate schedules to examine in the full edition as well.

These advantages notwithstanding, there are reasons why some small public libraries and school library media centers prefer to use LCSH. These reasons are explored and explained in more detail in the next chapter.

Conclusion

The process of assigning Sears subject headings to materials requires care and thought, but is relatively uncomplicated. As a cataloger works with the list and becomes familiar with its terminology and style, the task of assigning headings becomes faster and easier. Try assigning subject headings to the exercises in Figure 7.5. Although the exercises are for hypothetical materials, they have been created to represent types of materials common to small general collections. Answers may be found in Appendix B on page 247.

FIGURE 7.5

1. TITLE: *Wee places in the bens and glens*

    SUMMARY: A list of bed and breakfast accommodations in Scotland

2. TITLE: *What's with this weather?*

    SUMMARY: A discussion about rain, hail, sleet, and snow

3. TITLE: *Religion's impact on society*

    SUMMARY: A book about how religion affects social conditions

4. TITLE: *Lacrosse: a national sport*

    SUMMARY: A DVD about lacrosse

5. TITLE: *The effectiveness of bilingual education*

    SUMMARY: Parents, teachers, politicians, and students explore major issues in bilingual education

6. TITLE: *Doing business in China*

    SUMMARY: A CD containing basic Chinese words, phrases, and sentences that might be useful for an English-speaking businessman in China

7. TITLE: *The rebellion that became a revolution*

    SUMMARY: A history of the American Revolution

8. TITLE: *The California homeowner's directory*

    SUMMARY: A directory of retailers in California arranged by cities and towns

9. TITLE: The *Toronto yellow pages*

    SUMMARY: The Toronto telephone directory

10. TITLE: *We can do better for the homeless*

    SUMMARY: A proposal to a municipal government written by a community group about providing the homeless with opportunities to develop marketable manual skills and improvements in mental health

Recommended Reading

American Library Association. Subject Analysis Committee. *Guidelines on Subject Access to Individual Works of Fiction, Drama, Etc.*, 2nd ed. Chicago: American Library Association, 2000.

Fountain, Joanna F. *Subject Headings for School and Public Libraries: An LCSH/Sears Companion*, 2nd ed. Westport, CT: Libraries Unlimited, 2005.

Hoffman, Herbert H. *Small Library Cataloging*, 3rd ed. Lanham, MD: Scarecrow Press, 2002.

Intner, Sheila S., et al., eds. *Cataloging Correctly for Kids: An Introduction to the Tools*, 4th ed. Chicago: American Library Association, 2006.

Roe, Sandra K. "Subject Access Vocabularies in a Multi-type Library Consortium." *Cataloging & Classification Quarterly* 33, no. 2 (2001): 55–67.

Simpson, Carol. "Just When You Thought It Was Safe to Catalog. . . ." *Library Media Connection* 23, no. 1 (August/September 2004): 42–43.

Weihs, Jean. "Musings on an Unscientific Survey of *Sears* Use." *Technicalities* 24, no. 3 (May/June 2004): 5–7.

Notes

1. "Preface," *Sears List of Subject Headings*, 18th ed., ed. Joseph Miller (Bronx, NY: H. W. Wilson, 2004), p. vii. This and other factual information in this section are drawn largely from this source.

2. *Sears List of Subject Headings*, p. xvii.

3. Authorized subject headings from the list, such as **Dogs—Training**, are given in bold print throughout this chapter. Hypothetical or unauthorized subject headings are given in quotation marks.

4. *Sears List of Subject Headings*, p. xxxiv.

5. *Sears List of Subject Headings*, p. xlv.

6. Alphabetization in Sears follows the rules of the *ALA Filing Rules* (Chicago: American Library Association, 1980). In a nutshell, this means heading words are filed exactly as they appear (for example, Dr. is filed as "D," "r," period, not as "Doctor"), word by word, and punctuation is ignored.

7. *Sears List of Subject Headings*, p. 156.

8. *Sears List of Subject Headings*, p. xlii.

9. *Abridged Dewey Decimal Classification and Relative Index*, 14th ed. (Dublin, OH: OCLC Forest Press, 2004).

10. *Sears List of Subject Headings*, p. xl.

11. *Sears List of Subject Headings*, p. xli.

12. *Sears List of Subject Headings*, p. 365.

13. *Sears List of Subject Headings*, p. 528.

14. *Sears List of Subject Headings*, pp. xxii–xxiii.

15. Ibid.

16. *Sears List of Subject Headings*, p. 376.

17. *Sears List of Subject Headings*, p. 358.

18. *Sears List of Subject Headings*, p. 665.

19. *Sears List of Subject Headings*, pp. xxv–xxxii.

20. *Sears List of Subject Headings*, p. xliii.

21. *Sears List of Subject Headings: Canadian Companion*, 6th ed., ed. Lynne Lighthall (Bronx, NY: H. W. Wilson, 2001).

8

Library of Congress Subject Headings

Introduction

Library of Congress Subject Headings (LCSH)[1] was first published in 1909 under the title *Subject Headings Used in the Dictionary Catalogues of the Library of Congress*. Originally it was based on a list of subject headings compiled and issued by the American Library Association (ALA) called *The List of Subject Headings for Use in Dictionary Catalogs*. Before the initial publication of its own list of subject terms, LC's subject catalogers worked with the ALA list as they cataloged books for the LC's collections, adopting many headings exactly as they appeared, modifying others, and creating new headings when they did not find the terms they needed. This resulted in a pragmatic compilation of subject headings derived from the contents of the books in LC's collection.

The first edition of LCSH was issued in parts over a period of five years. Supplements continued updating this edition for another five years. A second edition was published in 1919. For the next half century, new editions appeared approximately once a decade, cumulating all the changes (additions, deletions, and modifications) that had taken place since the previous edition. The eighth edition (1975) was the first to bear the current title, *Library of Congress Subject Headings*. In 1988, following LCSH's conversion to a computerized database, new editions of the printed book version began appearing annually. Although initially LCSH might have been thought of as a monograph given irregular updates by its publisher, today it is a continuing resource, identified by the ISSN 1048-9711. (In contrast, the latest edition of *Sears List of Subject Headings* is a monograph, identified by the ISBN 0-8242-1040-9.)

LCSH is used in many places throughout the world, stating on LC's website it "is the only subject headings list accepted as the world wide standard."[2] Its wide appeal is attributable to four factors: (1) that LC collects many more books in nearly all subjects than other general libraries and is likely to provide all or nearly all the terms other libraries need; (2) that LC does a fine job of maintaining and distributing the ever-growing list of authorized subject headings and cross-references; (3) that its quality as a search tool is consistent and reliable; and (4) that although the cost of using LCSH has risen in recent years, it is not an expensive tool given all the work it entails—work that libraries choosing to adopt it need not do for themselves.

Principles of LCSH

1. *A practical list, not a thesaurus.* From its inception, LCSH has been a practical compilation of authorized terms and cross-references used to describe the contents of LC's books, not an attempt to provide a universal thesaurus following the rules such an undertaking would require. Like Sears, LCSH does not display the full hierarchy of subject areas from the broadest terms to the narrowest. Moreover, LC's catalog does not update earlier records containing an authorized heading when that heading is changed or deleted, or when another related term is added. During more than a century of growth and development, headings have been created according to the theories and ideas of many catalogers and heads of subject cataloging. Some preferred one mode of syntax (such as inverted adjectives) whereas some preferred other forms (such as direct word order), and no attempt has been made to ensure complete consistency throughout the list.

2. *Precoordination.* Like Sears, subdivided subject headings are given in LCSH in their authorized forms. This means they are *precoordinated*, or put together in advance for the cataloger. Authorized subject headings are main headings and, if LC catalogers deem it necessary, have authorized subdivisions added to them. Sometimes subdivisions have their own authorized subdivisions as well, and these will appear in the list following the subdivision to which they apply. Catalogers cannot take two main subject headings and put them together in heading-subheading combinations.

3. *Literary warrant.* On its "American Memory" website, LC states: "New subject headings are created when catalogers feel there is a sufficient mass of material to need increased specificity and not before there is a physical item in hand to catalog."[3] Thus, subject headings are created *after* material exists that requires their use. Headings that might be needed in the future are not established before the materials appear. The material (or literature) justifies (or warrants) the creation of the subject heading; ergo *literary warrant* prompts the establishment of headings.

4. *Specific and direct entry.* David Judson Haykin and Richard S. Angell, two of LC's cataloging heads from 1941 to 1952 and 1952 to 1966, respectively, did much to interpret and explain the principles of LCSH. They opted to follow Cutter's directive to assign subject headings to books that exactly represented their contents. They avoided assigning terms that were broader than the subject (such as "Dogs" for a book about poodles), or narrower than the subject (such as "Toy poodles," "Miniature poodles," and "Standard poodles" for a book about all types of poodles) as well as subordinating specific headings under broader ones (such as "Dogs—Poodles"). Cataloging theorists refer to subject headings that exactly match the scope and depth of subject matter being represented as being *coextensive* with the subjects; and Cutter, Haykin, and Angell all subscribed to the principle of coextensivity. Combining coextensivity with the principle of direct entry results in gathering fewer items under each heading than if the opposite principles were observed. This is appropriate when dealing with large collections for which distinguishing subject matter that is not exactly alike is more desirable than gathering as much material as possible under each heading.

5. *Preference for stability.* Whereas Sears is quick to adopt current terminology for concepts and alter spellings to conform to current preferences, LCSH is more likely to opt for stability in both areas. In the precomputer world of card catalogs, changing subject headings was a difficult and time-consuming job, requiring that individual changes be made to each and every card bearing a revised heading. If a changed term were part of many headings (such as "Moving pictures," "Animals in moving pictures," "Children in moving pictures," "Lawyers in moving pictures," etc.), the task multiplied exponentially. In addition, librarians had to face the problem of integrating the changes into the catalogs of thousands of individual libraries. The "American Memory" website states:

> When searching for older materials, especially before 1975, be aware that current subject terms may not have been used. *When a new term is created, it is not always added to the records of all previously cataloged titles.* To use the online catalog effectively, you must also search those terms marked "Former heading" in the *Library of Congress Subject Headings* as well as by call numbers and keywords.[4] (emphasis added)

Even in the current automated environment in which it is theoretically possible to change all occurrences of a term with one set of keystrokes, the practical facts on the ground are somewhat more complicated and it is rarely that easy. This may be why, in the earlier manual environment, LC seemed to drag its feet when catalogers lobbied for changes, such as those from "Aeroplanes" to **Airplanes** or "Moving pictures" to **Motion pictures**.

6. *Preference for accurate, formal terminology.* Cutter's rules dictate choosing terminology for subject headings most likely to be used by searchers. But, who is a searcher? LC's interpretation of the catalog user, if seen as a point along a continuum stretching from total novice to complete expert, seems to fall closer to expert than novice, and for good reason. A century ago, most people searching LC's catalogs were LC's own librarians, congressional researchers, or other scholars. The likelihood of searchers being young, in the early stages of their education, or unspecialized information seekers was slim. It made sense for LC to select as subject headings the most precise, accurate, unambiguous terms used by scholars, not popular buzzwords or catchphrases used by the general public.

   Since LC's catalog became available on the World Wide Web, however, the range of searchers has broadened considerably, and the image of whom the subject catalog serves has changed. Still, every effort is made to choose terms that are accurate, precise, and unambiguous, which often turn out to be formal or technical terms rather than popular terms, although terminology in common use is considered and may be used if it is appropriate.

7. *Supervision over the inclusion of new headings.* Unlike Sears, which recommends that local catalogers add subject headings as they need them, users of LCSH in local libraries are expected to make do with the headings that appear in the list and not add their own. Local librarians are, however, encouraged to send proposals to LC to add new headings to the list when they believe they have encountered enough literature that uses the terms to warrant their addition to LCSH.[5] When proposals for new headings are received and considered at LC by its Cataloging Policy and Support Office, they may be accepted, rejected, or sent back to their authors for more documentation.

Format of the List

LCSH is published in print and electronic forms. The printed version, issued annually, consists of five oversized volumes bound with distinctive red covers. Access to the electronic version, part of *Classification Web*, which is updated continuously and has considerably more functionality than simple listing, is available by subscription from LC's Cataloging Distribution Service. A list of subject authorities is also available free of charge on the World Wide Web at http://authorities.loc.gov/. This last version includes name, name-title, and series titles as well as topical subject authority records.

Authorized headings in LCSH are printed in boldface type where they appear in the main list. When they are given under other headings as cross-references, however, they appear in roman print. Roman print also is used for main headings and cross-references that are not authorized for use. Authorized subdivisions appear under the main headings they modify in boldface type, for example —**Georgia (Republic)** appears under the main heading **Art metal-work, Medieval**. A few terms are authorized as both main headings and subdivisions; for example, the word "Catalogs." A "see also" (SA) instruction under the main heading **Catalogs** (given in boldface type) authorizes using Catalogs (printed in roman type) as a subdivision under names of individual artists, craftspersons, persons doing business as sellers under their personal names, and corporate bodies, and under individual objects.[6]

For the first time in the twenty-sixth edition, the list of more than 3,200 (since raised to 3,900) *free-floating subdivisions* was incorporated into volume 1 of the printed edition of LCSH.[7] Formerly, this list of terms had to be purchased as a separate publication. It is also available online. The twenty-sixth edition stated in the "Introduction of Free-Floating Subdivisions" that this is "the first list of the subdivisions to appear with notes regarding their usage since the list of 'Most Commonly Used Subdivisions' was published in the 8th edition of *Library of Congress Subject Headings* 1975." The name *free-floating* suggests that catalogers may use the terms whenever they see fit to modify any authorized headings, but this is not so. Each free-floating subdivision has rules for its use; for example, under —**Missing in action**, LCSH instructs, "Further subdivide by subdivisions used under classes of persons," and "Use as a topical subdivision under individual wars."[8]

In addition to the list of subject headings and cross-references (whose total number is approaching 300,000) and free-floating subdivisions, the first volume of the printed edition of LCSH gives a brief history of the list; explains the components of the entries, the categories of headings that are included in the list and omitted from the list; and covers the special set of subject headings authorized for use with children's materials, explained in more detail later in this chapter.

The free online listing of LCSH headings is searchable directly by a topical word, name, or title, and retrieves the term itself along with a menu that includes the encoded authority record, the scope notes, and the cross-references. In contrast, searching topical terms through the subscription service *Classification Web* allows the searcher to see the information in thesaurus format, which facilitates the three levels of hierarchy to be viewed clearly, and enables the heading to be seen in bibliographic records via hyperlinks. Both Dewey Decimal and Library of Congress Classification numbers can be viewed in records to which a particular heading has been assigned, which goes far beyond the provision of Library of Congress Classification numbers for about 35 percent of LCSH records in the printed list. (Dewey Decimal Classification numbers are not given in the printed list.)[9]

Form of Entries: In the printed edition of LCSH, entries appear three columns to a page, printed in small type on thin paper. Entries for authorized subject headings (see Figure 8.1) begin with the heading itself, in bold print, followed by the instruction that the heading may be subdivided geographically if that applies, and, for a little more than one-third of the

FIGURE 8.1   (Note: Two columns are shown here and in figures 8.2 and 8.3 because showing three columns results in print too small to read easily.)

Shark cartilage
Xiphoid process
—**Diseases**   *(May Subd Geog)*
  NT   Dysostosis
      Osteogenesis imperfecta
—**Tumors**   *(May Subd Geog)*
  NT   Enchondroma
      Osteochondroma
Cartilage cells
  UF   Chondrocytes
  BT   Cells
  RT   Bone cells
Cartilage development
  USE   Chondrogenesis
Cartilage lichens
  USE   Ramalina
Cartilaginous fisheries
  USE   Elasmobranch fisheries
Cartilaginous fishes
  USE   Chondrichthyes
Cartilaginous ossification
  USE   Endochondral ossification
Cartilago epiphysialis
  USE   Growth plate
Cartland family   *(Not Subd Geog)*
Cartledge family   *(Not Subd Geog)*
Cartmall family
  USE   Cartmel family
Cartmel family   *(Not Subd Geog)*
  UF   Cartmall family
      Cartmell family
      Cartmill family
Cartmell family
  USE   Cartmel family
Cartmen
  USE   Carters
Cartmill family
  USE   Cartmel family
Cartographers   *(May Subd Geog)*
  [GA197.5-GA198]
  UF   Mapmakers
  BT   Earth scientists
  NT   Artists as cartographers
      Women cartographers
Cartographic historians   *(May Subd Geog)*
  [GA197.5-GA198]
  UF   Map historians
  BT   Historians
Cartographic materials   *(May Subd Geog)*
  BT   Nonbook materials
  NT   Cataloging of cartographic materials
      Globes
      Maps
      Remote-sensing images
Cartography   *(May Subd Geog)*
  [GA101-GA1776]
  Here are entered works on the general science of mapmaking, including map projection and the mapping of large areas. Works on the mapping of small areas and the drawing of maps in elementary schools are entered under Map drawing.
  UF   Cartography, Primitive
      [Former heading]
      Chartography
      Map-making
      Mapmaking
      Mapping (Cartography)
  BT   Maps
      Mathematical geography
      Surveying
  RT   Map projection
      Maps
  SA   *subdivision* Cartography *under individual wars, e.g.* World War, 1939-1945—Cartography
  NT   Agricultural mapping
      Avalanche mapping
      Aztec cartography
      Cave mapping
      Color in cartography
      Contours (Cartography)

Digital mapping
Environmental mapping
Eskimo cartography
Geological mapping
Geomorphological mapping
Grids (Cartography)
Indian cartography
Map printing
Map scales
Maps—Reproduction
Maps, Military
Military topography
Mountain mapping
Multimedia cartography
Orthophotomaps
Otomi cartography
Rectifiers (Photogrammetry)
Soil mapping
Stereoplanigraph
Topographical drawing
Vegetation mapping
—**Automation**
—**Computer programs**
—Conventional signs
  USE   Maps—Symbols
—**Conversion tables**
  [GA23]
  BT   Cartography—Tables
—**Data processing**
—**History**
  UF   Maps—History
—**Laser use in**
  UF   Laser mapping
  BT   Lasers
—Symbols
  USE   Maps—Symbols
—**Tables**
  UF   Cartography—Tables, etc.
      [Former heading]
  NT   Cartography—Conversion tables
—Tables, etc.
  USE   Cartography—Tables
—Terminology
  USE   Maps—Terminology
Cartography, Aztec
  USE   Aztec cartography
Cartography, Eskimo
  USE   Eskimo cartography
Cartography, Indian
  USE   Indian cartography
Cartography, Journalistic
  USE   Maps in journalism
Cartography, Otomi
  USE   Otomi cartography
Cartography, Prehistoric   *(May Subd Geog)*
  UF   Prehistoric cartography
Cartography, Primitive
  USE   Cartography
Cartography in art   *(Not Subd Geog)*
Cartomancy
  USE   Fortune-telling by cards
Cartometry
  BT   Area measurement
      Length measurement
      Maps
Carton de Wiart family   *(Not Subd Geog)*
Cartons
  [HF5770 (Commerce)]
  [TS1200 (Manufacture)]
  UF   Paper boxes
  BT   Boxes
      Paper containers
—**Law and legislation**   *(May Subd Geog)*
Cartoon artists
  USE   Cartoonists
Cartoon captions
  UF   Captions, Cartoon
  BT   Caricatures and cartoons

headings, a suggested number from the Library of Congress Classification associated with the subject. Like Sears subject headings, the next paragraph gives instructions about using the heading, if one is provided. In subsequent paragraphs, cross-references appear in the following order: Use For (UF), Broader Term (BT), Related Term (RT), See Also (SA), and Narrower Term (NT). Subdivided headings follow, with the entry for each authorized subdivided heading following the same form as for main headings.

The type of subdivision affects how it is listed, with chronological subdivisions first, topical subdivisions second, and geographical subdivisions last (see Figure 8.2).[10]

When one or more of the entry elements do not apply to a particular heading or subdivision—for example, if it has no application instructions and/or no cross-references of a specific type—that element or elements are omitted.

In some instances, more than one classification number is applicable to materials given a particular subject heading, and two classification numbers appear, as in the example in Figure 8.3. Classifiers are alerted to the fact that HE374-HE377 is used when the emphasis is on bridges in transportation and TG is used when the emphasis is on engineering of bridges.

All potential authorized subject headings are not given in LCSH; instead, several categories of headings that can be assigned are not included, such as name headings. For personal names, corporate body names, geographic names, uniform titles, and series titles used as subject headings, catalogers are expected to check a name authority file used to establish descriptive access points (see pp. 68–71, where name authorities are discussed) and use the authorized forms given in the 1XX field of the MARC Authorities format. Names of events, buildings, and so on are found there as well, and the authorized forms for them are accepted as subject headings.

Two other categories of authorized headings are not given in LCSH: free-floating phrase headings, such as **[Name of City] Metropolitan area**, and selected music headings for which the scope notes of existing headings provide authorization. Headings that follow the pattern **[Topic] in art**, **[Topic] in literature**, **[Topic] in motion pictures**, and the like, are another kind of pattern for unlisted headings that can be established locally. Rules for applying this type of heading are found in *Subject Cataloging Manual: Subject Headings.*[11]

Types of Subject Headings

LCSH headings have varying syntax. Like Sears, many are single nouns such as **Automation**. Charles Cutter believed single unambiguous nouns were ideal subject headings. Some one-word headings are verbs; for example, **Racing**. They represent activities rather than things. A good many subject headings are two-word phrases given in direct order. These can be modified nouns or verbs, such as **Automobile dealers** and **Automatic indexing**, respectively. Unlike Sears, some two-word headings are modified nouns or verbs in indirect or inverted order, which brings the word modified to the first position in the string of words and the adjective following it after a comma, even though this is not the way one would speak the phrase; for example, **Automobiles, Racing** and **Security, International**. In order to search indirect order headings in an OPAC (Online Public Access Catalog), one must ask for the terms as keywords.

Some single-word headings require explanation to be understood clearly. In LCSH, the explanation is often provided in the form of parenthetic modifiers, which make an enormous difference in meaning. Consider the widely divergent meanings of **Cookies**, used alone to refer to small edible sweets, and **Cookies (Computer science)**, which refer to the Internet's automatic tracking programs. However, qualifiers are not the only method used in LCSH to explain away possible ambiguity. Scope notes are also used for this purpose, as in the follow-

FIGURE 8.2

Bronze sculpture, Baroque   *(May Subd Geog)*
  UF Baroque bronze sculpture
Bronze sculpture, Basque   *(May Subd Geog)*
  UF Basque bronze sculpture
Bronze sculpture, Canadian
  (May Subd Geog)
  UF Canadian bronze sculpture
Bronze sculpture, Chilean   *(May Subd Geog)*
  UF Chilean bronze sculpture
Bronze sculpture, Classical   *(May Subd Geog)*
  UF Classical bronze sculpture
Bronze sculpture, Danish   *(May Subd Geog)*
  UF Danish bronze sculpture
Bronze sculpture, English   *(May Subd Geog)*
  UF English bronze sculpture
Bronze sculpture, European   *(Not Subd Geog)*
  UF European bronze sculpture
Bronze sculpture, Flemish   *(May Subd Geog)*
Bronze sculpture, French   *(May Subd Geog)*
  UF French bronze sculpture
Bronze sculpture, German   *(May Subd Geog)*
  UF German bronze sculpture
  NT Christussäule (Bronze sculpture)
      Goethe-Schiller-Denkmal (Weimar,
        Thuringia, Germany)
      Max-Joseph-Denkmal (Munich,
        Germany)
      Rathausbrunnen (Kempten, Germany)
      Willy Brandt Skulptur (Berlin,
        Germany)
Bronze sculpture, Greek   *(May Subd Geog)*
  [NB140]
  UF Greek bronze sculpture
  NT Artemision bronze statues
      Praying boy (Statue)
  —Expertising   *(May Subd Geog)*
Bronze sculpture, Hellenistic
  (May Subd Geog)
  UF Hellenistic bronze sculpture
Bronze sculpture, Hungarian
  (May Subd Geog)
  UF Hungarian bronze sculpture
Bronze sculpture, Indic   *(May Subd Geog)*
  UF Indic bronze sculpture
Bronze sculpture, Italian   *(May Subd Geog)*
  UF Italian bronze sculpture
Bronze sculpture, Japanese   *(May Subd Geog)*
  UF Japanese bronze sculpture
Bronze sculpture, Mexican   *(May Subd Geog)*
  UF Mexican bronze sculpture
Bronze sculpture, Norwegian
  (May Subd Geog)
  UF Norwegian bronze sculpture
Bronze sculpture, Polish   *(May Subd Geog)*
  UF Polish bronze sculpture
Bronze sculpture, Renaissance
  (May Subd Geog)
  UF Renaissance bronze sculpture
Bronze sculpture, Roman   *(May Subd Geog)*
  UF Roman bronze sculpture
  · NT Jüngling von Salamis (Statue)
      Marcus Aurelius Statue (Rome, Italy)
  —Expertising   *(May Subd Geog)*
Bronze sculpture, Scottish   *(May Subd Geog)*
  UF Scottish bronze sculpture
Bronze sculpture, Spanish   *(May Subd Geog)*
  UF Spanish bronze sculpture
Bronze sculpture, Tibetan   *(May Subd Geog)*
  UF Tibetan bronze sculpture
Bronze spears   *(May Subd Geog)*
  BT Bronze implements
      Spears
  NT Dōhoko
      Dōka
      Dōken
Bronze Star (U.S.)
  USE Bronze Star Medal (U.S.)

Bronze Star Medal (U.S.)
  UF Award of the Bronze Star (U.S.)
      Bronze Star (U.S.)
  BT United States. Army—Medals,
      badges, decorations, etc.
Bronzed cowbird   *(May Subd Geog)*
  [QL696.P2475 (Zoology)]
  UF Molothrus aeneus
      Red-eyed cowbird
      Tangavius aeneus
  BT Molothrus
Bronzed skin
  USE Addison's disease
Bronzes   *(May Subd Geog)*
  [NK7900-NK7999 (Art)]
  [TS570 (Technology)]
  BT Art
      Art metal-work
      Bronze
      Decoration and ornament
  NT Bronze amulets
      Bronze bells
      Bronze boxes
      Bronze crosses
      Bronze figurines
      Bronze fonts
      Bronze implements
      Bronze mirrors
      Bronze mortars
      Bronze mounts
      Bronze sculpture
      Gilt bronzes
      Jewish bronzes
  —19th century
  —20th century
  —Expertising   *(May Subd Geog)*
  —Inscriptions
      UF Inscriptions on bronzes
      BT Inscriptions
  —Oriental influences
  —Private collections   *(May Subd Geog)*
  —China
  ——To 221 B.C.
      USE Bronzes, Chinese—To 221 B.C.
  ——Ch'in-Han dynasties, 221 B.C.-220 A.D.
      USE Bronzes, Chinese—Qin-Han
           dynasties, 221 B.C.-220 A.D.
  —Greece
  —Iran
      NT Wade cup
  —Italy
  —Middle East
      UF Bronzes—Near East
          [Former heading]
      NT Bronzes, Seljuk
  —Near East
      USE Bronzes—Middle East
  —Nigeria
      UF Bronzes, Nigerian
          [Former heading]
Bronzes, African   *(Not Subd Geog)*
  UF African bronzes
Bronzes, American   *(May Subd Geog)*
  UF American bronzes
Bronzes, Ancient   *(May Subd Geog)*
  —Japan
      NT Bronzes, Yayoi
Bronzes, Baroque   *(May Subd Geog)*
  UF Baroque bronzes
Bronzes, Bini   *(May Subd Geog)*
  UF Bini bronzes
      Bronzes, Bini (African people)
          [Former heading]
Bronzes, Bini (African people)
  USE Bronzes, Bini
Bronzes, Buddhist   *(May Subd Geog)*
  UF Buddhist bronzes
Bronzes, Byzantine
  UF Byzantine bronzes
Bronzes, Celtiberian   *(May Subd Geog)*
  UF Celtiberian bronzes

FIGURE 8.3

Bridge crane industry   *(May Subd Geog)*
   [HD9705]
   BT   Construction equipment industry
Bridge cranes
   BT   Cranes, derricks, etc.
         Electric cranes
   NT   Gantry cranes
Bridge failures   *(May Subd Geog)*
   UF   Bridges—Failure
         Collapse of bridges
   BT   Bridges—Accidents
         Structural failures
   —New Zealand
         NT   Tangiwai Rail Disaster, Tangiwai,
               N.Z., 1953
   —Scotland
         NT   Tay Bridge Disaster, Dundee,
               Scotland, 1879
Bridge family   *(Not Subd Geog)*
   UF   Bridges family
         Brydges family
Bridge floors
   USE   Bridges—Floors
Bridge for three players
   USE   Three-handed bridge
Bridge lighting
   USE   Bridges—Lighting
Bridge lights (Navigation)   *(May Subd Geog)*
   [VK1247-VK1249]
   BT   Bridges
         Lighthouses
Bridge of Lions (Saint Augustine, Fla.)
   This heading is not valid for use as a geographic
subdivision.
   UF   Lions Bridge (Saint Augustine, Fla.)
   BT   Bridges—Florida
Bridge players   *(May Subd Geog)*
   UF   Contract bridge players
         Players, Bridge
         Players, Contract bridge
   BT   Card players
   NT   Women bridge players
Bridge railings
   UF   Bridges—Railings
         Railings, Bridge
   BT   Bridges
Bridge rectifiers
   [TK7872.R35]
   UF   Rectifiers, Bridge
   BT   Bridge circuits
         Electric current rectifiers
Bridge River (B.C.)
   BT   Rivers—British Columbia
Bridge River Valley (B.C.)
   UF   Bridge Valley (B.C.)
   BT   Valleys—British Columbia
Bridge Valley (B.C.)
   USE   Bridge River Valley (B.C.)
Bridge whist   *(May Subd Geog)*
   [GV1281]
   UF   Bridge (Game)
   BT   Whist
   NT   Auction bridge
         Contract bridge
         Domino bridge
         Five-suit bridge
         Pirate bridge
         Poker-bridge
Bridgeman family
   USE   Bridgman family
Bridgeport, Lake (Tex.)
   UF   Lake Bridgeport (Tex.)
   BT   Lakes—Texas
         Reservoirs—Texas
Bridgeport State Park (Wash.)
   BT   Parks—Washington (State)
Bridgeport Township Site (Mich.)
   BT   Michigan—Antiquities

Bridger Bowl (Bozeman, Mont.)
   UF   Bridger Bowl Ski Area (Bozeman,
         Mont.)
   BT   Ski resorts—Montana
Bridger Bowl Ski Area (Bozeman, Mont.)
   USE   Bridger Bowl (Bozeman, Mont.)
Bridger Canyon (Mont.)
   BT   Canyons—Montana
Bridger family   *(Not Subd Geog)*
   UF   Bridgers family
Bridger Jack Mesa Wilderness (Utah)
   UF   Bridger Jack Mesa Wilderness Study
         Area (Utah)
   BT   National parks and reserves—Utah
         Wilderness areas—Utah
Bridger Jack Mesa Wilderness Study Area (Utah)
   USE   Bridger Jack Mesa Wilderness (Utah)
Bridger National Forest (Wyo.)
   UF   Bridger-Teton National Forest (Wyo.)
   BT   Forest reserves—Wyoming
         National parks and reserves—Wyoming
Bridger Pass (Wyo.)
   UF   Bridger's Pass (Wyo.)
   BT   Mountain passes—Wyoming
Bridger Pass Overland Trail (Colo. and Wyo.)
   UF   Ben Holladay's Overland Stage Line
         (Colo. and Wyo.)
         Holladay's Overland Mail Road (Colo.
         and Wyo.)
   BT   Overland Trails
Bridger-Teton National Forest (Wyo.)
   USE   Bridger National Forest (Wyo.)
         Teton National Forest (Wyo.)
Bridger Wilderness (Wyo.)
   BT   National parks and reserves—Wyoming
         Wilderness areas—Wyoming
Bridgers family
   USE   Bridger family
Bridger's Pass (Wyo.)
   USE   Bridger Pass (Wyo.)
Bridges   *(May Subd Geog)*
   [HE374-HE377 (Transportation)]
   [TG (Engineering)]
   UF   Bridges, Highway
         Express highways—Bridges
         Highway bridges
   BT   Transportation
   RT   Viaducts
   NT   Bridge lights (Navigation)
         Bridge railings
         Bridges, Arched
         Causeways
         Culverts
         Drawbridges
         Elevated highways
         Ferry bridges
         Footbridges
         Historic bridges
         Ice crossings
         Military bridges
         Pontoon bridges
         Railroad bridges
         Skywalks
         Suspension bridges
         Toll bridges
         Transporter-bridges
   —Abutments
         [TG325]
         UF   Abutments, Bridge
               Bridge abutments
   —Accidents   *(May Subd Geog)*
         [TG470]
         BT   Disasters
         NT   Bridge failures
   —Aerodynamics
         BT   Aerodynamics
   —Bailey construction
         USE   Bridges, Prefabricated

891

Fig. 8.3—Continues

FIGURE 8.3 *(continued)*

Bridges *(Continued)*
—Bearings *(May Subd Geog)*
　[TG326]
　UF Bearings, Bridge
　　Bearings (Bridges)
　　Bridge bearings
　BT Bearings (Machinery)
—Construction
　USE Bridges—Design and construction
—Decks
　USE Bridges—Floors
—Design
　USE Bridges—Design and construction
—Design and construction
　UF Bridge construction
　　[Former heading]
　　Bridges—Construction
　　Bridges—Design
　　[Former heading]
——Costs
　　UF Bridges—Estimates and costs
　　　[Former heading]
——Estimates *(May Subd Geog)*
　　UF Bridges—Estimates and costs
　　　[Former heading]
—Drainage systems
　UF Bridges—Floors—Drainage
　　systems
　BT Drainage
—Earthquake effects *(May Subd Geog)*
—Estimates and costs
　USE Bridges—Design and
　　　construction—Costs
　　Bridges—Design and
　　　construction—Estimates
—Failure
　USE Bridge failures
—Flood damage *(May Subd Geog)*
　BT Flood damage
　NT Scour at bridges
—Floors
　[TG325.6]
　UF Bridge floors
　　Bridges—Decks
　　Decks (Bridges)
　BT Floors
　NT Bridges, Steel plate deck
——Drainage systems
　　USE Bridges—Drainage systems
——Joints
　　BT Joints (Engineering)
——Snow and ice control
　　USE Bridges—Snow and ice control
—Foundations and piers
　[TG320]
　UF Bridges—Piers
　　Piers (Bridge)
　BT Foundations
　　Hydraulic structures
　　Masonry
　RT Caissons
　　Cofferdams
　NT Scour at bridges
—Ice control
　USE Bridges—Snow and ice control
—Law and legislation *(May Subd Geog)*
　BT Highway law
—Lighting *(May Subd Geog)*
　UF Bridge lighting
—Live loads
　UF Bridges—Moving loads
　　Live loads (Bridges)
　　Moving loads (Bridges)
　BT Bridges—Vibration
　　Structural dynamics
—Maintenance and repair
　UF Bridges—Repairing
　NT Bridges—Snow and ice control
—Moving loads
　USE Bridges—Live loads

—Navigation clearances
　(May Subd Geog)
　UF Navigation clearances (Bridges)
　　Navigational clearances (Bridges)
　BT Bridges, Movable
　　Inland navigation
—Piers
　USE Bridges—Foundations and piers
—Railings
　USE Bridge railings
—Repairing
　USE Bridges—Maintenance and repair
—Snow and ice control
　(May Subd Geog)
　UF Bridges—Floors—Snow and ice
　　control
　　Bridges—Ice control
　　Ice control on bridges
　　Snow control on bridges
　BT Bridges—Maintenance and repair
　　Slush on pavements, runways, etc.
　　Snow removal
—Surveying
—Trestles
　USE Trestles
—Vibration *(May Subd Geog)*
　[TG265]
　NT Bridges—Live loads
—War damage *(May Subd Geog)*
　UF Bomb damage to bridges
　　War damage to bridges
　BT War—Economic aspects
—Welded joints
　BT Welded joints
——Cracking *(May Subd Geog)*
　　UF Cracking of welded joints in
　　　bridges
　　　Fatigue cracking of welded joints
　　　in bridges
　　BT Fracture mechanics
—Welding *(May Subd Geog)*
　BT Welding
—Alaska
　NT Miles Glacier Bridge (Alaska)
—Alberta
　NT Clover Bar Bridge (Edmonton,
　　Alta.)
　　Ellerslie Road/Blackmud Creek
　　Crossing (Edmonton, Alta.)
—Arkansas
　NT Highway 82 Bridge (Ark. and
　　Miss.)
—Australia
　NT Batman Bridge (Tas.)
　　Glebe Island Bridge (Sydney,
　　N.S.W.)
　　Ross Bridge (Ross, Tas.)
　　Sydney Harbour Bridge (Sydney,
　　N.S.W.)
　　Tasman Bridge (Hobart, Tas.)
——Tamar River (Tas.)
　　UF Tamar River (Tas.)—Bridges
　　　[Former heading]
—Austria
　NT Reichsbrücke (Vienna, Austria)
—Bangladesh
　NT Bangabandhu Bridge (Bangladesh)
—Brazil
　NT Costa e Silva Bridge (Brazil)
　　Ponte do Imperador (Brazil)
——Guanabara Bay
　　UF Guanabara Bay (Brazil)—
　　　Bridges
　　　[Former heading]
—British Columbia
　NT Lions Gate Bridge (Vancouver,
　　B.C.)
　　Point Ellice Bridge (Victoria, B.C.)
——Capilano River
　　UF Capilano River (B.C.)—Bridges
　　　[Former heading]

ing example, found immediately after the heading **Gems**: "Here are entered antiquarian or artistic works on engraved stones and jewels. Mineralogical and technological works on potential and actual engraved stones and jewels are entered under **Precious stones**."[12]

Numerous two-word headings filling the pages of LCSH are surnames followed by the word "family"; for example, **Diamond family**. Often, these headings are followed by long lists of Used For cross-references giving the name in unauthorized alternative spellings, all of which are gathered under the one authorized spelling. **Diamond family** has seven such references (Diamant family, Diamante family, Diman family, Dimand family, Dimon family, Dimond family, and Dymond family) as well as one Related Term reference to **Dement family**, whose members might or might not be related to the Diamond family.

LCSH has many modified noun and modified verb headings consisting of three or more words. Examples include **Women automobile industry workers** and **All terrain vehicle trails**. Some multiword headings consist of two nouns, a noun and a verb, or two verbs connected by *and*, such as **Cities and towns**, **Boats and boating**, and **Gliding and soaring**, respectively.[13] A good many multiword headings consist of two concepts connected by prepositions, such as **Peat as fertilizer**, **Folklore in motion pictures**, **Ports of entry**, **Transference (Psychology) in children**, and so forth. More complex multiword headings may include combinations of modified terms and phrases connected by prepositions or conjunctions, such as **Mail receiving and forwarding services** and **Game and game-birds, Dressing of**. (This last example illustrates combining multiple words and inverted order.) A few multiword headings are merely lists of related terms; for example, **Comic books, strips, etc.**

Cross-References

Like Sears, six types of cross-references are listed in LCSH: USE, Use For (UF), Broader Term (BT), Narrower Term (NT), Related Term (RT), and See Also (SA), explained in this section. Some references are reciprocal, meaning that if a cataloger makes one of a reciprocal pair, he or she must also make the other. The first, the USE reference, leads someone from an unauthorized term to the authorized heading. For example, the unauthorized phrase "Biology and law" is followed by a USE reference that says, "USE **Law and biology**." The second type of cross-reference is the reciprocal of the USE heading and is known as a "Use For" reference, abbreviated UF. An example is the UF reference at **Law and biology** that tells the cataloger to use this term in place of Biology and law. Every USE reference generates a reciprocal UF reference under the authorized heading. The point in listing unauthorized terms with their USE references is to prompt catalogers to add these cross-references to the catalog at the time the authorized terms are established, because searchers are likely to use them in seeking materials. If the references are made, anyone searching the unauthorized terms gets the message to look instead under the authorized terms; if not, he or she gets no answer, no reason for the lack of response, and no assistance about what to do next.

Two types of cross-references, Broader Term (BT) and Narrower Term (NT) references, indicate subject relationships at different levels of specificity. As with USE and UF references, BT references always generate NT reciprocals in LCSH and vice versa. These references mean exactly what they say: BTs listed under a subject heading will give headings at the next broader level of subject specificity, whereas NTs listed under a subject heading will give headings at the next narrower level. Entire subject hierarchies are not shown, but BTs and NTs reveal three levels at once. For example, the subject heading **Marathon running** lists **Running races** as a BT and **Rogaining** as an NT, showing the subject hierarchy as follows: **Running races** (broadest level); **Marathon running** (next-narrower level); **Rogaining** (narrowest level).[14] One can check to see whether there are terms broader than **Running** races and narrower than **Rogaining**. Doing so reveals that **Running races** has BTs for **Racing** and **Track and field**, whereas **Rogaining** has no NTs, although it does have a Related Term (RT) reference to **Orienteering**. **Rogaining** is the narrowest term in its hierarchy. Following **Racing**, one sees it has the BT **Sports**; **Sports** has the BT **Recreation**; **Recreation** has the BT **Manners and customs**; and **Manners and customs** has two BTs, **Civilization** and **Ethnology**. **Civilization** has a BT to **Auxiliary sciences of history**, whereas **Ethnology** has BTs to **Anthropology** and **Human beings**. **Auxiliary sciences of history** has no BTs, so it is the top of its hierarchy, although it does have an RT to **History**. Thus, one entire subject hierarchy that includes **Running races**, though it is not the only possible hierarchy for that term, would be:

> **Auxiliary sciences of history**
>> **Civilization**
>>> **Manners and customs**
>>>> **Recreation**
>>>>> **Sports**
>>>>>> →**Running races**
>>>>>>> **Marathon running**
>>>>>>> **Rogaining**

When no BTs appear under a heading, one can assume it is the broadest level in the subject hierarchy; when no NTs appear, one can assume it is the narrowest. Standard practice for LCSH as well as for Sears has long been that catalogers should make all associated NTs as "see also" references in the catalog when a subject heading is established, but none of the BTs. The rationale for this practice assumes a person searching a term is aware of the broader levels of the subject area, but not necessarily of the more specific levels. BTs are listed merely for educational purposes, to help a cataloger looking for possible subject headings or a library patron seeking potential search terms find something broader than the term he or she is examining.

RT (Related Term) references also indicate subject relationships, but at more or less equivalent levels of specificity. RTs always generate RT reciprocals with the terms they reference. Sometimes, RTs are similar to one another in meaning and other times they are opposites. For example, the RTs **Parks** and **Playgrounds** mean similar things; whereas the RTs **Hours of labor** and **Weekly rest day** have opposite but related meanings. One can assume that a searcher interested in material found using one heading of either of these pairs might be interested in material found using its RT. Subject cataloging practice is to make all RT references as "see also" references.

The final type of cross-reference is the See Also (SA) reference, also called a general reference. SAs are references to groups of headings, not individual headings, although they may give specific examples. SA instructions may lead from a broader heading to a group of specific headings one would find under it, from a generic heading to headings beginning with the same word, or to subdivisions. Examples of these uses of SA are, respectively:

- Under **Animal products**, SA *individual products, e.g.* Hides and skins; Wool
- Under **Optics**, SA *headings beginning with the word* Optical
- Under **Athletics**, SA *subdivision* Sports *under names of individual educational institutions, military services, and ethnic groups, e.g.,* Harvard University—Sports; United States. Army—Sports

As with Sears, LCSH cross-references expand the vocabulary of the subject catalog and make it possible for searchers to find materials even when they do not know the authorized subject headings. This contributes to the user-friendliness of the catalog and adds desirable flexibility without losing the gathering function of a controlled vocabulary. Cross-references enable the catalog to add new terminology without requiring immediate changes in established headings. They allow time to see whether new terminology does, indeed, completely replace the old, and would warrant a change in the authorized heading, or if the new terminology is, itself, replaced by something else.

Subdivisions

Subdivided headings are common in LCSH. As mentioned earlier in the chapter, subdivisions authorized for use appear in the list in boldface type under the heading they modify, preceded by a long dash, whereas subdivisions unauthorized for use but appropriate as cross-references are listed in roman print. Authorized subdivisions can have their own suggested classification numbers, geographic subdivision note, cross-references, and, sometimes, they themselves are subdivided; for example, **Fire departments—Equipment and supplies** has the subdivision **—Valuation**. This allows a cataloger to assign the more specific heading **Fire departments—Equipment and supplies—Valuation**. He or she cannot, however, add **—Valuation** to **Fire departments** alone or to any of the other subdivisions under **Fire departments**.

Many LCSH headings are following by the instruction *(May Subd Geog)* indicating that catalogers can create their own geographic subdivisions for those terms. For the most part, geographic subdivision is made at the country level. If the desired geographical entity is smaller than the country level (at the state, province, or city level), the name of the country must be interposed before the name of the smaller place, resulting in what is called *indirect geographic subdivision*. Indirect geographic subdivision having the country as the gathering element ensures that searchers will find topics limited to places within its borders after the topics pertaining to the country as a whole. There are exceptions to this rule, however, with Canada, the United States, and United Kingdom the main ones. For them, the province, state, or constituent country, respectively, is the gathering element.[15] A library with extensive holdings about agriculture might display the following list of subject headings (Note: This is a hypothetical list, not taken from any existing library catalog):

Agriculture

Agriculture—Brazil

Agriculture—Canada

Agriculture—China

Agriculture—China—Hubei (Province)

Agriculture—England

Agriculture—Massachusetts

Agriculture—Massachusetts—Berkshire County (Mass.)

Agriculture—Québec (Province)

Agriculture—United States

If policy makers at LC determine that geographical subdivision would be inappropriate, the negative instruction *(Not Subd Geog)* appears, emphasizing that it is forbidden. When no instruction appears regarding geographic subdivision, it means the heading has not been considered for that type of subdivision. Catalogers following LC policy would not act unilaterally to subdivide it without instructions from LC. If a sufficiently large body of materials that seem to require the geographic subdivision of a topic begins appearing in a library catalog department, that library's cataloger can ask LC to review the heading for geographic subdivision, providing the needed documentation along with the request.

LCSH provides pattern headings for twenty-four topical areas, authorizing the same sets of subdivisions for terms that match the pattern words; for example, **Chemicals**, **Industries**, and **Wars**. For a few of the topical areas, more than one option is provided; for example, musical instruments can be subdivided either like **Piano** or like **Clarinet**, and organs and regions of the body can be subdivided either like **Heart** or like **Foot**, depending on which is the best match for the topic of the catalog record being created. Thus, if the instrument for which the subdivision was needed were a glockenspiel, one would choose from **Piano**'s subdivisions; and if the part of the body being subdivided were the pancreas, one would seek a subdivision found under **Heart**.

Instructions in some SA references authorize the headings under which they are found to be used as subdivisions with other terms, for example, at **Biography**, the note says: "SA *subdivision* Biography *under names of countries, cities, etc., names of corporate bodies, uniform titles of sacred works, and under classes of persons, ethnic groups, individual and groups of animals, and historic events.*"[16] Similar instructions also can appear as USE references; for example, "Juvenile drama" is given in the main list in plain print, because it is not authorized as a main heading, but the reference under it says: "USE *subdivision* Juvenile drama *under names of countries, cities, etc., under names of individual persons and corporate bodies, and under classes of persons, ethnic groups, and topical headings.*"[17]

LCSH furnishes more than 3,900 authorized subdivisions consisting of general terms called "free-floating" subdivisions and rules for their assignment. The free-floating subdivisions and their rules appear in *Subject Cataloging Manual: Subject Headings*, in *Free-floating Subdivisions: An Alphabetical Index*, and in LCSH itself in a section titled "Introduction to Free-Floating Subdivisions," which was introduced in the twenty-sixth edition.[18] Some free-floating subdivisions consist of a string of multiple subdivisions. An example of this is **—Politics and government—[period subdivision]—Philosophy**, which can be added to names of countries, cities, and so on and is really a string of three subdivisions. Applying it would produce the following subject heading:

United States—Politics and government—19th century—Philosophy

To sum up, main headings may be subdivided in four ways: an instruction to subdivide geographically may appear with the heading; authorized subdivisions may appear under the heading; the heading may fit one of the twenty-four pattern headings; or the heading may be eligible to be subdivided with one of the free-floating subdivisions. Subdivisions enable catalogers to achieve a high level of precision in describing library materials in catalog records and, as a result, improve the catalog's ability to reveal what materials actually cover. For searchers who may not be able to peruse the materials in person but need to request them via interlibrary loans or who might have to pay for their delivery, this is a distinct advantage. Subdivisions are also useful in dividing a very large number of entries into smaller, more manageable groups, such as one might find in a large U.S. library catalog under the broad heading **United States—Politics and government**. This improves the relevance of materials retrieved by searchers, which is important for good service.

Applying LCSH

Complete guidance in applying LCSH can be found in *Subject Cataloging Manual: Subject Headings.* In general, application policies are similar to applying Sears (or perhaps it is more accurate to say that Sears's application policies are similar to LCSH's) and include the following:

1. Determine the subject(s) of the item being cataloged by examining its subject-rich elements (title, table of contents or menu, preface, introduction, "about" file, summary, index), considering these from a user's viewpoint.

2. Write the subject(s) down in your own words.

3. Match each subject with authorized headings in LCSH, assigning the one(s) that most closely represents it.

4. Assign as many subject headings per item as are needed to represent its contents accurately. For years, the standard practice was to assign a heading for a subject that occupied at least 20 percent of the content of the item being cataloged, which translated to a maximum of five subject headings per item. More recently, LC has opted to increase the number of headings assigned without requiring that an item have a specific proportion of content to justify them, leaving it up to the cataloger to decide what is needed. Figure 8.4 is an example of an item with many subject headings.

As with the assignment of Sears subject headings, subject catalogers using LCSH also consider the following matters when they assign subject headings:

1. Choose the most specific heading available, not a broader heading.

2. Give the most specific heading available directly, not as a subdivision of a broader heading.

3. Consider items already in the collection relating to the subject of the item being cataloged and try to collocate it with existing holdings on the same subject.

4. Generally, treat items first by topic, then by time period, by geographical focus, or by form, unless LCSH's scope notes instruct doing otherwise.

5. Consult *Subject Cataloging Manual: Subject Headings* for LC's policies on treatment of nonbook materials, selected genres of literature, and selected topical areas.

Canadian Subject Headings

Canadian Subject Headings (CSH) is a list of English-language subject headings, compatible with *Library of Congress Subject Headings,* used to access and express the subject content of documents on Canada and Canadian topics. It is no longer published in a paper format and has been superseded by *CSH on the Web,* a free, up-to-date access to over 6,000

FIGURE 8.4

This example is an illustration of:
- edited work entered under title
- several other title information
- subsidiary responsibility
- publishing date not listed, copyright date given
- series statement
- contents (index) note
- ISBN qualified
- large number of Library of Congress subject headings
- personal name added entries
- corporate body added entries
- title added entry
- series added entry
- 2nd level cataloging

The 9/11 investigations : staff reports of the 9/11 Commission :
  excerpts from the House-Senate joint enquiry report on 9/11 :
  testimony from fourteen key witness, including Richard Clarke,
  George Tenet, and Condoleezza Rice / edited by Steven Strasser
  ; with an introduction by Craig R. Whitney. -- New York :
  Public Affairs Press, c2004.
  xxxvi, 580 p. : ill. ; 21 cm. -- (Public Affairs reports)

  Includes index.
  ISBN 1-58648-279-3 (pbk.).

  1. National Commission on Terrorist Attacks upon the United
States. 2. Qaida (Organization). 3. United States. Central
Intelligence Agency. 4. United States. Federal Bureau of
Investigation. 5. September 11 Terrorist attacks, 2001.
6. Terrorism -- Government policy -- United States. 7. War on
Terrorism, 2001-. 8. Political violence -- United States.
9. Governmental investigations -- United States. 10. National
security -- United States. 11. Intelligence service -- United
States. I. Strasser, Stephen. II. Whitney, Craig R.
III. National Commission on Terrorist Attacks upon the United
States. IV. United States. Congress. Senate. Select Committee on
Intelligence. Joint inquiry into intelligence community
activities before and after the terrorist attacks of September
11, 2001. V. Title: Nine/eleven investigations. VI. Series.

Fig. 8.4—Continues

English-language subject authority records (www.collectionscanada.ca/csh/index-e.html).
The records are available in both the MARC 21 format and thesaurus display. There is a
monthly list of new and revised headings and an alphabetical list of subdivisions. The database, updated monthly, provides a large number of references, scope notes, and instructions
setting topics in their Canadian context. The list of subdivisions provides French-language
equivalents, and the database provides a link to *Répertoire de vedettes-matière* for equivalent
French-language headings.

FIGURE 8.4 *(continued)*

(chief source of information)

(title page)

The **9/11** Investigations

(information on verso)

Staff Reports of the 9/11 Commission

———

Excerpts from the House-Senate
Joint Inquiry Report on 9/11

———

Testimony from fourteen key witnesses, including
Richard Clarke, George Tenet,
and Condoleezza Rice

EDITED BY
STEVEN STRASSER

WITH AN INTRODUCTION BY
Craig R. Whitney of *The New York Times*

PublicAffairs
NEW YORK

Many Canadian topics are better described using CSH. The 1989 massacre of students in Montreal, an incident that is remembered annually across Canada, is an example. The CSH heading is **Montréal École Polytechnique Women Students Massacre, Montréal, Québec, 1989**. It would be difficult to construct this heading from LCSH using its pattern example of **Saint Bartholomew Day, Massacre of, France, 1572**.

Subject authority records for *Canadian Subject Headings* are also available in the AMICUS database. Registered AMICUS users can download CSH authority records in the MARC 21 format from AMICUS. (Although users must register to obtain entry to the AMICUS database, its use is free of charge.)

Problems with LCSH

For small libraries, the principal problem with LCSH headings is that they are too specific and, therefore, fail to collocate enough materials under the assigned headings to furnish a satisfying array of hits for subject searchers. It is difficult to avoid all problems with low levels of collocation; but, on the other hand, small libraries that purchase small numbers of materials having broad coverage of a subject area (as contrasted with large libraries that purchase thousands of titles, many of which cover very narrow and detailed subject matter) would be correct in assigning broad headings to their materials. Thus, this problem would resolve itself to some degree.

For libraries of all sizes, the sheer size and complexity of LCSH is daunting for subject catalogers who must learn to follow the application rules, choose appropriate headings from among a large number of similar-sounding possibilities, struggle with terminology they may not recognize easily (such as **Cheirodendron** or **Feldspathoid**), and suffer along when desired headings are absent from the list because the materials collected in their libraries differ in content from LC's holdings.

Problems described in previous editions of this book—such as the tendencies to put up with outdated language in headings, to delay establishing needed new headings, and to reflect an unduly conservative view of the world—have been or are in the process of being addressed in a timely manner. LCSH has increased the number of scope notes and other instructions for the benefit of non-LC subject catalogers, making it easier to use than ever. Decisions that increase user convenience, such as printing the list of free-floating subdivisions in the list, make it possible for a library to adopt LCSH without committing itself to the purchase of numerous auxiliary tools.

Perhaps the conversion of LCSH to an online database and its development into a networked tool is one factor in encouraging its staff to respond more quickly to change, once a change is deemed appropriate. In the past, the physical burden and cost of manual labor involved in altering numerous headings one by one may have made even the most desirable changes seem difficult to implement. LC seems to be more aware and considerate of its outside users, formatting its tools with greater attention to ease of use and eliminating some of the frustrating inconsistencies that formerly plagued the list. LC has enjoyed success in expanding its user group (for example, the British Library adopted LCSH after many years of intensive work on a different controlled vocabulary system, called PRECIS).

In addition to the suggestions of its own staff members, LC participates in and receives proposals for change from the Subject Analysis Committee of the American Library Association.[19] The Committee maintains many subcommittees and task forces, each devoted to a particular problem or issue. Members are appointed on the basis of their interest and expertise, and their reports often are instrumental in adding new headings to LCSH, changing existing headings, or modifying its application policies. For example, a subcommittee of the Subject Analysis Committee succeeded in ridding the list of sexist headings intimating that it is unusual for women to be doctors, authors, or other kinds of professionals. The offensive "Women as [professionals]" headings were deleted from the list and, instead, headings for such topics are constructed on the model **Women authors**, **Women doctors**, **Women lawyers**, and so on. Subsequently, catalogers sensitive to gender equality also saw that the presence of heading pairs that singled out only women ("Authors" and "Women authors," for example) was a different kind of unequal treatment. They lobbied again to have gender-specific headings for both sexes and LC complied in some, though not all, areas. LCSH currently has headings for both men and women authors, and has eliminated some headings for women professionals, such as women doctors. (The heading that now covers that subject is **Women in the health professions**.) Some might see inequality in the terminology used, for example, **Male authors** and **Women authors**, or **Male actors** and **Actresses**. It seems reasonable to ask why "Men authors" is not the counterpart to **Women authors** or, as an alternative, why "Female authors" is not the counterpart to **Male authors**. Perhaps, those questions take the issue of gender equality in subject headings a step too far, even for advocates.

Other groups have also lobbied LC successfully to obtain needed headings (such as the Music Library Association) or, alternatively, created their own thesauri to supplement LCSH (such as the organizations that sponsored thesauri for moving image materials or the *Art & Architecture Thesaurus*). These terms are accommodated by special encoding protocols in the MARC format and have been successfully integrated in catalogs along with standardized headings from LCSH.

Why Use LCSH?

The most obvious answers to this question are "Because it is there, and because the work is done by LC, the world's largest cataloging authority." The mere fact that librarians need not develop their own list and all the cross-references that go with it, or devote the time and effort needed to maintain a local list over time is answer enough for most librarians. Moreover, adopting LCSH enables them to copy subject headings from catalog records in standard sources, such as LC's MARC database, OCLC, and other bibliographic networks, and ensures that locally assigned subject headings conform to regional, national, and international standards.

It is true that LCSH includes a large number of headings that would never be of use to catalogers in small public libraries or school library media centers, but their presence in the list is easy enough to ignore. LC's penchant for technical terminology and inverted order for selected phrase headings can be addressed by means of local USE references, requiring minimal effort to create and maintain.

A great advantage of using LCSH is that it is the vocabulary of choice for numerous institutions that do large amounts of original cataloging. Not only can their subject heading assignments be copied by local catalogers when they copy entire catalog records, but they can be emulated when local catalogers do original cataloging for material covering similar subject areas. Catalogers whose libraries adopt LCSH can benefit from manuals, workshops, and other training materials intended for the rest of the large community of LCSH users.

LC's Annotated Card Program

In 1965, LC responded to an expressed need on the part of librarians working with children and youth for modified subject headings for their materials by initiating its Annotated Card (AC) Program. Materials designated for young readers were given the following variant treatments:

1. Subdivisions indicating age levels, such as **—Juvenile literature**, were dropped (see Figure 8.5).

2. Selected subject headings were added, revised, or simplified to make them more appropriate to children's vocabularies and children's materials.

3. Subdivision practice was modified, making it permissible to give subject access to individual works of fiction and to biographies in fields in which LCSH had no established term for persons in that field.

4. Summaries were provided in the descriptive cataloging.

When a catalog record contains AC headings (see Figure 12.13 on page 250), they are found in the usual MARC format subject fields (650, 651, etc.) with the second indicator coded "1" instead of "0." In printed versions of catalog records containing AC headings, for example, in the CIP records found on the verso of a book (see Figure 8.5), the headings are enclosed in square brackets. Summaries are always given in the body of the record.

The list of AC headings appears at the beginning of the first volume of LCSH, along with a brief history of the initiative, and brief descriptions of the categories of headings,

FIGURE 8.5

This example is an illustration of:
- edition statement
- publishing date not listed, copyright date given
- dimensions where the width of the item is greater than the height
- summary
- ISBN qualified
- both Library of Congress and LC annotated card subject headings
- Library of Congress annotated card program CIP
- title added entry
- 2nd level cataloging

```
Heller, Ruth.
   "Galápagos" means "tortoises" / written and illustrated by Ruth
Heller. -- 1st ed. -- San Francisco : Sierra Club Books for
Children, c2000.
   41 p. : col. ill. ; 24 x 27 cm.

   Summary: Rhyming text and illustrations present the
characteristics and behavior of animals found on the Galápagos
Islands, including the giant tortoises, blue-footed boobies, and
land iguanas.
   ISBN 0-87156-917-5 (alk. paper).
```

Tracing with Library of Congress subject headings
```
   1. Zoology -- Galápagos Islands -- Juvenile literature.
I. Title.
```

Tracing with Library of Congress annotated card subject headings

```
1. Zoology -- Galápagos Islands.  I. Title.
```

Fig. 8.5—Continues

application policies, subdivisions, references, scope notes, and AC products. Regarding this last mentioned item, catalog records containing AC headings may be obtained as part of the MARC 21 database available via FTP and via *Classification Web*, the World Wide Web subscription service. Updates to AC headings are also found at the end of LC's *Weekly Lists*.

Conclusion

LCSH remains the subject heading list in widest use among U.S. and Canadian libraries, despite its problems and idiosyncrasies. Network records almost always contain LCSH subject headings. The desire to exploit the power of cataloging networks or outsource local cataloging in order to contain costs, speed cataloging production, and meet cataloging standards has prompted many librarians and media specialists to give up previously used systems

FIGURE 8.5 *(continued)*

(chief source of information)

(title page)   *(information on verso)*

"GALÁPAGOS"
Means "Tortoises"

Written and illustrated by
Ruth Heller

Sierra Club Books for Children
San Francisco

With much love to
Philip
and
to all the splendid
Galápagos
guides
and
every
blue-footed booby
besides.

Special thanks to Susan Guevara
for sharing her first-class photographs.

The Sierra Club, founded in 1892 by John Muir, has devoted itself to the study and protection of the earth's scenic and ecological resources — mountains, wetlands, woodlands, wild shores and rivers, deserts and plains. The publishing program of the Sierra Club offers books to the public as a nonprofit educational service in the hope that they may enlarge the public's understanding of the Club's basic concerns. The point of view expressed in each book, however, does not necessarily represent that of the Club. The Sierra Club has some sixty chapters in the United States and Canada. For information about how you may participate in its programs to preserve wilderness and the quality of life, please address inquiries to Sierra Club, 85 Second Street, San Francisco, CA 94105, or visit our website at http://www.sierraclub.org.

First Edition

Published by Sierra Club Books for Children
85 Second Street, San Francisco, California 94105
www.sierraclub.org/books

Published in conjunction with Gibbs Smith, Publisher
P.O. Box 667, Layton, Utah 84041
www.gibbs-smith.com

Sierra Club, Sierra Club Books, and the Sierra Club design logos are registered trademarks of the Sierra Club.

Library of Congress Cataloging-in-Publication Data
Heller, Ruth
    "Galápagos" means "tortoises" / written and illustrated by Ruth Heller. — 1st ed.
        p. cm.
    Summary: Rhyming text and illustrations present the characteristics and behavior of animals found on the Galápagos Islands, including the giant tortoises, blue-footed boobies, and land iguanas.
    ISBN 0-87156-917-5 (alk. paper)
    1. Zoology — Galápagos Islands Juvenile literature. [1. Zoology — Galápagos Islands.] I. Title.
QL345.G2H45 2000
591.98663 — dc21   99-28983

Printed in Hong Kong
10 9 8 7 6 5 4 3 2 1

and adopt LCSH. A noteworthy example of such a decision occurred a few years when the Hennepin County Library (Minnetonka, Minnesota) joined the OCLC bibliographic network. Simultaneously with joining the network, the library ended its practice of augmenting cataloging copy containing LCSH-assigned subject headings by creating and assigning its own subject headings.

The decision to adopt LCSH should rest on the size and nature of a library's collection, and the patrons for whom the catalog is intended. If the collection is unspecialized, exceeds 20,000 volumes,[20] and is used by an audience of nonspecialists, LCSH is the logical choice for an all-purpose, standardized subject authority. The delicate balance between gathering materials on like subjects and distinguishing materials on unlike subjects for large numbers of searchers of different types is difficult to achieve, but LCSH has a generally positive track record in doing so for more than a century. This may be the most convincing evidence in its favor.

Try assigning LCSH headings to the hypothetical titles that follow in Figure 8.6. The answers will be found in Appendix B on page 248.

FIGURE 8.6

1. TITLE: *Wee places in the bens and glens*

   SUMMARY: A list of bed and breakfast accommodations in Scotland

2. TITLE: *What's with this weather?*

   SUMMARY: A discussion about rain, hail, sleet, and snow

3. TITLE: *Religion's impact on society*

   SUMMARY: A book about how religion affects social conditions

4. TITLE: *The rebellion that became a revolution*

   SUMMARY: A history of the American Revolution

5. TITLE: *The effectiveness of bilingual education*

   SUMMARY: Parents, teachers, politicians, and students explore major issues in bilingual

education

6. TITLE: On the hustings

   SUMMARY: A book of political cartoons about politics

7. TITLE: Pesky visitors to the wheat field

   SUMMARY: A DVD about the methods to use in keeping wheat healthy without using pesticides

8. TITLE: *The California homeowner's directory*

   SUMMARY: A directory of retailers in California arranged by cities and towns

9. TITLE: *My war to save the world*

   SUMMARY: Reminiscences of a veteran who was with the Canadian army in Europe during

World War II

10. TITLE: *We can do better for the homeless*

   SUMMARY: A proposal to a municipal government written by a community group about

providing the homeless with opportunities to develop marketable manual skills and improvements in

mental health

11. TITLE: *When breast cancer strikes: A Chicago story*

   SUMMARY: A history of the progress in diagnosing breast cancer in Chicago

Recommended Reading

American Library Association. Subject Analysis Committee. *Guidelines on Subject Access to Individual Works of Fiction, Drama, Etc.*, 2nd ed. Chicago: American Library Association, 2000.

Chan, Lois Mai. *Library of Congress Subject Headings: Principles and Application*, 4th ed. Westport, CT: Libraries Unlimited, 2005.

Fountain, Joanna F. *Subject Headings for School and Public Libraries: An LCSH/Sears Companion*, 2nd ed. Westport, CT: Libraries Unlimited, 2005.

Ganendran, Jacki. *Learn Library of Congress Subject Access*. Lanham, MD: Scarecrow Press, 2000.

Intner, Sheila S., et al., eds. *Cataloging Correctly for Kids: An Introduction to the Tools*, 4th ed. Chicago: American Library Association, 2006.

Knowlton, Steven A. "Three Decades Since "Prejudices and Antipathies": A Study of Changes in the *Library of Congress Subject Headings*." *Cataloging & Classification Quarterly* 40, no. 2 (2005): 123–145.

Mann, Thomas. "Research at Risk." *Library Journal* 130, no. 12 (July 2005): 38–40.

Robare, Lori, ed. *Basic Subject Cataloging Using LCSH*. Washington, DC: ALCTS/SAC-PCC/SCT Joint Initiative on Subject Training Materials; Library of Congress Cataloging Distribution Service, 2004. 2 volumes: Trainee's Manual and Instructor's Manual.

Roe, Sandra K. "Subject Access Vocabularies in a Multi-type Library Consortium." *Cataloging & Classification Quarterly* 33, no. 2 (2001): 55–67.

Stone, Alva T., ed. *The LCSH Century: One Hundred Years with the Library of Congress Subject Headings System*. New York: Haworth Information Press, 2000.

Notes

1. Library of Congress, Cataloging Policy and Support Office, Library Services, *Library of Congress Subject Headings*, 29th ed. (Washington, DC: Library of Congress Cataloging Distribution Service, 2006). Though this edition will be somewhat dated at the time this book is published, the general stability of LCSH makes it possible to reference for this chapter. Individual headings and subdivisions chosen as examples have been checked against the online authority file for accuracy as of January 2007.

2. http://www.loc.gov/cds/lcsh.html (Viewed January 18, 2007).

3. http://memory.loc.gov/ammem/awhhtml/awgc1/lc_subject.html (Viewed November 29, 2005).

4. Ibid.

5. For specific information on who may make new subject heading proposals and how to do so, see the PowerPoint presentation on the LC website at www.loc.gov/catdir/pcc/saco/SACO-MLA_2004_files/slide0160.htm (Viewed December 7, 2005).

6. *Library of Congress Subject Headings* (2006), 29th ed., p. 1096.

7. Ibid., pp. SD-i to SD-97.

8. Ibid., p. SD-57.

9. Information about *Classification Web* functionality given by Bruce Chr. Johnson, Library of Congress, Cataloging Distribution Service, to Sheila S. Intner, via email February 1, 2006.

10. In terms of LCSH's computer programming, a subject heading with the first subfield y files before the same subject heading with the first subfield x, which, in turn, files before the same subject heading with the first subfield z. In the illustration, "Bronzes," the first subdivisions are chronological and file before the topical subdivisions, which, in turn, file before the geographic subdivisions.

11. Library of Congress, *Subject Cataloging Manual: Subject Headings*, 5th ed. (Washington, DC: Library of Congress, Cataloging Distribution Service, 1996). Updated information is available in later issues of *Cataloging Service Bulletin* and at the Library of Congress website: www.loc.gov.

12. *Library of Congress Subject Headings* (LCSH), p. 2723.

13. Readers should note the overlap in a few of these LCSH examples with the examples given in Chapter 7 taken from *Sears List of Subject Headings*. The choices were deliberate, highlighting the fact that some headings are common to both lists.

14. LCSH, p. 4108.

15. Library of Congress, Office for Subject Cataloging Policy, *Subject Cataloging Manual: Subject Headings*, 5th ed. (Washington, DC: Library of Congress, Cataloging Distribution Service, 1996–) provides more detailed instructions on geographic subdivision and lists exceptions in addition to these three.

16. LCSH, p. 739.

17. LCSH, p. 3627.

18. LCSH, pp. SD-i to SD-97.

19. The Subject Analysis Committee (SAC) is a committee of the Cataloging and Classification Section of the Association for Library Collections & Technical Services (ALCTS), and ALCTS is a division of the American Library Association (ALA), not a committee directly under the governance of ALA as a whole. Thus, the Committee's true hierarchy from top to bottom is ALA/ALCTS/CCS/SAC. To facilitate ease of reading, the hierarchy is telescoped here.

20. Twenty thousand volumes is the recommended collection size limit for users of *Sears List of Subject Headings*.

9

Classification Systems

Introduction

Classification is the name applied to the subject-oriented arrangement of materials in a collection, either physically, on library shelves, or virtually, in bibliographies, catalogs, database indexes, and other finding tools. In North American libraries, classification is used primarily to arrange materials on shelves. In Europe and elsewhere around the world, it is used to organize major bibliographies and library catalogs as well as to place materials on shelves. Some North American bibliographies, such as H. W. Wilson's *Public Library Catalog*, are arranged in classified order. This chapter will examine the principles of library classification and their applications in libraries.

Organizing Attributes

Anyone who has tried to locate one item within a collection of many hundreds or thousands of similar items knows how difficult it is, even when one recalls an approximate location in which to look. Small libraries and media centers that typically have collections numbering in the ten thousands[1] would do the public a disservice if they did not arrange their materials in a useful order on the shelves. *Small* is a relative term and so is *useful*. Applying an organizing attribute does not guarantee an arrangement is useful. The resulting arrangement must meet the needs and expectations of the public for whom it is intended.

The following eight attributes have been or are being used in classifying library materials.

1. *Date acquired.* Libraries once put materials on their shelves in the order in which they were acquired. As each item entered the library, it was assigned a number in a single sequence from one to infinity, called an accession number, that was recorded in a list known as an accession list. (This process, called *accessioning*, used to be the first step in processing library materials.) The accession list was of perpetual interest as a record of exactly how a library's collection was built, item by item; and if some items were later discarded, the discard dates might be recorded next to the accession numbers, but the listings, evidence of previous ownership, remained. If one wanted an item in a collec-

tion arranged by accession number, one had to know its number. Browsing through many pages of acquisitions to find it could take a long time if the collection were large and the searcher had no idea when the item had been purchased. Although not strictly an accession order system, the practice of many libraries of placing new materials in a special section of shelves reflects this attribute.

2. *Fixed-order.* Typically, accession number arrangements also employed the principle of fixed order. As each new item arrives, it is shelved after those that were previously acquired. Once placed, it would not be moved again. With fixed-order schemes, once one learns where an item is, one can return to it expeditiously. Although one might think this principle has long been discarded, it is alive and well in some collections of nonprint materials. It tends to be used for closed stack collections in which requested items are paged by staff members, and browsing, on the part of either patrons or staff members, is not an option.

3. *Genre and form.* The famous library at Alexandria in the ancient world was supposed to have been classified by literary genres—poetry in one place, speeches in another, plays in a third, and so on. Today, one sees echoes of the genre attribute in collections of fiction (often subdivided further into novels, short stories, mysteries, westerns, science fiction, fantasy, etc.), biographies, and periodicals. Another form often used to classify library materials is physical form. Separate shelf arrangements are provided for books, sound recordings, videos, direct access electronic resources, maps, and the like. Classification by form is advantageous because types of shelving appropriate to each form can be deployed in different areas of the library. It also avoids the need to repackage materials to intershelve items whose sizes and shapes vary widely. Grouping by form may also be used to further subdivide collections of musical recordings on sound tape, sound disc, videotape, and videodisc; or art collections that include paintings, sculptures, slides, photographs, videotapes, videodiscs, and films.

4. *Size.* Medieval libraries often shelved books by size (folios in one place, quartos in another, octavos in still another, etc.), which economized on the amount of space they occupied. Closed stack collections for which space is limited often use that attribute today as well. Echoes of size-order arrangements are also found in many libraries' use of special sections for oversized materials.

5. *Alphabetical order.* Alphabetical order is used often by public libraries in shelving fiction and biography, but members of the public need to know that fiction arrangements alphabetize the authors' surnames and biography arrangements alphabetize the subjects' (that is, the biographees') surnames. Many public and academic libraries shelve periodicals alphabetically by title. They believe the time and cost of classifying them is not worth the resulting convenience for browsers of placing subject-oriented periodicals together with related monographs. Without question, no single choice suits every searcher best. People accustomed to finding periodicals together in one alphabetical arrangement might not be pleased if the periodicals were distributed across the entire collection according to their subject matter.

6. *Main entries.* Few library collections are arranged by main entry, although it is not unheard of; but the great *National Union Catalog* of the United States was arranged that way until the 1980s.[2] The rule of thumb for many items was that authors were the main entries of their publications, but frequent exceptions to it caused problems. Only librari-

ans with thorough knowledge of the cataloging rules could be sure of an item's main entry, and even they were sometimes confounded by tricky interpretations.

7. *Subject arrangement.* Subject content is the organizing attribute most frequently used for library collections, whether to arrange the physical items on shelves or to list the bibliographic information in bibliographies, catalogs, and similar finding tools. Knowledge can be divided according to the focus of study; for example, into humanities (subjects that focus on human culture, such as religion and philosophy, literature, the arts, and history), social sciences (subjects that focus on society's organized activities, such as sociology, political science, law, and economics), and natural sciences (subjects that focus on natural phenomena and activities, such as mathematics, physics, chemistry, geology, biology, etc.). Often, knowledge is divided into commonly recognized fields of study, such as those that make up university departments. What is important about subject classification is that the division of subjects must be exhaustive (that is, cover all topics), unambiguous (that is, identified clearly), and mutually exclusive (that is, there must be no doubt about where one subject ends and another begins).

8. *Relative location.* The eighth and last of the classificatory attributes is the idea that materials may be moved around from one part of a shelf arrangement or database compilation to another depending on their relationships to one another. When subject classification is the guiding principle, as new materials or entries are added to collections, the relationships of individual items to the rest may change. The attribute of relative location permits them to be moved to preserve the subject relationships.

Classification in North American Libraries

North American libraries generally use classification systems to arrange materials on library shelves according to their subjects. Classification is not used to arrange public catalogs, which, in North American tradition, are alphabetical. The most popular systems used in practice are the Dewey Decimal Classification (DDC) and the Library of Congress Classification (LCC). Both organize knowledge into disciplines (main classes) and assume relative, not fixed, location. DDC divides knowledge into ten main classes, LCC into twenty-one, deriving more main classes by separating some fields of study that DDC treats as part of a broader discipline. For example, DDC has one main class (3xx) that includes sociology, political science, economics, law, and education. LCC has four main classes (H, J, K, L) covering those same fields of study.[3]

DDC and LCC practices dictate choosing a classification number that exactly matches the subject covered by an item, called a *coextensive* number (e.g., an item titled *Principles of Chemistry* is assigned a number for chemistry, but an item titled *Principles of Inorganic Chemistry* is assigned a narrower number that covers only inorganic chemistry and excludes organic chemistry). Should the content of an item cover more than one subject (e.g., an item titled *Principles of Chemistry and Physics*), it still is assigned only one number. To decide what the number should be, classifiers are expected to examine how much of the item is devoted to each subject. If one subject predominates (it occupies more space in the item), the classification number for that subject is assigned. (If *Principles of Chemistry and Physics* has 100 pages about chemistry and 200 about physics, it receives a number for physics.) If two or three subjects are covered equally, in LCC the classification number assigned reflects the subject presented first in the work; but in DDC the classification number reflects the number that comes first in the classification schedule. Therefore, the appropriate DDC number for the example is the number for physics. If more than three subjects are covered, a broader number is assigned that includes all the individual subjects.

Librarians assume all copies of a title are assigned the same classification number. As a result, one cannot buy two copies of *Principles of Chemistry and Physics* and assign the number for chemistry to one and the number for physics to the second. Both copies are assigned the same number, which is determined by one of the subjects having more space than the other or, if the space is equally divided between them, by the order that the subjects are presented in the work for LCC and by the order they are presented in the classification schedule by DDC.

Comparison of DDC and LCC

DDC and LCC are covered in some detail in Chapters 10 and 11, respectively, and are not described here. Readers may wish to skip this section until they have finished reading those chapters and come back to it afterward. The general comparison offered here is based on features of the two systems that are common knowledge among those who, having used libraries in elementary and secondary schools, colleges or universities, and public libraries, are likely to have encountered and used both systems. DDC and LCC share many characteristics as well as having certain fundamental differences.

In North America, DDC is popular mainly in school library media centers and public libraries of all sizes, whereas LCC is used mainly in college and university libraries. Having made the statement, however, the authors hasten to add it is not a hard and fast rule and there are many exceptions (e.g., the University of Toronto Faculty of Information Studies Library uses DDC and the Boston Public Library uses LCC). During the latter third of the twentieth century, a number of college and university libraries shifted to LCC from DDC, in part to make it possible for their classifiers to copy the more numerous LCC numbers from bibliographic network catalog records and in part to address the issues that arise in classifying very large collections. As academic library collections grew to 1 million volumes or more, classification options other than those they were using seemed more effective.

Similarities of DDC and LCC: DDC and LCC both consist of schedules of numbers representing all topics in all disciplines in the universe of knowledge. These kinds of systems are called *enumerative*, because all the classes are provided (that is, enumerated), and the classifier examines the array to find the slot that fits each item being classified. By contrast, if one classifies an item using a nonenumerative or *faceted* system (also called *synthetic*), one takes appropriate numbers from each of the facets and combines (or synthesizes) them to build the number.

DDC and LCC also share some of their history and outlook. DDC is older, but both classifications originated well over a century ago and reflect a late nineteenth/early twentieth century perception of the relationships among disciplines.[4] Both began in the United States and have biases toward the United States, North America, and Western culture in general.[5] Beyond this, they also reflect perceptions of knowledge tinged by white, male, Anglo-Saxon, Christian biases. Efforts have been made by editors of both classifications to internationalize their approach to subjects and de-emphasize the biases, but many examples still exist and are difficult to erase entirely.[6]

Both classifications are updated on a continuous basis, with new, deleted, and changed numbers published online (see Chapters 10 and 11). New printed editions of DDC and LCC schedules are issued irregularly.

To sum up, DDC and LCC have the following similarities:

1. Scope   3. History and worldview
2. Enumeration   4. Updating

Differences Between DDC and LCC: The principal difference between DDC and LCC is their size. LCC has many more enumerated numbers, which is obvious when one considers its forty-plus printed volumes in contrast to DDC's four volumes. DDC employs more number building than does LCC through the use of auxiliary tables and repetitions of specific patterns of subdivision and sub-subdivision for numerous subjects, but its numbers do not match LCC's level of specificity although, theoretically, they could.

A second visible difference between the classifications is their notation. DDC's consists only of Arabic numbers; LCC's is alphanumeric, using both capital letters and Arabic numbers. The single character system is called *pure notation*; the multiple character system is called *mixed notation*. LCC's notation tends to be more flexible and economical than DDC's, because the number of characters it can combine and permute is larger (thirty-six for LCC versus ten for DDC). As a result, LCC numbers for the same topics can be much shorter.[7] (See Figure 11.3 on page 191. Note that the LCC is E161.5; the rest of the number is the shelf mark.)

A third and more significant difference between the two classifications is their structural approach. DDC is hierarchical and, for the most part, short numbers express broader topics, whereas long numbers represent narrower ones. The decimal point in DDC[8] means the number sequence puts narrow topics after the broader ones to which they relate; for example, the narrowest topic in the following array has the most numbers:

306	culture and institutions
306.3	economic institutions
306.36	systems of labor
306.362	slavery
306.36203	slavery in the ancient world
306.362038	slavery in ancient Greece
306.3620385	slavery in ancient Athens

LCC, on the other hand, is a practical arrangement of LC's collection. It is not hierarchical, although some of its number spans do exhibit hierarchy. LCC often subdivides topics by alphabetizing their geographical or topical aspects. It also requires the publication of items on new topics before it establishes numbers for them, whereas DDC is more flexible. If it is clear that new topics have emerged, DDC numbers for them may be developed independently of the publication of specific items.

DDC provides mnemonics (memory aids) that operate throughout its schedules, such as the use of "9" for the history/biography/geography of a subject and numbers from its auxiliary table 2 for geographic locations. One learns that -951 at the end of a DDC number probably means "China" and -92 means biography. Schedules for LCC main classes are developed independently of one another and LCC has no universal mnemonics. LCC main classes have few, if any, internal mnemonics that apply throughout a class.

DDC has a single relative index that lists topics and numbers for the entire classification, whereas LCC indexes are specific only to individual volumes. Similarly, DDC has six auxiliary tables that apply to the entire classification, whereas LCC has myriad tables in every volume, but few of them apply to more than one span of numbers. Numbers from DDC tables are concatenated to numbers from the schedules (called "base" numbers) to subdivide them. Numbers from LCC tables may be either added arithmetically or concatenated to base numbers, depending, generally, on whether the table number is a digit (for example, 3 or 3.5) or a cutter number (that is, C3 or C3.5).

To sum up, differences between DDC and LCC include the following:

1. Size and specificity
2. Notation
3. Structural approaches
4. Mnemonics
5. Indexing
6. Tables and their application

Call Numbers: Other Shelf Marks

Collection Designations: If part of a library's collection is to be housed separately from the main collection, a collection designation is often added to the call number. Generally, collection designations appear first in call numbers, preceding the classification number and all other shelf marks. Collection designations are used to identify different units in a system or buildings in a complex (main library vs. branches; individual media centers in a school district), departments within a building (reference vs. circulating; adult vs. children's; music vs. English department), and/or material forms (for example, books vs. videos).

If two copies of an item are purchased, for example, one for a main library collection and one for a branch, the main library and/or branch designations are likely to appear first, followed by the same call number. (Or, perhaps, only branch materials are given collection designations. Materials without collection designations belong to the main library.) Or, if one copy is purchased for the reference collection and a second for the circulating collection, the designations identifying them will precede the rest of the call number. Or, if two copies of Shakespeare's *Hamlet* are purchased, one recorded on a sound disc and one on a video DVD, the former might be given the collection designation "Sound" or "CD" and the other "Video" or "DVD." Sometimes several collection designations must be combined; for example, a branch library's DVD or a second, circulating copy of an Art Department Library reference tool.

It aids members of the public when collection designations are clear and understandable. Reference departments, for example, might be identified as "R" or "Ref.," but if a branch of the library were known as the "Refectory" branch, it would be confusing to use the same abbreviation for it as for the reference department. Assuming the longer abbreviation were used, a reference item in the Refectory branch would be identified as "Ref./Ref." Similarly, the choice of identifications for nonprint media collections should not be confusing. Physical forms of materials have proliferated to the point that using abbreviations is difficult and submedia need to be identified as well (for example, sound tapes and sound discs, videotapes and videodiscs, etc.) The authors recommend using whole words, such as "Sound," "Video," "Maps," and so forth, in place of letters or alphanumeric combinations that must be deciphered.

In the OCLC bibliographic network, collection designations are given in a different field than shelf marks that follow the classification number. The former appear in field 049 as collection addresses; the latter appear in subfield b of the classification number field as shelf addresses within a particular collection.

Cutter Numbers: Charles Cutter initiated the practice of creating brief alphanumeric symbols consisting of an initial letter followed by one or more digits representing subsequent letters to substitute for full names or other words. The result is to alphabetize them using fewer characters than if they were spelled out in full. The symbols are known as cutter numbers and the practice of assigning them is called *cuttering.*

LCC classification includes cutter numbers in the classification as well as using them for shelf marks. In LCC call numbers, the shelf mark "I58" stands for the name "Intner." Very small libraries may substitute letters alone, calling them cutter letters instead of cutter numbers; for example, Intner's book could be cuttered "I," "In," or "Int."

Only LC can establish official cutter numbers, but any librarian can create local cutters at any time for use in local libraries. Later, if a librarian discovers that LC has cataloged the same item using a different cutter number, he or she can choose to change the local number to conform to LC or continue to use the locally assigned number. Conforming to LC avoids potential conflicts in the future, but it takes time and costs money to change. Departing from LC requires no action, but risks the possibility that LC will assign the same number to a different item, creating more differences as time passes and forcing the local library to create new local cutters for every item it catalogs. If librarians can live with their self-induced need for more local cutters, the local catalog can continue to avoid conflicts. Which of the two choices results in the least additional work is unknown.

Cutter numbers can be created in two ways: published lists enumerate two- and three-digit cutter numbers that librarians can copy,[9] or, alternatively, librarians can construct cutter numbers using LC's cuttering rules (see page 205).

If one adopts a published list, but encounters a name or word that is not listed, a number is interpolated for the item that maintains alphabetic consistency, as in the following hypothetical example: A local library buys a book by Alma McCostrel, but the list gives only M33 for McConnell and M34 for McCottrell. The local librarian interpolates a cutter that falls between the two published numbers—M335—for McCostrel's book. Not only does M335 fall between M33 and M34, but it leaves room to add M331 for McConnelly, M332 for McConnough, M333 for McConyers, and so on. The foregoing example is hypothetical, but the fact that cutter numbers are filed as decimals is not. It is the feature that allows for interpolation.

Dates: Dates used as shelf mark elements are publication dates. LC policy, which once added publication dates to call numbers solely for editions subsequent to the first editions of a title, changed toward the end of the twentieth century to add them to all materials cataloged. Currently, the publication years, given in arabic numerals, are added to LCC call numbers after the cutter numbers regardless of how editions are expressed in the items themselves; that is, whether they are numbered (2nd, 3rd, etc.), named (revised, enlarged, etc.), or actually identified by years of publication (2007 edition).

Title Letters: In order to distinguish among the works of prolific authors, composers, and the like, letters from significant words in individual titles may be added in order to form unique call numbers that alphabetize the person's works on the shelf. Title letters usually are lowercased. The number of letters to be added is a matter of local policy, but it is wise to add enough to avoid potential conflicts, even though it may not be practical to add a great many. Choosing the appropriate title words to use as shelf marks may require extra thought if classifiers are faced with many items by the same author with titles such as "The Mystery of the . . . ," or "The Lonely Planet Guide to . . . . "

The assignment of shelf marks for materials classified using DDC is not the same as those assigned to LCC. In Figure 9.1 the LC cataloging-in-publication gives the complete LCC with appropriate shelf marks, while the DDC is given without shelf marks. This is because the items that LC catalogs are part of its collection and, therefore, have a place on

FIGURE 9.1

```
This example is an illustration of:
    • work emanating from a corporate body entered under title
    • other title information
    • subsidiary responsibility
    • place of publication not given, but known
    • distributor
    • contents (bibliography and index) note
    • two ISBNs
    • ISBNs qualified
    • Library of Congress and Sears subject headings the same
    • added entry for illustrator
    • added entry for corporate body
    • Dewey decimal classification with prime marks
    • Library of Congress classification
    • Canadian CIP
    • 2nd level cataloging
```

```
Research ate my brain : the panic-proof guide to surviving
    homework / Toronto Public Library ; art by Martha Newbigging.
    -- [Toronto] : Annick Press : Firefly Books [distributor],
    c2005.
    96 p. : ill. ; 22 cm.

    Includes bibliographic references and index.
    ISBN 1-55037-939-9 (bound). -- ISBN 1-55037-938-0 (pbk.).

    1. Homework -- Handbooks, manuals, etc.  2. Research --
Methodology -- Handbooks, manuals, etc.  I. Newbigging, Martha.
II. Toronto Public Library.
```

Recommended DDC: 371.3'028'1
Recommended LCC: LB1048.R48 2005

Fig. 9.1—Continues

LC's shelves for which a cutter number is established, whereas the DDC is not used by LC to house its collection, but is added solely as an aid to catalogers.

There are two methods that DDC-classified libraries use as shelf marks. Larger libraries generally use the cutter tables listed in footnote 9 on page 164. Smaller collections add call letters—the first one, first two, or first three letters of the main entry (excluding initial articles). Like LC, the only deviation from this policy is for biography wherein the cutter number or call letters of the biographee are listed before those of the author.

Policy Issues

Choice of Classification System and Application Practice: The most important policy decision in connection with classification is the choice of the system the library uses to arrange its materials. A collateral, but equally important, decision is whether to apply the same system to all materials or to use different systems of classification for some. The authors

FIGURE 9.1 *(continued)*

(chief source of information)

(title page)

Research Ate My Brain

THE PANIC-PROOF GUIDE TO SURVIVING HOMEWORK

TORONTO PUBLIC LIBRARY
ART BY MARTHA NEWBIGGING

ANNICK PRESS LTD.
Toronto • New York • Vancouver

(information on verso)

We acknowledge the support of the Canada Council for the Arts, the Ontario
Arts Council, and the Government of Canada through the Book Publishing
Industry Development Program (BPIDP) for our publishing activities.

Cataloging in Publication

Research ate my brain : the panic-proof guide to surviving homework /
Toronto Public Library : art by Martha Newbigging.

Includes bibliographical references and index.
ISBN 1-55037-939-9 (bound). —ISBN 1-55037-938-0 (pbk.)

1. Homework—Handbooks, manuals, etc. 2. Research—Methodology—
Handbooks, manuals, etc. I. Newbigging, Martha II. Toronto Public Library

LB1048.R48 2005   371.3'028'1   C2005-902816-5

The text was typeset in Galliard.

Distributed in Canada by: Published in the U.S.A. by Annick Press (U.S.) Ltd.
Firefly Books Ltd.   Distributed in the U.S.A. by:
66 Leek Crescent   Firefly Books (U.S.) Inc.
Richmond Hill, ON   P.O. Box 1338
L4B 1H1   Ellicott Station
                                    Buffalo, NY 14205

Printed and bound in Canada by Friesens, Altona, Manitoba.

Visit us at: www.annickpress.com
· ·
With special thanks to Ab. Velasco.
· ·

In *Research Ate My Brain*, you will find a list of recommended websites
for research. With the exception of RAMP, Science Net, and Virtual
Reference Library, these websites are not endorsed by Annick Press or
Toronto Public Library.

Also, please note that although these websites were current and
functional when this book went to press, Web addresses do change all
the time. If you come across a dead link, try typing just the first part of
the address – up to the first slash (/) – where applicable. This takes
you to the site host's home page.

---

recommend using one system for all library collections, whether or not they are shelved
together. The advantages are many: classifiers and patrons alike become familiar with the
system and can use it more effectively, and instructional programs have greater benefits; if
collections are open to the public, browsing efficiency is enhanced; searching by classification number in online catalogs is more productive; discovery of materials in a variety of
collection areas is facilitated; and patrons often care more about the subject matter covered
than the type of materials they find. Nevertheless, some libraries choose to use different
classifications with different types of materials. Those most frequently exempted from the

main classification system are nonbook materials, microforms, government documents, and, in public libraries in particular, fiction and biographies.

If a library chooses to use DDC, it must decide immediately whether to use the full edition or the abridged edition. Very small libraries (fewer than 20,000 items) may be satisfied with the abridged numbers, which generally run no more than 5 digits and are matched to headings in *Sears List of Subject Headings*. Figure 5.10 on page 82 displays a short Dewey number that is different in the abridged and unabridged editions. The abridged Dewey number in Figure 9.2 may be too long for the needs of a small library and, if the library does not have many items on social groups relating to women, the number could be shortened to 305.4.

A second set of decisions should be made about how to apply DDC's options for biography and, outside the United States and Canada, for languages and literatures. If a library chooses to use LCC, a set of decisions should be made about what to do about cuttering when previously established cutter numbers are not available for authors, titles, and topics. The LC policy manuals titled *Subject Cataloging Manual: Classification* and *Subject Cataloging Manual: Shelflisting* can be of help in making these decisions.

Decisions also need to be made in advance about how to implement changes to DDC and LCC schedules. This is a more critical issue for DDC libraries, because DDC revises its schedules more frequently than LCC does, but new, deleted, and revised numbers appear from time to time in LCC as well (for example, shifting law numbers from other subject schedules to class K and reassigning the numbers in the JX schedule). Plans for implementation should be made before changes occur, not in a crisis response to the sudden appearance of new materials with changed numbers that fail to collocate with existing collections.

Choice of Shelf Marks: The choice of which shelf marks to employ and how they are to appear on the spines of books or boxes of other forms of materials should be made after consideration of the size and distribution of collections, not merely continuing to follow whatever tradition was in place at a particular library. If a collection is small, fewer marks may be necessary to identify individual items. If a collection was once small but has grown to the point where the marks in current use do not distinguish items sufficiently, changes can make the shelving arrangement function better.

An anecdote illustrates problems that ignoring shelf marks can cause. A very large university library collection that had been classified with DDC switched to LCC, but left its shelf marks unchanged. As a result, music materials that had previously been assigned the collection designation "D" for "departmental library," which was the name given much earlier to the university's sole stand-alone departmental library, were being mistaken for history materials in LCC's class D. Classifiers had to change the shelf marks to clear up the confusion among members of the shelving staff and to ensure that music materials were shelved in the university's music library and history materials in the main library.

Unique Call Numbers: There is no hard and fast, universally accepted rule that each item in library collections must be given a unique call number. Libraries that want each title (not item) in their collection to have a unique call number are likely to assign all shelf marks described above (collection designations, cutter numbers, dates, and title marks). Doing this can be expected to provide a unique call number for each title. Then, if copy numbers are added, each item bears a unique call number. (Before items were bar coded, most libraries simply designated them "copy 1," "copy 2," etc., in the order in which they were added to the collection. Today, they are bar coded, and some people think the copy numbers have disappeared, but that is wrong. Each bar code is a unique number and identifies the particular copy to which it is given. To some degree, bar codes echo the much earlier practice of assigning an accession number to each item added to a library's collection.)

In libraries that do not have unique call numbers, several items can share the same call

FIGURE 9.2

This example is an illustration of:
- joint responsibility
- more than one other title information statement
- subsidiary responsibility
- text mostly illustrations
- contents (bibliography and index) note
- ISBN qualified
- Library of Congress subject headings
- Sears subject headings
- personal name added entries
- title added entry
- Dewey decimal classification with prime marks
- abridged Dewey decimal classification with prime marks
- Library of Congress classification
- Canadian CIP
- 2nd level cataloging

Macdonald, Jeanne.
  Toronto women : changing faces, 1900-2000 : a photographic journey / photographic research by Jeanne MacDonald and Nadine Stoikoff ; text by Randall White. -- Toronto : Eastendbooks, 1997.
  144 p. : chiefly ill., ports. ; 28 cm.

  Includes bibliographical references and index.
  ISBN 1-896973-04-3 (pbk.)

Tracing with Library of Congress subject headings

  1. Women -- Ontario -- Toronto -- History -- 20th century -- Pictorial works. I. Stoikoff, Nadine. II. White, Randall. III. Title.

Tracing with Sears subject headings

  1. Women -- Toronto (Ont.) -- History -- 20th century -- Pictorial works. I. Stoikoff, Nadine. II. White, Randall. III. Title.

Recommended DDC: 305.4'09713'5410904

Recommended abridged DDC: 305.4'09713

Recommended LCC: HQ1460.T6W44 1997

Fig. 9.2—Continues

FIGURE 9.2 *(continued)*

(chief source of information)

(title page)

Toronto Women
Changing Faces 1900-2000
A PHOTOGRAPHIC JOURNEY

Photographic Research by
Jeanne MacDonald and Nadine Stoikoff

Text by
Randall White

eastendbooks
Toronto 1997

(information on verso)

Designed by Andy Tong

Printed in Canada by Metrolitho

Front cover: *Toronto Women* illustration © Andrew Judd
Back cover: On the waterfront at Fisherman's Island, City of Toronto Archives,
William James Fonds, SC 244-177
On the waterfront at Balmy Beach, Susanne Milligan, Photographer

Canadian Cataloguing in Publication Data

MacDonald, Jeanne, 1943–
    Toronto women : changing faces: 1900–2000

Includes bibliographical references and index.
ISBN 1-896973-04-3

1. Women – Ontario – Toronto – History – 20th century – Pictorial works.
I. Stoikoff, Nadine. II. White, Randall. III. Title.

HQ1460.T6W44 1997   305.4'09713'5410904   C97-932004-6

eastendbooks is an imprint of Venture Press
45 Fernwood Park Avenue
Toronto, Canada
M4E 3E9
(416) 691-6816 [telephone]
(416) 691-2414 [fax]

---

number. Fewer shelf marks are assigned—only a cutter letter for the initial letter of the main entry, perhaps—and items on the same subjects with similar descriptive features (such as main entry personal authors whose surnames begin with the same letter) are shelved together at random. As long as it does not involve too many duplications, this is not a problem for browsers or librarians seeking a particular item. Retrieving a particular desired item does mean examining a few books, videos, recordings, or whatever form of item it is, to find the right one, but the process is likely to take a few minutes at most if no more than a few items must be examined. Problems occur, however, if large numbers of items all bear the same call number and many must be examined to locate the correct item. For example, it may not be very difficult to spot the Dickens title one seeks, even if all Charles Dickens's many novels are shelved in one group randomly. One can browse that single sequence quickly. But if Dickens's novels were randomly intershelved with a great many more novels by dozens of other authors whose surnames begin with "D," it might take a long time and be very tedious to search the books one by one to find the desired item.

The size of the collection and convenience of patrons should be the guiding principles for making decisions about unique call numbers. Easing classifiers' work by letting them skip some of the shelf marks is inappropriate and not recommended.

Conclusion

The North American tradition of keeping materials on shelves open to the public, who can browse them to find a desired item, makes classification by subject a powerful access tool for patrons. Online searchers can use call numbers to find useful materials when they do not know exactly what they want, but know the general subject area in which they are interested. Because call number access tends to be somewhat broader than subject headings or keywords, it is a good method of getting an overview of a subject area. Thus, call number access is a viable alternative to searching by keywords, authorized subject headings, authors, and titles.

Organizing attributes other than subject content discussed in this chapter include accession order, size, alphabetizing elements, genre and form, and main entries. In addition, the difference between fixed and relative location order is described.

Two popular classification systems used in North American libraries, DDC and LCC, are discussed and compared, as well as other elements added to classification numbers to create call numbers. These last, which are determined by local policies, include collection designations, cutter numbers, dates, and title marks. Local policies determine which classification(s) libraries use and how they apply them as well as whether or not materials have unique call numbers. Unique call numbers, which are not a requirement in shelving materials, are likely to require more shelf marks, including copy numbers that identify individual items uniquely, rather than allowing multiple titles to share the same call numbers. Collection size and patron convenience are important to consider in deciding how to identify and shelve library materials.

Decisions regarding classification and shelving made in a library should be carefully documented in writing and maintained in a file with other cataloging (in the broad sense) policies and procedures. Members of the staff and patrons can examine the written record to learn what to do as well as to understand why things are done that way. This ensures continuity when veteran classifiers leave and are replaced by new people.

Let us examine the two major classification systems in use in North America today. The next two chapters cover DDC and LCC in more detail.

Recommended Reading

Broughton, Vanda. *Essential Classification*. New York: Neal-Schuman Publishers, 2004.

Chan, Lois Mai, et al., eds. *Theory of Subject Analysis: A Sourcebook*. Littleton, CO: Libraries Unlimited, 1985.

Scott, Mona L. *Conversion Tables*, 3rd ed. Westport, CT: Libraries Unlimited, 2005. (3 volumes: LC-Dewey; Dewey-LC; Subject Headings LC and Dewey.)

Taylor, Arlene G. *The Organization of Information*, 2nd ed. Westport, CT: Libraries Unlimited, 2003.

Notes

1.   *Small* is a relative term. *Sears List of Subject Headings*, which is explicitly designed for small libraries, claims to be appropriate for collections of up to 20,000 titles. Sheila S. Intner and Josephine Riss Fang, in *Technical Services in the Medium-Sized Library* (Hamden, CT:

Shoe String Press, 1991), defined medium-sized public libraries by a population served of between 50,000 and 150,000 people. According to that definition, small libraries serve fewer people. The medium-sized libraries Intner and Fang studied held between 34,000 and 380,000 titles.

2.   When this great national bibliography was computerized, a decision was made to switch to a sequential numbering system linked to multiple indexes. Although the new system required two searches to locate an item, it was preferable to the former main entry only arrangement.

3.   In LCC, H covers both sociology and economics; J covers political science; K covers law; L covers education.

4.   An example of outdated worldview is the placement of psychology as a subdivision of philosophy rather than science or medicine, as is common thinking in the twenty-first century.

5.   Geographical subdivision of topics often put the United States, North America, and Western Europe before other countries and regions of the world, and the subdivisions for the United States, North America, and Western Europe tend to be better developed. To some degree, this is a result of *literary warrant*, the need to arrange more materials covering the United States and so on, than those that cover other countries and regions.

6.   One example in LCC is the placement of sexuality under "women" in a subdivision titled "The family. Marriage. Women" (HQ). There is no comparable subdivision for "men." Gender neutrality is absent; everything related to sex is subsumed under women, including deviance, sexual perversion, and so forth.

7.   Michael Gorman poked fun at this feature of DDC, observing that treatises on extremely narrow topics issued as short pieces with narrow spines require very long DDC numbers to achieve the requisite degree of specificity. The long numbers do not fit well on the narrow spines. Michael Gorman, "The Longer the Number, the Narrower the Spine," *American Libraries* 12, no. 8 (September 1981): 498–499.

8.   Interestingly, LCC also employs a point, but not a decimal point. Its point appears before the first cutter number, whether this cutter is part of the classification number or the shelf marks.

9.   Charles Ammi Cutter, *Two-Figure Author Table* (Chicopee Falls, MA: H. R. Huntting; distr. Westport, CT: Libraries Unlimited, 1969–); Charles Ammi Cutter, *Three-Figure Author Table* (Chicopee Falls, MA: H. R. Huntting; distr. Westport, CT: Libraries Unlimited, 1969–); *Cutter-Sanborn Three-Figure Author Table*, Swanson-Swift revision (Westport, CT: Libraries Unlimited, 1969). Cutter tables are also available online.

10

The Dewey Decimal Classification

Background and History

The Dewey Decimal Classification (DDC) was devised in the early 1870s by Melvil Dewey[1] and was initially applied to library collections at Amherst College, where Dewey served as college librarian. He tested the system at Amherst for three years before publishing it and making it available to other libraries. DDC enjoyed immediate success and was adopted widely in North America and elsewhere around the world. It is used to organize the *British National Bibliography* and arrange materials in numerous libraries in the United Kingdom. It was the basis for the Universal Decimal Classification, translated into French and developed into a faceted classification by Paul Otlet and Henri LaFontaine. DDC is said to be the world's most popular classification.[2]

Currently in its twenty-second edition, DDC was first published in 1876 under the title *Classification and Subject Index for Cataloguing and Arranging the Books and Pamphlets of a Library.* The classification has grown enormously since its inception. The initial edition, which was all that was needed to arrange Amherst College's entire collection, contained 1,000 three-digit numbers and had no auxiliary tables. In the twenty-second edition, numbers in the main schedules occupy two large volumes totaling nearly 1,800 pages. Each page contains many numbers and each number is made up of anywhere from three to ten (or more) digits. In addition to the main schedules, six auxiliary tables occupy well over 500 pages in a separate volume. Numbers from the tables are concatenated to numbers from the main schedules, elongating them further.

According to Comaromi,[3] for many years, Dewey and succeeding DDC editors May Seymour and Dorcas Fellows continued expanding selected topics and adjusting the juxtapositions of topics in response to users' requests, but made few major changes. In 1951, however, the fifteenth edition, produced under the direction of Esther Potter, was a sea change. Comaromi reports,

> ... the fifteenth edition was historically the most important edition of the DDC—not for what it was, but for what is made possible. It ushered in some modern

terminology and common spelling. It dispensed with much of the dead wood, unfortunately cutting out much living timber in the bargain. It dispensed with the overly detailed sections which no longer deserved inclusion in a book classification which the DDC had come to be. . . . It embodied some of the best ideas in typography, printing, and binding, becoming for the first time a handsome book. . . . It was a giant step in the direction of keeping pace with knowledge, a trend that has continued, though not so violently, in subsequent editions. At the same time, of course, integrity of numbers was compromised.[4]

The original fifteenth edition, rejected by DDC users, was quickly revised and republished in 1952.

Since the 1960s, new editions have been criticized for different reasons, but a strong, solid base of DDC users, particularly in North American public libraries and school library media centers, holds firm and is augmented by large numbers of libraries internationally. Translations of the full and abridged editions into languages other than English now exceed thirty, and DDC is used to organize the national bibliographies of more than sixty countries.[5] The balance of this chapter is devoted to examining the principles underlying DDC as well as the forms in which it appears, the opportunities for DDC copy classification, and its schedules and tables.

Principles

Seven principles underlie the organization and structure of DDC: (1) decimal division, (2) classification by discipline, (3) hierarchy, (4) mnemonics, (5) literary warrant, (6) enumeration, and (7) relative location. These are explained below.

1. *Decimal division.* Decimal division or division by tens is the primary method of dividing subjects used by DDC. It merits attention because it is a familiar and useful method of dividing things. Most people refer to dividing by tens as using "round" numbers. However, decimal division also is the source of troubling limitations, because subjects do not necessarily divide neatly into ten subdivisions. Think, for example, of the number of languages into which the broad class of Literature is divided or the number of countries into which the broad class of History is divided. As a result of the decimal principle, first level divisions of Literature may appear as three digits (810 = American literature and 820 = English literature), four digits (839.7 = Swedish literature), five digits (891.86 = Czech literature), six digits (891.992 = Armenian literature), and so on.

2. *Classification by discipline.* The primary attribute applied in dividing knowledge is discipline, represented by the ten main classes. Although this may seem natural to readers of this book because it is a familiar way of doing things, it is not the only possibility. Knowledge could be divided first by a different element, such as time period or geographic location, and only after that by discipline, genre, form, and other attributes. Also, DDC's main classes do not coincide with most university disciplines, which usually number a great many more than ten, or the traditional triumvirate: Humanities, Social Sciences, Sciences.

3. *Hierarchy.* The principle of moving from broad categories to narrower ones and from these to still narrower ones until the narrowest possible category is reached is frequently encountered in classification, but DDC emphasizes it and it is obvious in many complex

numbers. Ideally, the hierarchy built into DDC numbers identifies topics at the same level and clarifies which are broader and narrower merely by noting the number and character of the digits in the class. In practice, this functions only part of the time, because all topical areas do not divide neatly into tens, as mentioned in principle 2, above. In Literature, a number with three digits might be at the same classificatory level as a second number with five digits; for example, British fiction is 823, but Russian fiction is 891.43. An example hierarchy may be seen in the DDC number for a teacher's guide for harvest songs: 781.524607, parsed as follows:

7	the arts, fine and decorative arts
78	music
781	general principles and musical forms
781.5	kinds of music
781.52	music for specific times
781.524	music for the seasons
781.5246	fall (autumn) including harvest
781.524607	education, research, related topics

4. *Mnemonics.* Dewey was enamored of time-saving devices and incorporated them into his classification wherever he could. Specific groups of numbers can represent the same topic in multiple places throughout the classification. A familiar example is the number "9," which stands for Geography and History in many instances: 900 = all Geography and History; 759 = Painting limited to a specific location. By adding 9 to the number for Cooking 641.5 = 641.59 makes it specific to a particular geographic location. Another example of mnemonics is found in the numbers for geographic locations: 44 = France when added to 641.59 as in French cooking, 641.5944. Another example of the mnemonic 44 is found in the number for Travel in France, 914.4, 91 = Travel in general, but adding 44 limits it to Travel in France.

5. *Literary warrant.* This principle dictates that classes are created only after materials exist that require them. Because DDC is a universal classification, one might think that classes for all the subjects that might ever be written about are already established, but no classification of limited size can anticipate or list all topics, and DDC is no exception. When new subjects appear, numbers for them are established, sometimes causing disruptions in the part of the classification where they occur. "Computers" is a good example of a topic that was established when the need for it emerged. In the nineteenth and earlier editions of DDC, computers occupy a tiny class (001.64) under the larger topic of "Research" (001). In the twentieth and later editions, Computers were relocated and expanded to occupy three newly established sections of their own: 004–006.

6. *Enumeration.* This principle dictates the listing of precoordinated class numbers for complex topics. Enumeration can be contrasted to the principle of faceting or synthesis in which topical elements (or facets) are provided that classifiers or searchers must combine (or synthesize) to build complex topics. While this principle still generally guides DDC, recent editions incorporate more instances of number building and fewer instances of enumeration because the former is more economical of page space. Enormous expansion of some subject areas in recent years would require tremendous increases in enumerated

numbers to represent them, whereas instructions to apply existing expansion techniques without actually enumerating each of them does not.

7. *Relative location.* At one time in the United States, Canada, and elsewhere, library books were shelved in fixed locations. Once an item was given its place on the shelves, it would never be moved to any other, no matter what new materials were added to the collection. DDC operates on the principle that as new materials are added and shelved, existing items will be moved as well to keep materials on the same subjects together. The DDC number merely identifies a shelf location relative to other items in the collection. Readers should not think that fixed location classification has disappeared entirely. It is not unusual for materials shelved in the order they are acquired, also called accession number arrangements, for small collections of nonbook materials such as videotapes, toys, and realia.

None of the seven principles operates everywhere, perfectly, throughout the DDC system. They are observed as far as possible when they do not conflict, create unwanted juxtapositions of subjects, or otherwise interfere with practical considerations. Enumeration may be abandoned to save space; mnemonics are superseded when necessary; and other principles are modified when it is important to do so. Nevertheless, the principles govern many of the decisions made by DDC's editors with regard to class numbers and relationships.

An eighth principle—integrity of numbers—was promised by Dewey to DDC users in the early days of the classification. This meant that, once assigned, numbers representing a particular topic would not change. Changing classification numbers creates significant work in a library trying to keep all of its materials shelved in a consistent, up-to-date manner. At the least, call number labels and markings in or on materials must be changed; catalog records must be altered to display new call numbers; and materials must be moved to their new locations. Sometimes, large spans of numbers have been changed to reflect profound changes in a subject area, a practice once called *phoenixing.* A phoenixed schedule was discarded entirely and rebuilt (one might say "risen from the ashes," like the mythical bird). At several points in DDC's history, users rebelled at having to absorb too many changes.[6] In recent years, the term was replaced by the milder phrase "complete revision" and the practice was modified, though not abandoned totally.

Format of the Classification Numbers

DDC is divided, first of all, into 10 main classes, 100 divisions, and 1,000 sections. *Main classes* consist of spans of 100 whole numbers from XX0 to X99 (see the list of main classes below), wherein "X" stands for any digit between zero and nine. *Divisions* consist of spans of 10 whole numbers from XX0 to XX9, such as 000–009, 520–529, and so forth. *Sections* include one whole number and all the decimally extended classification numbers falling between it and the next higher whole number, such as 071 (Newspapers in North America) or 641 (Food & drink). Thus, listed within the single section 415 (Grammar and syntax of standard forms of language) are 15 decimally extended "subsections," including nouns (415.5), verbs (415.6), and more, two of these extending to four digits after the decimal point. Some sections are subdivided extensively, whereas others have few subdivisions and extend only one or two digits beyond the decimal point.

The term *schedule* is defined and used loosely by classifiers, and can indicate different kinds of number spans. Tens of thousands of categories are enumerated in the "main" schedules; that is, all the numbers listed in volumes 2 and 3 of the printed edition or, if one thinks of it in arithmetic terms, in the entire span of numbers from 000 to 999. These are also called, simply, "the schedules." Numbers within a main class are called that discipline's "schedules"; for example, the span from 200 to 299 is called the "religion schedules." Smaller spans of numbers are also referred to as schedules; for example, numbers from 340 to 349 are called the "law schedules," numbers from 780 to 789 are called the "music schedules," and the like.

The ten disciplines represented by DDC main classes are as follows:

Computer science, information, general works	(000–099)
Philosophy, parapsychology and occultism, psychology	(100–199)[7]
Religion	(200–299)
Social sciences	(300–399)
Language	(400–499)
Natural sciences and mathematics	(500–599)
Technology (Applied sciences)	(600–699)
The arts Fine and decorative arts	(700–799)
Literature (Belles-lettres and rhetoric)	(800–899)
History, geography, and auxiliary disciplines	(900–999)

Readers wishing to see lists of divisions and sections will find them in the first few pages of volume 2 of the printed edition, under the heading "Summaries."[8] Small summaries are found at the start of each new main class and sometimes at the beginning of a subclass or still smaller spans of numbers. Figure 10.1 shows the summary at the start of the 800s; Figure 10.2 shows the summary at the start of the 650s; Figure 10.3 shows a typical page covering toxicology that includes instructional notes and a mini-summary.

Indentations, bold and plain print, running headers, and special spacing are used to indicate the meanings of numbers on a page. In Figure 10.3, one sees the following DDC printing conventions: (1) the first three digits of each number on the page, 615, are given only at the top of the page; (2) square brackets around a number indicate it is obsolete; (3) a space is inserted between each group of three digits for clarity; (4) subtopics are indented under broader topics; (5) italics are used for "see" references; and (6) bold print is used for the broad topic "Toxicology" but plain print is used for the subtopics under it. Other marks of punctuation, including daggers, asterisks, parentheses, and angle brackets, are used to highlight number building techniques and/or special meanings or treatments for the numbers with which they are used.

Editions/Versions of DDC

DDC appears in two printed editions, the twenty-second full edition (DDC22) and the fourteenth abridged edition (ADDC14); and two electronic versions, *WebDewey* and *Abridged WebDewey*, corresponding to the two printed editions, respectively, that are available as subscriptions via the Internet. ADDC14 and its electronic counterpart are recommended for small collections, defined as containing up to 20,000 items.

DDC22 is available in four printed volumes, whereas its abridged counterpart is contained in one volume. DDC is updated continuously and authorized updates are immediately available on the Dewey website (*www.oclc.org/dewey*), but new issues of the full printed edition are on a seven-year publication schedule, and updated versions of both *WebDewey*

FIGURE 10.1

800

---

800 Literature (Belles-lettres) and rhetoric

Class here works of literature, works about literature

After general topics (800–809) the basic arrangement is literature by language, then literature of each language by form, then each form by historical period; however, miscellaneous writings are arranged first by historical period, then by form. More detailed instructions are given at the beginning of Table 3

Unless other instructions are given, observe the following table of preference, e.g., collections of drama written in poetry from more than two literatures 808.82 (*not* 808.81):

> Drama
> Poetry
>   Class epigrams in verse with miscellaneous writings
> Fiction
> Essays
> Speeches
> Letters
> Miscellaneous writings
> Humor and satire

Class folk literature in 398.2; class librettos, poems, words written to be sung or recited with music in 780.268; class interdisciplinary works on language and literature in 400; class interdisciplinary works on the arts in 700

See Manual at 800; also at 080 vs. 800; also at 741.6 vs. 800; also at 800 vs. 398.2; also at 800, T3C—362 vs. 398.245, 590, 636

SUMMARY

801–807	Standard subdivisions
808	Rhetoric and collections of literary texts from more than two literatures
809	History, description, critical appraisal of more than two literatures
810	American literature in English
.1–.9	Standard subdivisions; collections; history, description, critical appraisal of American literature in English
811	American poetry in English
812	American drama in English
813	American fiction in English
814	American essays in English
815	American speeches in English
816	American letters in English
817	American humor and satire in English
818	American miscellaneous writings in English

820	English and Old English (Anglo-Saxon) literatures
.1–.9	Standard subdivisions; collections; history, description, critical appraisal of English literature
821	English poetry
822	English drama
823	English fiction
824	English essays
825	English speeches
826	English letters
827	English humor and satire
828	English miscellaneous writings
829	Old English (Anglo-Saxon) literature
830	Literatures of Germanic languages German literature
.01–.09	Standard subdivisions of literatures of Germanic languages
.1–.9	Standard subdivisions; collections; history, description, critical appraisal of German literature
831	German poetry
832	German drama
833	German fiction
834	German essays
835	German speeches
836	German letters
837	German humor and satire
838	German miscellaneous writings
839	Other Germanic literatures
840	Literatures of Romance languages French literature
.01–.09	Standard subdivisions of literatures of Romance languages
.1–.9	Standard subdivisions; collections; history, description, critical appraisal of French literature
841	French poetry
842	French drama
843	French fiction
844	French essays
845	French speeches
846	French letters
847	French humor and satire
848	French miscellaneous writings
849	Occitan, Catalan, Franco-Provençal literatures
850	Literatures of Italian, Sardinian, Dalmatian, Romanian, Rhaeto-Romanic languages Italian literature
.1–.9	Standard subdivisions; collections; history, description, critical appraisal of Italian literature
851	Italian poetry
852	Italian drama
853	Italian fiction
854	Italian essays
855	Italian speeches
856	Italian letters
857	Italian humor and satire
858	Italian miscellaneous writings
859	Romanian and Rhaeto-Romanic literatures

860	Literatures of Spanish and Portuguese languages Spanish literature
.01–.09	Standard subdivisions of literatures of Spanish and Portuguese languages
.1–.9	Standard subdivisions; collections; history, description, critical appraisal of Spanish literature
861	Spanish poetry
862	Spanish drama
863	Spanish fiction
864	Spanish essays
865	Spanish speeches
866	Spanish letters
867	Spanish humor and satire
868	Spanish miscellaneous writings
869	Portuguese literature
870	Literatures of Italic languages Latin literature
.01–.09	Standard subdivisions of literatures of Italic languages
.1–.9	Standard subdivisions; collections; history, description, critical appraisal of Latin literature
871	Latin poetry
872	Latin dramatic poetry and drama
873	Latin epic poetry and fiction
874	Latin lyric poetry
875	Latin speeches
876	Latin letters
877	Latin humor and satire
878	Latin miscellaneous writings
879	Literatures of other Italic languages
880	Literatures of Hellenic languages Classical Greek literature
.01–.09	Standard subdivisions of classical (Greek and Latin) literatures
.1–.9	Standard subdivisions; collections; history, description, critical appraisal of classical Greek literature
881	Classical Greek poetry
882	Classical Greek dramatic poetry and drama
883	Classical Greek epic poetry and fiction
884	Classical Greek lyric poetry
885	Classical Greek speeches
886	Classical Greek letters
887	Classical Greek humor and satire
888	Classical Greek miscellaneous writings
889	Modern Greek literature
890	Literatures of other specific languages and language families
891	East Indo-European and Celtic literatures
892	Afro-Asiatic literatures Semitic literatures
893	Non-Semitic Afro-Asiatic literatures
894	Altaic, Uralic, Hyperborean, Dravidian literatures
895	Literatures of East and Southeast Asia Sino-Tibetan literatures
896	African literatures
897	Literatures of North American native languages
898	Literatures of South American native languages
899	Literatures of non-Austronesian languages of Oceania, of Austronesian languages, of miscellaneous languages

FIGURE 10.2

650   **Management and auxiliary services**

Class here business

See Manual at 330 vs. 650, 658

SUMMARY

650.01–.09	Standard subdivisions
.1	Personal success in business
651	Office services
.2	Equipment and supplies
.3	Office management
.5	Records management
.7	Communication Creation and transmission of records
.8	Data processing Computer applications
.9	Office services in specific kinds of enterprises
652	Processes of written communication
.1	Penmanship
.3	Keyboarding
.4	Copying
.8	Cryptography
653	Shorthand
.1	Basic shorthand practice
.2	Abbreviated longhand systems
.3	Machine systems
.4	Handwritten systems
657	Accounting
.04	Levels of accounting
.1	Constructive accounting
.2	Bookkeeping (Recordkeeping)
.3	Financial reports (Financial statements)
.4	Specific fields of accounting
.6	Specific kinds of accounting
.7	Accounting for specific phases of business activity
.8	Accounting for enterprises engaged in specific kinds of activities
.9	Accounting for enterprises of specific sizes or specific kinds of legal or ownership form
658	General management
.001–.009	Standard subdivisions
.01–.09	[Management of enterprises of specific sizes, scopes, forms; data processing]
.1	Organization and finance
.2	Plant management
.3	Personnel management (Human resource management)
.4	Executive management
.5	Management of production
.7	Management of materials
.8	Management of marketing
659	Advertising and public relations
.1	Advertising
.2	Public relations

.01–.09   Standard subdivisions

FIGURE 10.3

615	*Dewey Decimal Classification*	615

[.882]   Folk medicine

> Number discontinued; class in 615.88

[.886]   Patent medicines

> Relocated to 615.1

.89   Other therapies

.892   Acupuncture

> Including moxibustion, electroacupuncture
>
> Class here comprehensive works on acupuncture and acupressure
>
> *For acupressure, see 615.8222*

.895   Gene therapy

[.899]   Ancient and medieval remedies

> Ancient remedies relocated to 615.880901; medieval remedies relocated to 615.880902

.9   Toxicology

> Class here poisons and poisoning
>
> Class forensic toxicology in 614.13. Class effects of poisons on a specific system or organ with the system or organ, plus notation 071 from tables under 616.1–616.9, 617, 618.1–618.8, e.g., effect of poisons on the liver 616.362071
>
> *See Manual at 615.7 vs. 615.9*

SUMMARY

615.900 1–.900 9	**Standard subdivisions**
.901–.909	**[Industrial toxicology; incidence, prevention, tests, analysis, detection, treatment of poisoning]**
.91	**Gaseous poisons**
.92	**Inorganic poisons**
.94	**Animal poisons**
.95	**Organic poisons**

.900 1   Philosophy and theory

.900 2   Miscellany

[.900 287]   Testing and measurement

> Do not use; class in 615.907

.900 3–.900 9   Standard subdivisions

---

and *Abridged WebDewey* are mounted quarterly.[9] (An earlier electronic version of DDC, issued by subscription in the form of a CD-ROM called *Dewey for Windows*, was discontinued February 28, 2005, when the Internet-based versions superseded it.)

The printed and electronic versions are not identical, though some key features are the result of differing capabilities inherent in their physical formats. DDC22 includes the following material:

Volume 1. Prefatory information, including a list of new features in the edition; an extensive introduction; options; a glossary and index to the introduction and glossary; the manual; the six auxiliary tables; a list of relocations and discontinuations; and a list of reused numbers

Volume 2. The three summaries (10 main classes, 100 divisions, 1,000 sections); the schedules for main classes 000, 100, 200, 300, 400, and 500

Volume 3. The schedules for main classes 600, 700, 800, and 900

Volume 4. The relative index

WebDewey includes the following material:

1. All the content from DDC22 plus quarterly updates to it
2. Updated mappings for headings in the list of *People, Places & Things*[10] to DDC22 numbers
3. Thousands of LC's *Library of Congress Subject Headings* (LCSH) that have been statistically mapped to Dewey numbers found in catalog records in OCLC's *World-Cat* database (the network's union catalog)
4. Thousands of terms from the relative index and "built numbers" (that is, numbers constructed by classifiers and DDC experts) not given in the printed edition
5. Links from the mapped Library of Congress subject headings (see feature 3, above) to their LC subject authority records
6. A selection of subject heading mappings from the (U.S.) National Library of Medicine's *Medical Subject Headings*

Added to the special features in the electronic versions of DDC that assist local classifiers in finding appropriate numbers for materials being classified originally, all the advantages of computerized searching accrue to users of the electronic versions as well.

Copy Classification

Since the 1930s, classifiers at the Library of Congress have assigned Dewey numbers to a selection of the titles cataloged there, averaging between 20,000 to 30,000 titles a year in the first few decades to about 100,000 to 110,000 titles a year since 1975.[11] Many classifiers use the Dewey numbers provided by LC in the cataloging-in-publication information located on the verso of the title pages of books, or in the catalog records contributed to bibliographic network records. When this is done, certain conventions followed by larger institutions need to be understood. The most important of these is the method used to show where numbers have been expanded. An apostrophe (also called a *prime mark* or *hash mark*) is placed at the end of the basic number and again after each complete expansion (see Figure 10.4). By knowing where the expansions begin and end, a library can opt to copy what is most appropriate to its needs. One library might use the entire number with all its expansions; a second library might want only the basic number, excluding the expansions; and a third might prefer something in between, such as accepting the first expansion, but nothing more.

Some agencies prefer that numbers not get too long and institute policies to limit them. Such policies should involve the addition or omission of *expansions*, rather than a designated number of digits. The expansions are meaningful expressions of subject matter and should not be cut off in the middle, causing a loss of meaning. For example, the DDC number for the topic "Models of helicopters" is 629.1331352—without doubt, a very long number. A small library having a policy of using a maximum of five numbers would cut off the number after the first "3," leaving an item about helicopter models in 629.13. Doing that, however, destroys the meaning of the basic topic, "Aircraft models," represented by the slightly longer number 629.1331, and puts the material in the much broader subject of "Aeronautics." Assigning 629.13 would mix together materials about real planes and helicopters with materials

FIGURE 10.4   Different Methods of Showing Prime Marks

Title of book: 100 Canadian heroines : famous and forgotten faces

DDC number in Library and Archives Canada CIP 920.72'0971

DDC number in LC MARC record 920.72/0971/03 *

*Authors' note: This figure illustrates the importance of checking classification numbers found in CIP or other cataloging copy sources before assigning them. LC has added -03 from Table 1 for dictionaries, encyclopedias, and concordances. This book containing 100 short biographies does not really fit into any of these three categories.

about model aircraft, which seems less desirable than separating them, even in a library or media center with a small collection of materials about aircraft.

A second convention that needs to be noted is the fact that some libraries furnish more than the class number, adding shelf marks such as cutter numbers and call letters to it. When using another library's catalog records, shelf marks should be ignored unless it is a local policy to follow these practices, also. If so, then classifiers must be careful about *whose* practices they follow. In some places, the initial letter of the main entry is used in place of a cutter number. In others, two- or three-digit cutter numbers are used, some copied from lists of cutters,[12] and others created by following LC's rules (see p. 205 for an explanation of rules for creating cutter numbers). It would be confusing to adopt all of these practices simultaneously. Letters or numbers that indicate an item is part of a reference collection, or a departmental or branch collection, and dates indicating different editions of a work, are not part of DDC classification numbers, either, and should not be copied unless they are consistent with the practices of the classifier's library as well.

Small libraries and media centers that wish to limit the length of DDC numbers would do well to consider adopting the abridged edition, even though doing so might mean having to do additional checking for needed adjustments to numbers from CIP or network records that come from the full edition. (See Figure 10.5 on the next page for a comparison of the full and abridged Dewey number.) Starting with a known number and adjusting it is easier than figuring out where to classify an item from scratch, and many numbers from the full edition need only minor revision. So long as classifiers using the abridged edition understand that "revision" and "adjustment" mean doing more than lopping off digits, local arrangements remain consistent and standardized, and furnish good browsing.

In Figure 10.5 the difference between full and abridged Dewey numbers presents no decisions; these numbers are clearly set forth in the full and abridged DDC. Figure 8.5 on pages 145–146 demonstrates an instance in which a cataloger may wish to shorten a classification number. The full DDC listed in the CIP for this book is 591.9866'5; the abridged DDC is 591.9866, which a small library may believe is too long for its collection. If a library has few books about animals in South America, the number can be shortened to 591.98.

The Schedules

In this section, DDC's schedules are explored in more detail, noting a selection of the subjects included within each main class about which public libraries and school library

FIGURE 10.5

Information on all sides of the cardboard container:
    PUMPING HEART   HUMAN SCIENCE   LINDBERG
Information on container top and one side:
    Operating plastic model heart kit with transparent heart chambers
    Kit no. 1332
Information on one side:
    Operating plastic model kit for use by doctors, educators,
    students and schools for study demonstration purposes. Adult
    guidance is suggested for youngsters under ten years old.
    Copyright by Lindberg Products Inc., Skokie Illinois ...
Information on one side:
    Life-like continuous action pumps blood thru the visible heart
    chambers, just like a real heart. Complete assembly instructions
    are included in kit. Model is 11 1/8" high (28.3 cm.)
Information on assembly instructions:
    NATURAL HISTORY SCIENCE SERIES
    The visible PUMPING HEART
    Lindberg Products, Inc.   Skokie, Illinois   kit no. 1332

This example is an illustration of:
  • model
  • entry under title
  • general material designation
  • no statement of responsibility
  • date of publication unknown
  • series statement
  • accompanying material listed in note area
  • quoted note
  • intended audience
  • local holdings note
  • Library of Congress and Sears subject heading the same
  • added entry for additional title
  • series added entry
  • comparison of full and abridged Dewey Decimal
    classification
  • 2nd level cataloging

Pumping heart [model]. -- Skokie, Ill. : Lindberg, [20--].
   1 model (various pieces) : plastic ; 29 cm. high in container
31 x 24 x 7 cm. -- (Natural science series)

   Assembly instructions (4 p.) has title: The Visible pumping
heart.
   "Life-like continuous action pumps blood thru the visible heart
chambers"--Container.
   Intended audience: for use by doctors, educators, students and
schools for study demonstration purposes.
   Library's copy unassembled.

   1. Heart -- Anatomy. I. Title: Visible pumping heart.
II. Series.

DDC: 611.12
Abridged DDC: 611

media centers are likely to collect materials. Because of space limits, however, no attempt is made to list either all the topics within a main class or all the topics likely to be included in library and media center collections. Familiarity with each class is most readily gained through repeated use of its schedules and the tools that help interpret them: the DDC manual (incorporated into the printed edition), the library's shelf list, suggested numbers from CIP and other sources, and common sense.

000s: Computer science, information, general works includes works about knowledge in general. Many of these materials fall into the category of reference materials, such as general encyclopedias, almanacs, indexes, and catalogs. An option offers locating all indexes and bibliographies in the 000s whether they are general in coverage or deal with a specific topic, such as economics or education. The rationale for the practice is that it limits searching for sources in any field to a single span of shelves and enables reference librarians responding to patrons' questions on all sorts of topics to avoid going to shelves located all over the library to find sources. (The downside of the practice is that searchers interested solely in one topic, education, for example, must go to two different parts of the library to find bibliographic sources and other materials about education.) With the advent of online versions of these materials, physical location becomes less important; but, for the time being, access to them is not universal, and online versions located together makes them easier to browse. Popular topics located in the 000s include controversial knowledge (001.9), which includes UFOs, the Loch Ness monster, the Bermuda Triangle, and other natural and human-made mysteries; computer science (004–006); libraries and librarianship (020–028); and publishing (070–079).

100s: Philosophy, parapsychology and occultism, psychology is a sharply divided class with five divisions devoted to philosophy (100–149), including one that covers parapsychology and the occult (130–139); and five divisions to psychology (150–199). This juxtaposition of psychology with other systems of thought rather than under science or medicine, where it also could be placed, reflects the way it was viewed in the nineteenth century. Section 133, titled "Specific topics in parapsychology and occultism," contains some of the most popular topics in the 100s. It includes ghosts, haunted houses, fortune-telling, witchcraft and related magic arts,[13] horoscopes, and other psychic phenomena. Harry Potter might be classified here as easily as in English fiction (823). Specific philosophic schools (Platonism, Romanticism, Kantianism, Utilitarianism, etc.) and specific schools of psychology (Freudian, Adlerian, Jungian, etc.) are assigned numbers in the 100s. Ethics (170–179), a popular topic in the twenty-first century, including political, familial, occupational, and sexual ethics, are covered here, too.

200s: Religion remains focused mainly on Christianity, although recent efforts to reduce this bias have been successful. Once, 80 percent of the numbers in the 200s were devoted to Christianity. Currently, half the divisions are devoted exclusively to it (230–239, 240–249, 250–259, 270–279, and 280–289) and so are parts of other divisions, such as the New Testament (225–229). All other religions are relegated to eight sections in division 290–299. The two sections for Judaism (296) and Islam (297) were revised and expanded in the twenty-first edition. Additional changes appear in the twenty-second edition, mainly in the relocation, revision, and expansion of specific aspects of religion from 291 to 201–209. Religions of South American native origin (299.8) are also revised and expanded in the current edition.

300s: Social sciences covers subjects typically subsumed under this rubric, most of which are important in public library and media center collections. They include sociology and anthropology (301—more familiar, perhaps, as "social studies"), statistics (310),[14] political science (320), economics (330), law (340), public administration (350), social problems and services (360), education (370), and commerce (390). It also includes some subjects one might not think of immediately as social sciences: military science (355–359), folklore (398), and the customs of war and diplomacy (399). The juxtaposition of folklore, in which fairy tales of the Brothers Grimm and Hans Christian Andersen are classified, and war, including war dances and peace pipe ceremonies, might seem a little odd, but they can be seen as different kinds of social patterns. Gorier human customs such as suicide and cannibalism are located a few divisions away (394). Perhaps they are perceived as related more closely to death customs (393) than to war, although both suicide and cannibalism may be consequences of war. When folklore is scrutinized closely it can be bloody (think of the witch eating Little Red Riding Hood alive and the woodcutter slicing the witch open to free her!); thus, it is not surprising these sections are found to be near one another.

400s: Language is a straightforward class having one division covering language in general (400–409), one covering linguistics (410–419), and the rest devoted to the theory and structure of specific languages. Linguistics contains familiar topics such as dictionaries, grammar, and standard usage, but its numbers apply solely to works on these topics in general. For dictionaries, works on grammar, and works on usage that are limited to one language, a mnemonic pattern of numbers appears within the division for that language. For example, dictionaries in general (and polyglot dictionaries) are at 413; English dictionaries are at 423; Latin dictionaries are at 473. As one immediately sees, eight divisions cannot cover all the world's languages. Seven language families have their own divisions: English; German; French; Italian; Spanish and Portuguese; Latin; and Greek. All other languages are assigned longer numbers in the final division, 490–499. For example, Chinese dictionaries are at 495.13; Thai dictionaries are at 495.91013; and Yoruba dictionaries are at 496.3333.

500s: Natural sciences and mathematics begins with general theories and topics covering all science or, at least, several of the sciences (500–509), after which it proceeds to cover individual scientific disciplines one by one: mathematics (510–519); astronomy (520–529); physics (530–539); chemistry (540–549); earth sciences (550–559); paleontology (560–569); life sciences including biology (570–579); plants (580–589); and, in the final division, animals (590–599).

600s: Technology (Applied sciences) begins and ends with divisions for subjects most people would identify with the rubric "technology": general topics in technology (600–609); medicine (610–619); engineering (620–629); agriculture (630–639); chemical engineering (660–669); manufacturing of raw materials (670–679); manufacturing of products for specific uses (680–689); and buildings (690–699). In the middle of the class, however, are two divisions that fit the definition of applied "sciences," though most people might not identify them as such: home and family management (640–649) and management (650–659). Many subjects popular with both adults and young people who use small general libraries are found here. Among these are medicine and health, already mentioned; gardening (635); cooking and meal service (641–643); housekeeping (648); parenting (649); "business" management (640–648) and advertising (649); and carpentry (694). Engineering is a particularly crowded part of the classification and has expanded with each new edition since the mid-twentieth century. Transportation engineering and related areas such as aerospace and astronautics (629.04–629.8) have many subclasses and sub-subclasses consisting of nine or more digits, running on for page after page. Among the changes in DDC22 are twenty-seven new numbers for subtopics in cooking, from food additives (641.308) to five current health-conscious cooking styles (low-salt, 641.56323; low-carb, 641.56383; sugar-free, 641.53837; low-fat, 641.56384; and low-cholesterol, 641.563847) to cake decoration (641.586539).

700s: The arts. Fine and decorative arts includes many subjects popular with readers in school and public libraries that one would expect to find in this class, including landscape architecture and area planning (710–719), architecture (720–729), sculpture (730–739), drawing and painting (740–759), graphic arts (760–769), photography (770–779), and music (780–789). Some public libraries create special areas for their music and art collections with special shelving for large art books, art gallery style partitions for hanging paintings or displaying other art objects, and equipment for viewing slides and listening to recordings. Most of the 700s would be found in the special areas of these libraries. In the final division of the 700s are some subjects that seem different—"Recreational and performing arts." With due respect to the artistry these activities demand, the 790s are where materials are found about circuses, movies, and television (791); theater (792); ballet (792.8); folk dancing (793.3); magic (793.8); games of skill and games of chance (794–795); and all sorts of athletics, including baseball, football, basketball, soccer, swimming, horse racing, fishing, hunting, and sport shooting (796–799).

800s: Literature (Belles-lettres and rhetoric), like Languages, begins with a division for general topics not limited by country or language and, then, is arranged by a combination of the two elements. The first division is devoted to American literature (81X), followed by divisions for the following literatures: English (82X), German (83X), French (84X), Italian (85X), Spanish (86X), Latin (87X), and Greek (88X). The final division covers all other literatures, including those of the nations and languages of Asia, Africa, Eastern Europe, South America, Oceania, and elsewhere. Canadians classify literature a little differently. The policies of the Library and Archives Canada state: "Canadian literary works are distinguished by adding an uppercase 'C' to the appropriate DDC number. This is an option provided by the editors at 810 and 840, but it is LAC policy to add the 'C' prefix to distinguish Canadian literature in all languages throughout the literature schedules."[15]

900s: History, geography, and auxiliary disciplines is divided into three popular subject areas: history, geography/travel, and biography. Biography has some special rules that limit what is classified in the 900s. Biographies of people associated with a particular subject are classified with the subject; for example, musicians would be assigned 780.92. Numbers in the 900s cover collected biographies of people related by location (920.03–09) as well as the related topics of genealogy, names, and so forth (929). Geography/travel numbers begin at 910 for general topics, 911 for historical geography, and 912 for graphic representations such as maps. Travel to particular destinations is covered in 913–919, with the third digit and decimal extensions of it representing a place and, sometimes, a chronological period as well. History numbers begin again at 930 with history of the ancient world. Starting at 940 and continuing to the end of the class are numbers representing the history, by country and period, of Europe (94X), Asia (95X), Africa (96X), North America (97X), and South America (98X). In the final division, one finds the history of every other place in this world (990–998) and on extraterrestrial worlds (999). In the history schedules as with literature, Canadian policy sometimes differs from the printed schedule. Historic events shared with the United States and given numbers in U.S. history (973) are assigned alternate Canadian history numbers (971) by Canadian classifiers.[16] For example, the War of 1812, a war that each side claims it won, has only one entry in the relative index, 973.52. A note in the schedules gives 971.034 as an option.

Options

Cognizant of the role it plays in libraries beyond national borders, DDC offers an option that gives users outside the United States the opportunity to organize literature differently from the way prescribed by the schedules. The description of the treatment of Canadian literature and history described above is an example of these options.

Biography: DDC states that the preferred method of classifying a biography is to place it with the topic for which the person is closely connected. The biography of Mao Zedong in Figure 10.6 has been classified in the history of China during the period of the People's

FIGURE 10.6

This example is an illustration of:
- two authors
- other title information
- detailed pagination
- particular type of illustration noted
- title information note
- contents(bibliography and index) note
- Library of Congress subject headings
- added entry for joint author
- title added entry
- added entry for alternate title
- alternate Dewey decimal classification call numbers for biography
- Library of Congress CIP
- 2nd level cataloging

Chang, Jung.
  Mao : the unknown story / Jung Chang, Jon Halliday. -- New York : Knopf, 2005.
    vii, 814 p., [32] p. of plates : ill., maps ; 24 cm.

  At head of title on paper jacket: The unknown story.
  Includes bibliographical references and index.
  ISBN 0-679-42271-4.

  1. Mao, Zedong. 2. Heads of state -- China -- Biography.
3. China -- Politics and government, 1949-1976. I. Halliday, Jon.
II. Title. III. Title: The unknown story.

Recommended call number with DDC: 951.05′092 MAO CHA
Alternate: 923.1 MAO CHA
Alternate: 921 MAO CHA

In a Canadian library the publication, distribution, etc., statement would read: New York : Knopf; Toronto: Random House, 2005.

Authors' note: The LC CIP has "1st ed.", but this does not appear anywhere else in the prescribed sources of information and therefore should not be in the bibliographic record or should be added in square brackets.

Fig. 10.6—Continues

FIGURE 10.6 *(continued)*

(chief source of information)

(title page)   *(information on verso)*

THE UNKNOWN STORY

J   J
U   O
N   N
G   H
C   A
H   L
A   L
N   I
G   D
    A
    Y

ALFRED A. KNOPF
NEW YORK
2005

Originally published in Great Britain by Jonathan Cape, London.

www.aaknopf.com

Knopf, Borzoi Books, and the colophon are registered trademarks
of Random House, Inc.

Library of Congress Cataloging-in-Publication Data
Chang, Jung, [date]
Mao : the unknown story / Jung Chang and Jon Halliday.—1st ed.
p.   cm.
Includes bibliographical references and index.
ISBN 0-679-42271-4
1. Mao, Zedong, 1893–1976. 2. Heads of state—China—Biography.
I. Title: Unknown story. II. Halliday, Jon. III. Title.
DS778.M3C38 2005
951.05′092—dc22
[B]   2004063826

Manufactured in the United States of America
Published October 21, 2005
Reprinted Three Times
Fifth Printing, December 2005

Republic. However, DDC provides options for libraries that want to shelve their biographies together. DDC suggests the following options:

- Use the 920–928 schedule, for example, 923.1 (heads of state).
- Use 92 for individual biographies.
- Use B (indicating Biography) for individual biographies.
- Use 920.71 for biographies of men, 920.72 for biographies of women.

In addition, the following practice is used in many libraries:

- Use 920 for collected biographies and 921 for individual biographies.[17]

The Tables

DDC22 provides six auxiliary tables of numbers to be concatenated to numbers from the main schedules to further subdivide them, unlike the twenty-first edition and several of its predecessors, which had seven such tables. Table 1, Standard Subdivisions, is used often to narrow the meaning of numbers from the main schedules, and may be used with any number from the main schedules provided there is no instruction *not* to do so. The basic pattern of Table 1 numbers is:

-01 = Philosophy and theory of a subject

-02 = Miscellany

-03 = Dictionaries, encyclopedias, concordances

-04 = Special topics

-05 = Serial publications

-06 = Organizations and management

-07 = Education, research, etc.

-08 = History and description with respect to kinds of persons

-09 = Historical, geographic, persons (i.e., biographical) treatment

When -09 is added to a number to limit a subject to a particular location, the standard procedure is to specify the place by concatenating a number for it from Table 2, the list of numbers for geographic areas, historical periods, and persons. An explicit instruction is given at the start of –093–099 to add numbers that further specify location from Table 2.[18]

Sometimes, the main schedules dictate dropping the zero; for example, French cooking is not 641.50944 but 641.5944, as discussed earlier in the chapter. In this instance, the "944" is not an addition from Table 1, but a precoordinated number given in the 641s. However, when material covers a narrower subject such as the popularity of French cooking in the United States, which is also geographically limited, this time to the United States, the zero is included because the number for United States comes first from Table 1 and, then, from Table 2: 641.59440973. Similarly, Chinese cooking in France would be given 641.59510944 (see Figure 10.7).

Table 2, as already mentioned, contains numbers for geographic locations (-1 to -19 and -3 to -99), occupying the majority of pages for this table. It also has numbers representing chronological periods (-01 to -05) and biographical treatments, called "persons" (-2, -22).

Table 3 is, in fact, three separate tables applicable to selected topics in the arts, individual literatures, or specific literary forms. These tables may be used only when specifically instructed to do so by an instruction in the main schedules. Table 3A is used to express concepts for the single or collected works of an individual author. Table 3B is used to express concepts for collections of two or more authors and for rhetoric in specific literary forms. Table 3C is used for additional elements as instructed in Table 3B as well as for selected topics in 700.4, 791.4, and 808–809, when instructed to do so.[19]

Numbers from Table 4, Subdivisions of Individual Languages and Language Families, are used only as instructed with numbers 420 to 490 in the main schedules. Asterisks are given to the numbers in the main schedules to which Table 4 numbers apply, and an explanation is provided at the start of the 420s.

FIGURE 10.7

The chief source of information, the top sheet, has

Chef Wong Lee's
     C'EST BON CHINESE COOKING

Fusion Cooking
     What It Is & How To Do It Number 4

Dupuis Frères distributed in North America by Langlois Ltd

- -

This example is an illustration of:
- chart (flip chart)
- entry under title
- statement of responsibility part of title
- general material designation
- place of publication unknown
- distributor
- date probable decade
- series statement with other title information and numbering
- physical description note
- Library of Congress subject heading
- personal name added entry
- additional title added entry
- series added entry
- Dewey Decimal classification
- 2nd level cataloging

Chef Wong Lee's c'est bon Chinese cooking [chart]. -- [S.l.] :
  Dupuis Frères ; distributed in North America by Langlois,
  [200-?].
  1 flip chart (10 sheets) : double sided, col. ; 20 x 29 cm. --
(Fusion cooking : what it is & how to do it ; no. 4)

  Attached cardboard strips can be folded into a stand.

  1. Cookery, Chinese -- French style. I. Wong, Lee. II. Title:
C'est bon Chinese cooking. III. Series.

Recommended DDC: 641.59510944

Table 5, "Ethnic and National Groups, consists of numbers for persons of mixed ancestry (-05 to -09) followed by numbers for North Americans (-1); British, English, and Anglo-Saxons (-2); Germanic peoples (-3); modern Latin peoples (-4); Italians, Romanians, and related groups (-5); Spanish and Portuguese (-6); other Italic peoples (-7); Greeks and related groups (-8); and all other ethnic and national groups (-9). In this table, one sees repetitions, though not always exact, of the geographic mnemonics in the 400s and 800s, respectively; for example, 43X = German, 81X = American literature, and 82X = English literature. An instruction in Table 1 at -089 tells classifiers to add numbers to it from Table 5 to specify ethnic and national groups.[20]

Table 6 is a table of languages, as follows:

-1	=	Indo-European languages
-2	=	English and Old English (Anglo-Saxon)
-3	=	Germanic languages
-4	=	Romance languages
-5	=	Italian, Sardinian, Dalmatian, Romanian, Rhaeto-Romanic
-6	=	Spanish and Portuguese
-7	=	Italic languages (that is, Latin, etc.)
-8	=	Hellenic languages (that is, Greek)
-9	=	Other languages

Table 1 is the only table whose numbers may be used without a specific instruction to do so. In order to use a number from Tables 2 through 6, specific instructions to go to that table and add a number from it must appear with the number from the main schedules under consideration. In contrast, classifiers may add the standard subdivisions at will, unless they are told not to do so. Exceptions to these two basic rules about using numbers from the auxiliary tables are made for certain numbers in Table 1 that instruct classifiers to augment them by adding numbers from other tables (for example, -09 and -089).

The seventh auxiliary table, mentioned above, which has been dropped from the current edition, provided numbers for groups of people by characteristics such as age, sex, and so on. Where appropriate, numbers expressing these characteristics have been incorporated into the main schedules, obviating the need for the table.

Use of the tables enables classifiers to express more information in the classification number and construct narrower categories than they might if they used only the main schedules. This is advantageous for the classification of extremely large collections in which many materials would otherwise share one classification number. Further subdivision is desirable in such instances.

The Relative Index

One of Dewey's original ideas in the Decimal Classification was the Relative Index, which in the twenty-second edition occupies 928 pages in volume 4 of the printed version. This alphabetic listing of topics and associated classification numbers is a valuable tool for classifiers and searchers alike.

For classifiers, Dewey intended the index to be used as a final check after a number was assigned, not before the assignment, to locate a number without consulting the schedules. The most important classification decision was the main class to which an item belonged, not what number represented its subject. Once the main class was determined, a classifier could move down its hierarchy to locate the appropriate classification number, going from main class to division, from division to section, and then looking further within a section to the proper expression of the desired subject. It is difficult to persuade new classifiers that they should not simply consult the index and, if they find the term they seek, immediately assign the associated number. However, once they see how often a particular subject term turns out to be associated with several numbers and how often the meaning of a term in colloquial language differs from its meaning in the DDC, they begin to realize the value of approaching classification in Dewey's intended manner.

For searchers, the index can serve as a browsing tool, moving directly to a point in the classification where a topic seems to be located and, then, scanning forward and backward to ensure that all closely related material is examined. Searchers, also, may be led astray when a subject term can be interpreted in different ways. For example, the term "Hunger" can be interpreted as a subject in human physiology (612.391), psychology (152.1886), social theology (201.7638), Christianity (261.8326), and social welfare (363.8). A more complicated example, perhaps, is "Hydrangeas," which the index gives two interpretations even though both refer to the same flower. Hydrangeas as botanic entities is assigned 583.72, but as entities in floriculture is assigned 636.93372. In this example, it is easy to see how determining the main class first helps both a searcher and a classifier avoid the unwanted interpretation.

Conclusion

DDC is widely used to arrange materials on library shelves as well as to organize bibliographies, databases, and digital libraries. Its flexibility makes it possible to serve many purposes and provide appropriate levels of specificity for general collections of different sizes, and even for some special collections. Librarians who want something simpler than the basic numbers in the full edition can turn to the abridged edition. Librarians who want greater specificity can apply the tables to subdivide many areas of knowledge even further than they are divided in the main schedules. The use of digits rather than letters or combinations of letters and digits makes DDC easy to use regardless of the language one speaks or the script in which it is written. The addition of the decimal point after the third digit provides a psychological pause in our minds as we view a number. Most people think of long Dewey numbers such as 782.42162 (folk songs) as something in the 782s rather than the eight-digit string 78242162. The mnemonics, the Relative Index, and DDC's easily grasped overall logic contribute to its user-friendliness.

In the next chapter, a brief look is given to DDC's only major rival in North American libraries, the Library of Congress Classification. However, before turning to it, readers may want to try assigning numbers to the titles in the exercises in Figure 10.8. Answers to the exercises are found in Appendix B.

FIGURE 10.8   Exercises in Assigning DDC22 Numbers to 10 Titles in Various Disciplines

1. TITLE: *Cooking with spuds*
    SUMMARY: A cookbook of potato recipes.

2. TITLE: *The Oslo royals*
    SUMMARY: A history of Norway's Royal Family.

3. TITLE: *Bound in chains*
    SUMMARY: A picture book showing the daily life of slaves.

FIGURE 10.8 *(continued)*

4. TITLE: *The way things work*
    SUMMARY: A description of simple and complex mechanical devices from the incline plane to clocks and watches and central heating.

5. TITLE: *Beautiful museums and libraries*
    SUMMARY: A description of the architectural features of museum buildings and library buildings.

6. TITLE: *How our neighbors worship*
    SUMMARY: A basic description of Buddhism, Judaism, and Islam.

7. TITLE: *Bar tales: great lawyers in person*
    SUMMARY: Collected biographies of forty lawyers from Canada, the United States and the United Kingdom.

8. TITLE: *Diplomatic relations* à *la français*
    SUMMARY: A study of diplomatic relations with England from the French point-of-view.

9. TITLE: *Mythology and the Conquistadors*
    SUMMARY: An examination of Spanish-language mythology in Spain, Mexico, and Peru.

10. TITLE: *Port Elgin: from village to town*
    SUMMARY: The history of a town in Ontario.

Recommended Reading

Bowman, Jennifer H. *Essential Dewey.* New York: Neal Schuman Publishers, 2005.

Miksa, Francis L. *The DDC, the Universe of Knowledge, and the Post-Modern Library.* Albany, NY: Forest Press, 1998.

Neigel, Christina, ed. *Workbook for DDC 22: Dewey Decimal Classification Edition 22.* Ottawa: Canadian Library Association, 2006.

OCLC, Inc. *WebDewey Tutorial.* Available at www.oclc.org/dewey/resources/tutorial/default .htm (Viewed September 13, 2005).

Scott, Mona L. *Dewey Decimal Classification, 22nd Edition: A Study Manual and Number Building Guide.* Westport, CT: Libraries Unlimited, 2005.

Wiegand, Wayne A. *Irrepressible Reformer: A Biography of Melvil Dewey.* Chicago: American Library Association, 1996.

Wursten, Richard B., comp. *In Celebration of Revised 780: Music in the* Dewey Decimal Classification *Edition 20.* (MLA Technical Report no. 19.) Canton, MA: Music Library Association, 1990.

Notes

1.   Dewey was critical of English orthography as being extremely confusing and championed simpler spellings that facilitated pronunciation. In an attempt to achieve greater clarity, he

altered the spelling of his name to Melvil Dui. The abbreviated version of his surname has been dropped in favor of the original spelling, but "Melvil" became the preferred spelling of his forename and is the form that will be found in official publications and name authorities.

2.   www.oclc.org/dewey

3.   John Phillip Comaromi, *A History of the Dewey Decimal Classification: Editions One through Fifteen, 1876–1951* (Ann Arbor, MI: University Microfilms, 1969).

4.   Ibid., pp. 423–424.

5.   *Dewey Decimal Classification and Relative Index*, 22nd ed., ed. Joan S. Mitchell et al. (Dublin, OH: OCLC Forest Press, 2003), vol. 1, pp. xxxvii–xxxviii.

6.   The revised Music schedule (780) that appeared in the twentieth edition was the cause of much grumbling at the grassroots level and did not gain widespread acceptance easily. The ill-fated fifteenth edition, however, which contained an exceptionally large number of changes, was rejected by users and eventually recalled by Forest Press.

7.   This class had a different title in the twenty-first edition.

8.   *Dewey Decimal Classification*, vol. 2, pp. vi–xvi.

9.   www.oclc.org/dewey/versions/default.htm

10.   *People, Places & Things: A List of Popular Library of Congress Subject Headings with Dewey Numbers.* (Dublin, OH: OCLC, 2001).

11.   Gregory R. New, "Sources for Dewey Numbers," in *Cataloging Correctly for Kids*, 4th ed., eds. Sheila S. Intner et al. (Chicago: American Library Association, 2006), p. 86; *Dewey Decimal Classification*, p. xxxviii.

12.   Charles Ammi Cutter, *Two-Figure Author Table* (Chicopee Falls, MA: H. R. Huntting; distr. Westport, CT: Libraries Unlimited, 1969–); Charles Ammi Cutter, *Three-Figure Author Table* (Chicopee Falls, MA: H. R. Huntting; distr. Westport, CT: Libraries Unlimited, 1969–); *Cutter-Sanborn Three-Figure Author Table*, Swanson-Swift revision (Westport, CT: Libraries Unlimited, 1969). Cutter tables are also available online.

13.   The kind of magic classified in the 100s is the kind one would consider unreal. In contrast, "real" magic, once called "parlor magic," such as that presented by the legendary Harry Houdini or magician-entertainers such as The Magnificent Randi, is classified in the 790s with amusements.

14.   The statistics to which the 310s apply are demographic statistics such as found in the census, not the mathematics of statistics or probability theory, which are part of mathematics (510s).

15.   http://collectionscanada.ca/6/17/s17–208-e.html (Viewed January 6, 2007).

16.   Ibid.

17.   *Dewey Decimal Classification,* vol. 3, p. 849.

18.   *Dewey Decimal Classification*, vol. 1, p. 214.

19.   *Dewey Decimal Classification*, vol. 1, p. 616.

20.   *Dewey Decimal Classification*, vol. 1, p. 209.

11

The Library of Congress Classification

Introduction

The Library of Congress Classification (LCC) is the practical answer to a question that troubled administrators at LC at the turn of the twentieth century: How can LC's collections be arranged most effectively? Before exploring the answer, a little history about what prompted the question is in order. LC's original collection was destroyed by fire when the British burned down the Capitol during the War of 1812. Afterward, Thomas Jefferson sold Congress his personal library of about 7,000 volumes as the basis for rebuilding the collections. The books were organized according to Jefferson's own classification, which LC also adopted.[1] By the end of the century, the collections grew to approximately one million volumes, and it was increasingly difficult to fit new titles into the Jeffersonian scheme. When Herbert Putnam was named Librarian of Congress in 1899, one of his goals was to address this and other organizational issues.

At the turn of the twentieth century, Melvil Dewey's Decimal Classification was in its fifth edition and Charles Cutter's Expansive Classification, a popular rival of Dewey's, was in its sixth. Both schemes were considered for adoption by LC, but eventually rejected. LC wanted close classification designed for an exceptionally large collection and also wished to be able to make basic editorial decisions, not be required to conform to someone else's vision of how knowledge should be arranged. This prompted devising an entirely new scheme wholly controlled by LC. Putnam turned to Charles Martel, the chief cataloger, to lead the project, whose principal aim was to create a plan for the orderly arrangement of LC's current and future holdings.

LCC evolved into a loose federation of schedules. Each was initially developed by one or more subject experts and was designed to accommodate what LC owned at the time on that subject and might be expected to add in the years to come. Although several overarching principles are found throughout LCC, each schedule is an individual entity in which the division and organization of the subjects need not relate to that of any other schedule. Therefore, individual schedules may be in their first, second, third, or later editions. Since the late twentieth century, new editions are identified solely by the publication year (for example, at this writing, the S schedule, which covers agriculture, is in its 1996 edition; and the Z schedule, which covers library science and bibliography, is in its 2006 edition).

Like DDC, LCC is updated on a continuous basis. The latest decisions on new, revised, and deleted classification numbers are disseminated online at the Cataloging Policy and Support Office website as well as via new paper publications.[2]

Principles

Eight principles underlie the organization and structure of LCC.

1. *Literary warrant.* This principle, which dictates that classes or numbers be established only when materials exist that require them, is fundamental to LCC. The scheme was not designed primarily to organize knowledge, although it does that. Instead, it was intended to arrange LC's materials, which elevates the principle of literary warrant to first priority status. There is no need for LCC to provide numbers for topics that lie outside LC's collecting interests. On the other hand, those collecting interests are so numerous, broad, and varied, and LC collects so much more material than other libraries do, that general library classifiers can expect to find all the numbers they need in LCC.

2. *Classification by discipline.* Like DDC, LCC divides knowledge first into disciplines. In all, twenty-one single-letter main classes represent the disciplines in LCC, in contrast to only ten in DDC. See Figure 11.1 for LCC's interpretation of the principal disciplines into which knowledge can be divided.

3. *Close classification.* At the time LCC was being developed, the Library's collections had passed the one million mark. Yet, scholars needed to be able to make fine distinctions between documents on similar topics. A high level of detail and precision in classification is known as "close classification," and LCC was designed to provide it.

4. *Alphabetical arrangement.* One of LCC's basic tools in dividing topical areas is the use of alphabetical arrangements. These arrangements are notated by means of cutter numbers: translations of verbal terms into brief, alphanumeric terms consisting of the initial letter followed by one or more numbers representing the subsequent letters of the words. LCC cutter numbers may represent topics, title words, names, geographic locations, languages, and so on. For instance, in many places, the cutter number "U7" stands for the United States; in the N (Art) schedule, cutter numbers represent painters' names; in the S (Agriculture) schedule, cutter numbers represent different species of trees; in the PN (General English Literature) schedule, cutter numbers represent film title words; and in the Z (Library Science and Bibliography) schedules, "M28" stands for the MARC format. These examples are instances in which the cutter numbers are mnemonics for words, but some LCC cutter numbers are not linked to words at all, merely representing a particular kind of topical division. LC's rules for creating cutter numbers are found at the end of this chapter (p. 205).

5. *Geographical arrangement.* Geographical subarrangements are also heavily favored in LCC, sometimes in addition to and sometimes in place of alphabetical arrangements. This is logical for a system used by legislative researchers seeking information specific to various jurisdictions. When the geographical locations are expressed by means of cutter numbers, such as in the example of the United States above, the subarrangement

FIGURE 11.1   General Outline of LCC

A	General Works
B	Philosophy, Psychology, Religion
C	Auxiliary Sciences of History
D	History (General) and History of Europe
E/F	History: America
G	Geography, Anthropology, Recreation
H	Social Sciences
J	Political Science
K	Law
L	Education
M	Music and Books on Music
N	Fine Arts
P	Language and Literature
Q	Science
R	Medicine
S	Agriculture
T	Technology
U	Military Science
V	Naval Science
Z	Bibliography, Library Science, Information Resources (General)

is also alphabetical. When locations are expressed in numeric terms or through the use of other devices, alphabetization does not play a role. (See Figure 11.2 for an illustration of the different methods of representing geographic location.)

6. *Economy of notation*. LCC uses mixed notation, employing both alphabetic and numeric characters. This gives it far greater flexibility to represent a large number of classes with fewer characters than systems that employ pure notation. Although it is not always the case, frequently LCC requires fewer characters to represent topics at very narrow levels of hierarchy than are required by DDC. For example, in Figure 11.3 the LCC is E161.5 (.S77 1998 is the shelf mark) while the DDC is 910.8996073.

7. *Enumeration*. Similar to DDC, LCC enumerates a very large proportion of the classes it provides. At the same time, it minimizes the use of number building techniques that

FIGURE 11.2   Notation for Location using Sequential Numbers

Feminism in the United States	HQ1410
Feminism in Canada	HQ1453

Notation for location using cutter numbers:

Postal service in Toronto:	HE6656.T67

---

allow classifiers to synthesize their own class numbers. The enormous size of LCC is evidence of its major reliance on enumeration.

8. *Relative location*. Again, similar to DDC, LCC employs the principle of relative location, although its use of geographic and alphabetic subarrangements tends to fragment materials related to one another in a topical hierarchy.

In addition to the eight principles, Charles Martel designed a seven-point schema for arranging the genres of subject literatures that, while no longer followed, is visible in schedules established before the schema was abandoned.

1. *Form*, including periodicals, society publications, yearbooks, congresses, documents, directories, and the like.

2. *Theory and philosophy.*

3. *History and biography.*

4. *Treatises and general works.*

5. *Law*. LCC's law schedules (Class K) were among the last to be developed. Before they were published, the numbers for laws relating to a subject appeared within the subject's schedule. Later, when the K schedules were issued, these numbers were deleted from subject-specific schedules and relocated to K.

6. *Education*, including materials covering the study and teaching of a subject, research on the subject, and textbooks.

7. *Specific subjects and subdivisions.*

Martel's seven-point structure is sometimes repeated within a schedule many times within topics and subtopics at different levels of hierarchy, depending on the amount of material being arranged. For example, TH1 represents "Periodicals and societies" for building construction as a whole; TH1061 represents "Periodicals, societies, etc." for individual systems of building construction; and TH2430 represents "Periodicals, societies, congresses, etc." for roofing, which is a part of systems of building. However, there is no comparable form number for floors and flooring, a subtopic at the same hierarchical level as roofing. The creation of numbers depended on literary warrant; that is, the likelihood that LC would collect material requiring them. It seems that, in the case of floors and flooring, the amount of material in form categories (periodicals, society publications, congresses, etc.) collected at LC was not sufficient to warrant establishing a separate number.

FIGURE 11.3

This example is an illustration of:
- collection of works by different authors
- edited work
- title main entry
- other title information
- joint editors
- publication date not listed, copyright date given
- detailed pagination
- contents (bibliography) note
- two ISBNs listed on verso; the one given relates to the item in hand
- ISBN qualified
- Library of Congress subject headings
- added entries for editors
- bibliographic form of Griffin's name taken from Library of Congress CIP
- Dewey and Library of Congress classification numbers
- 2nd level cataloging

```
A stranger in the village : two centuries of African-American
   travel writing / edited by Farah J. Griffin and Cheryl J.
   Fish. -- Boston : Beacon Press, c1998.
   xvii, 366 p. ; 23 cm.

   Bibliography: p. 357-62.
   ISBN 0-8070-7121-8 (pbk.).

   1. United States -- Description and travel.  2. African-
Americans -- Travel -- History -- Sources.  3. Travelers'
writings, American -- African-American authors.  I. Griffin,
Farah Jasmine.  II. Fish, Cheryl J.
```

Recommended DDC: 910.8996073

Recommended LCC: E161.5.S77 1998

Fig. 11.3—Continues

Format of LCC Numbers

An LCC call number consists of a classification number to which are added one or more shelf marks, just as a DDC number does. The classification elements all have the following two parts:

- One, two, or, occasionally, three capital letters identifying the subject discipline (main class, first letter) and a broad subdivision within it (subclass, second and third letters). For example, K stands for law; KF stands for law of the United States; KFG

FIGURE 11.3 *(continued)*

(chief source of information)

(title page)   *(information on verso)*

A STRANGER IN
THE VILLAGE

TWO CENTURIES OF
AFRICAN–AMERICAN
TRAVEL WRITING

Edited by FARAH J. GRIFFIN
AND CHERYL J. FISH

BEACON PRESS
BOSTON

BEACON PRESS
25 Beacon Street
Boston, Massachusetts 02108-2892
www.beacon.org

Beacon Press books
are published under the auspices of
the Unitarian Universalist Association of Congregations.

03 02 01 00 99   8 7 6 5 4 3 2

This book is printed on recycled acid-free paper that contains at least 20 percent postconsumer waste and meets the uncoated paper ANSI/NISO specifications for performance as revised in 1992.

Text design by Margaret M. Wagner

Library of Congress Cataloging-in-Publication Data

A stranger in the village: two centuries of African-American travel writing / edited by Farah J. Griffin and Cheryl J. Fish.
p. cm.
Includes bibliographical references.
ISBN 0-8070-7120-X (cloth)
ISBN 0-8070-7121-8 (paper)
1. United States—Description and travel. 2. Afro-Americans—Travel—History—Sources. 3. Travelers' writings, American—Afro-American authors. I. Griffin. Farah Jasmine. II. Fish, Cheryl J.
E161.5.S77 1998
910'.8996073—dc21   98-5265

stands for the law of the state of Georgia. Most disciplines have a maximum of two capital letters, but the G (geography) and K (law) schedules have numbers that contain three.

- A sequential whole number from 1 to 9,999, sometimes, extended decimally, representing narrower subdivisions of the topic.

Some LCC classification numbers also may include the following:

- A cutter number that is part of the classification, not a shelf mark, representing a further subarrangement by a topic, a geographic location, a language, a form or genre, a time period, and so forth. (Note: The first cutter number in an LCC call number is preceded by a period. When the call number includes more than one cutter number, only the first is preceded by a period. The reason for this punctuation protocol has been lost.)

- A second cutter number, also part of the classification number, not a shelf mark, representing a specific kind of material.

- A date (for example, the dates of financial crises are part of class numbers for materials on those events).

Once the classification number is complete, a series of shelf marks is added to it that provides an exact address for the item on local library shelves. The first shelf mark is usually a cutter number representing the main entry of the work, although at times it may represent a different element, such as subject or geographic location. The cutter number is followed by one or more added marks, including publication dates, title marks, collection locations (often, these precede the classification number, as in the call number of a reference department copy of a book that begins with an "R," followed by a classification number and all the other shelf marks), copy numbers, and/or other elements mandated by local policies.

Editions/Versions of LCC

As previously mentioned, LCC is available online and in printed volumes. At this writing, a full set of LCC consists of forty-one volumes, published in various years (shown below in parentheses), as follows:

A	General works (1998)
B–BJ	Philosophy, Psychology (2000)
BL–BQ	Religion (General), Hinduism . . . etc. (2001)
BR–BX	Christianity, Bible (2000)
C	Auxiliary sciences of history (1996)
D–DR	History (General) & History of Europe (2001)
DS–DX	History of Asia, Africa, Australia, New Zealand, etc. (1998)
E–F	History: America (2000)
G	Geography, Maps, Anthropology, Recreation (2005)
G tables	Cutter numbers and tables for use with G (no date)
H	Social Sciences (2005)
J	Political Science (2006)
K Law	(General) (2005)
K tables	Form division tables for use with K (2005)
KB	Religious law (2004)
KD	Law of the UK and Ireland (1998)
KDZ, KG–KH	Law of the Americas, etc. (2000)
KE	Law of Canada (1999)
KF	Law of the USA (2005)
KJ–KKZ	Law of Europe (2000)
KJV–KJW	Law of France (1999)
KK–KKC	Law of Germany (2000)
KL–KWX	Law of Asia and Eurasia, etc. (2001)
KZ	Law of nations (1998)
L	Education (2005)
M	Music and Books on music (1998)
N	Fine arts (2007, projected publication date)
P–PZ tables	Language and literature tables (2006)

P–PA	Philology and Linguistics, Greek and Latin languages and literatures (1997)
PB–PH	Modern European languages (2005)
PJ–PK	Oriental philology and literature, etc. (2005)
PL–PM	Languages of Eastern Asia, Africa, etc. (2006)
PN	Literature (General) (2004)
PQ	French, Italian, Spanish, and Portuguese literatures (2004)
PR, PS, PZ	English and American literature, Juvenile belles lettres (2005)
PT	German, Dutch, and Scandinavian literature (2005)
Q	Science (2004)
R	Medicine (1999) [Note: Medical libraries may prefer using the classification of the National Library of Medicine's W schedule]
S	Agriculture (1996)
T	Technology (1999)
U–V	Military science, Naval science (1996)
Z	Bibliography, Library science, Information resources (2006)

Three of the volumes contain auxiliary tables to be used with specific schedules (G, K, P). Each printed schedule includes a preface that gives a thumbnail history of its development; a synopsis listing the primary divisions of the class or subclass; an outline, summarizing the main subdivisions of the class; the schedule itself; auxiliary tables used in more than one place in the schedule;[3] and an index.

The online version of LCC is *Classification Web*, an online reference tool that enumerates LCC numbers and LC subject headings. It is obtained by subscription from LC's Cataloging Distribution Service (CDS) and is updated on a continuous basis.[4] Other classification tools available from CDS include the online *LC Classification Outline* and two guides for patrons: a printed pocket guide and a poster suitable for mounting on the walls of library stacks.

LC offers two auxiliary tools that are intended to help classifiers apply LCC according to LC policies: *Subject Cataloging Manual: Classification* and *Subject Cataloging Manual: Shelflisting*. At this writing, these manuals, issued separately in oversized three-ring binders, are soon to be superseded by a single "volume" covering both classifying and shelflisting.[5]

Copy Classification

Libraries that arrange their materials using LCC and adhering strictly to LC policies can adopt the LCC call numbers found in CIP and LC-contributed catalog records in network databases directly, without alteration. A number of LCC-arranged collections, however, use the classification number without change, but alter the shelf marks to conform to their local policies. Tinkering with shelf marks can be counterproductive, because doing so takes time and some level of expertise, if only in knowing what the local policies are and how to follow them. The less one tinkers with a source's call number the quicker, easier, and less costly it is to classify materials; therefore, the authors suggest librarians scrutinize any local departures from LC policies carefully to be sure they are worth the time, effort, and money that they cost the library.

Copying call numbers from network catalog records contributed by libraries other than LC can sometimes be risky if the contributors depart widely from LC's policies. A wise librarian might check a series of titles originating from a particular source to be certain they follow similar policies before adopting all their call numbers. Small differences are not rare, and many of them do not have much of an impact on searching; but when they occur in crowded parts of the schedules or in literature collections, major departures from LC practice can prove troublesome in the long run, because complicated shelflisting from scratch inevitably is required.

Interpreting the LCC call number also takes a little practice, unless the copy classifier is looking at a MARC record. The classification number in MARC records appears in MARC subfield "a" and the shelf marks in subfield "b," and there is no question about which is which. But, in CIP, the entire call number appears as a string of characters, often, but not always, including a space before the start of the shelf marks. Sometimes, the call number appears in very tiny print and/or the space is hard to see, so the classifier must decide where the classification number ends and the shelf marks begin. Generally speaking, shelf marks begin with the last cutter number. When there is one cutter number, it marks the start of the shelf marks. When there are two or more cutter numbers, the final one marks the start of shelf marks, while any that precede it are part of the classification number.

The Schedules

Perhaps, because the main classes into which LCC divides knowledge are narrower in scope than DDC's main classes, it is easier to understand the coverage of individual schedules, but some subject placements seem odd to people living in the twenty-first century. Brief descriptions of the subject matter covered in LCC's main classes follow.

A, *General Works*, includes familiar genres of reference works (encyclopedias, dictionaries, indexes), newspapers, and general periodicals. It also includes collecting, museums, and museum techniques, and scholarship and learning in general, but not education, which is addressed in class L.

B, *Philosophy, Psychology, Religion*, begins with philosophy in general, including logic (B–BD); then, in BF, treats psychology, parapsychology, and the occult; returns briefly to the philosophic topics of aesthetics (BH) and ethics (BJ); then shifts to religion in general (BL) and individual religious groups (BM–BX).

Classes C through F comprise the history group, including historical sciences (C); European history, geography, and regional descriptions (DA–DR); and the history, geography, and regional descriptions of the rest of the world's regions (DS–DX). C includes archaeology; coins, medals, and inscriptions; and heraldry, as well as biography in general (CT). Biography associated with a particular subject, however, is classified with the subject. D, E, and F used to be known as "old world" (D) and "new world" (E–F) history, but currently they are identified solely by region. E and F, which do not have two-letter subclasses, tend to occupy a large proportion of North American libraries, because they deal with American history. DX, the final subclass of D, provides numbers for classifying "Gypsies," which, to some degree, perpetuates their isolation.

G, *Geography*, includes general geography and description of regions in general, although such topics relating to a specific country or region are classified elsewhere, in D–F. Atlases, maps, and globes are classified in G. Cartography is also covered here (GA). Subclasses provide numbers for physical geography (GB), oceanography (GC), environmental sciences (GE), and human ecology (GF). Topics included in G for less obvious reasons are anthropology (GN), folklore (GR), customs (GT), and recreational activities (GV). GV has numbers for outdoor activities such as camping and mountain climbing, physical education, and all kinds of games and amusements, dancing, and performing arts. Hunting and fishing, however, are not in GV with outdoor sports, but in class S, with animal culture.

H, *Social Sciences*, begins with categories for social science in general (H) and demographics (HA), followed by economics (HB–HD), transportation (HE), commerce and finance (HG–HJ), and sociology and related subjects (HM–HX). Topics classified in H include controversial ones such as sexuality (HQ), race (HT), and crime (HV), as well as socialism, communism, and anarchism, in general (HX).

J, *Political Science*, first covers topics in general: legislative and executive papers (J), political science (JA), political theory (JC), and political institutions and public administration (JF). Then, subclasses cover the political institutions and public administration of specific locations: North America (JJ), the United States (JK), Canada and Latin America (JL), Europe (JN), and the rest of the world (JQ). Local governmental institutions, colonies and the movement of people among countries, and international relations are classified in JS, JV, and JZ, respectively. Subdivision JX, which once covered international law, is obsolete, its numbers moved to appropriate parts of class K.

K, *Law*, is organized by geographic location beginning with the United Kingdom and Ireland (KD) after first providing numbers for law in general (K). The numbers for law of Canada (KE), law of the United States (KF), and associated subclasses for individual Canadian provinces and U.S. states often occupy the largest part of the K shelves in North American libraries.

L, *Education*, covers education in general (L), its history (LA), and its theories (LB), before turning to more practical topics. Special aspects of education (LC) include social aspects, types of education, and the education of particular groups of persons. Individual educational institutions are classified in LD–LG. Activities such as school publications, social societies, and textbooks are classified in LH, LJ, and LT, respectively.

M, *Music and Books on Music*, is a brief class, covering music itself (that is, works containing musical notation for performance, in M), works about music (ML), and works intended for instruction and study (MT). The large and important body of literature on music criticism is classified in ML.

N, *Fine Arts*, covers visual arts first (N), followed by subdivisions for architecture (NA), sculpture (NB), drawing (NC), painting (ND), print media (NE), and decorative arts (NK). A subdivision for fine arts in general closes the class in NX.

P, *Language and Literature*, is deceptively simple sounding when, in fact, the class has an enormous scope, filling several volumes of schedules. Following numbers for philology and linguistics in general that also includes extinct languages (P), the rest of this enormous class is divided by language. Nineteen subclasses contained in nine separate volumes cover classical languages (PA), modern European languages (PB, PC, PD, PE, PF, PG, PH), Oriental languages and literatures (PJ, PK, PL, PM), English literature (PN, PR, PS, PZ), and modern European literatures (PQ, PT). Some of the nomenclature has changed in recent years; for example, Greek and Roman supersedes classic languages, Romanic supersedes Romance, and Uralic supersedes Finno-Ugrian and Basque.

Q, *Science*, begins with general science and then enumerates individual sciences, including mathematics (QA), astronomy (QB), physics (QC), chemistry (QD), geology (QE), natural history and biology (QH), botany (QK), zoology (QL), human anatomy (QM), physiology (QP), and microbiology (QR). Computer science and electronic data processing are classified here, subsumed under mathematics (QA76).

R, *Medicine*, tends to be used primarily by general libraries with small collections of medical materials. Large specialized medical collections are more likely to be classified with the National Library of Medicine Classification (NLM), using class W in place of R. The NLM classification is far more detailed. In LCC, the R schedule begins with general medicine (R), followed by public aspects of medicine (RA), Pathology (RB), internal medicine (RC), surgery (RD), and various medical specialties (RE, RF, RG, RJ, RK, RL, RM, RS). Nursing is located in RT, and botanic and homeopathic systems of medicine, which might be considered "alternative" systems, at RV and RX, respectively. RZ classifies "other systems of medicine," which include chiropractic, osteopathy, and mental healing.

S, *Agriculture*, covers plant and animal culture, both land and water based. It also includes forestry (SD). The first subclass for generalities (S) covers soil and land conservation as well as irrigation, fertilizers, machinery, and related engineering. Other subclasses provide numbers for plant culture (SB), animal culture (SF), aquaculture (SH), and hunting (SK), which are classified here, not in GV with other outdoor recreations.

T, *Technology*, begins with general numbers classifying topics that embrace multiple engineering disciplines (T). These are followed by subdivisions covering individual branches of engineering (TA–TP). Photography is classified in TR, manufactures in TS, handicrafts in TT, and home economics, which includes cookbooks, in subclass TX.

U, *Military Science*, begins with military science in general (U), armies (UA), administration (UB), maintenance and transportation (UC), and branches of the army, including infantry (UD), cavalry (UE), artillery (UF), engineering and air forces (UG), and other services (UH). Military history, however, is classified with history in D–F, not in class U.

V, *Naval Science*, is similar to class U, starting with naval science in general (N) and followed by navies (VA), administration (VB), maintenance (VC), naval seamen (VD), marines (VE), naval ordnance (VF), minor services of navies (VG), navigation and merchant marine (VK), and naval architecture and shipbuilding (VM). Like military history, naval history is classified in D–F.

Z, *Bibliography, Library Science, Information Resources (General)*, was the first LCC schedule to be developed, but was revised in 2006. The first part of the schedule consists of three broad sections: numbers for books in general, history of books, writing, and the book trades; numbers for libraries and library science; and numbers for bibliographies, divided into broad types of collections, including national bibliographies and personal bibliographies. One double-letter subclass, ZA, titled Information resources (General), is used to classify twenty-first-century topics, including information services, information centers, information super-highway, government information, and information in specific formats and media.

Tables and Subdivision in LCC

Tables used in LCC apply to a single schedule or, in many instances, to a single number or limited span of numbers. For classifiers using the printed version of LCC, most of the latter type of tables are printed together with the numbers they subdivide. For the most part, they are easy to decipher and apply, and additional help can be found in *Subject Cataloging Manual: Classification*. Tables used in many places throughout a schedule (LCC calls these *auxiliary tables*) appear at the end of the schedule itself or, for the G, K, and P schedules, in separate volumes. These volumes of tables are needed to build specific numbers for topics covered within those three disciplines. Online users can click on links to the tables, which are identified by schedule and table numbers (for example, table H5 is the H schedule's table 5).

Tables in LCC take several forms. Some tables provide an array of whole numbers and/or whole numbers with decimal extensions that are added arithmetically to a base number to create more narrowly defined subarrangements of topics (see Figures 11.4 and 11.5).

Other tables consist of cutter numbers intended to follow a number from the schedules, subdividing it further by topic or geographic location. A different type consists of special "A" and "Z" cutter numbers that do not represent characters in words, but define categories or forms, as in the examples in Figure 11.6.

FIGURE 11.4

HQ	THE FAMILY. MARRIAGE. WOMEN	HQ

Women. Feminism
   By region or country -- Continued
1451-1870.7   Other regions or countries (Table H9)
         Add country number in table to HQ1450
         Under each:
      Apply Table HQ1451/1 for 10 number countries
              Table for women, feminism
              (10 no. countries)

1   *Periodicals. Serials*
             History.- General and modern
               For ancient, medieval and renaissance
               history, see HQ 1127+
3   *General works*
             Biography of reformers, feminists, etc.
5.A3   *Collective*
5.A4 -Z   *Individual, A -Z*
             Reform literature, emancipation
6   *Early through 1870*
7   *1871-*
9.A -Z   *By state, province, etc., A -Z*
10.A -Z   *By city, A Z*

FIGURE 11.5

H31	TABLE FOR PUBLIC FINANCE PERIODICALS BY COUNTRY (EXCEPT THE UNITED STATES)	H31

.A1-.A199	General serials
.A2-.A299	Budget. Appropriations and expenditures
.A3-.A399	Revenue. Taxation
.A3995	Expenditures. Government spending policy
.A4-.A499	Public debts
.A6-.A699	Accounts. Audits
	For accounting and auditing methodology in the public sector, see HJ9701+
.A7-.A799	Colonies
.A8-.Z	By state or province, A-Z
	For local finance, i.e. counties, boroughs, communes, municipalities, etc., see HJ9350+

FIGURE 11.6

H46	TABLE FOR PROTECTION, ASSISTANCE, AND RELIEF OF SPECIAL CLASSES, BY REGION OR COUNTRY (2 NOS.)	H46

1.A1-.A19	Periodicals, Serials
1.A2-.A29	Societies. Associations
	For local societies and associations, see the locality
	Documents
1.A3-.A39	Serials
1.A4	Monographs. By date
1.A5-.A59	Collected works (nonserial)
1.A6	General works. History, etc.
1.A7-Z	By state, province, etc., A-Z
2.A-Z	By city, A-Z

Subdivision in LCC often involves dividing topics by geographic focus. When cutter numbers are used to identify locations, the arrangement organizes these locations alphabetically. Unless otherwise specified, geographic subdivision is done at the country level. When numbers are used to identify locations, the arrangement could be alphabetic, but is more likely to be organized in a geographic progression or, sometimes, by LC's preference for particular locations. Materials subdivided by location often emphasize the United States, North America, and Europe, putting these locations first or giving them the most detailed lists of numbers.

For any topic to be subdivided geographically, LC's experts decide the extent to which materials pertaining to particular countries need subdivision. Literary warrant—that is, the volume of material and the topics likely to be addressed by authors—is the determining factor. As a result, LCC sometimes offers table options in which each option provides a different array of subtopics. If a country requires a great deal of subdivision, a larger array is applied; if a country requires less or very little subdivision, smaller arrays are applied. Thus, classifiers speak of a country as being an "n"-number country, where "n" stands for the total number of subtopics in the applicable table (see Figure 11.7).

Canadian Accommodations

LC does not use the two schedules developed by the Library and Archives Canada (LAC) for materials relating to Canadian history (*Class FC: A Classification for Canadian History*[6]) and Canadian literature (*Class PS8000: A Classification for Canadian Literature*[7]), both of which are available on the LAC website.[8] These LAC schedules supply more specific classification numbers for Canadian content than do the main LCC schedules.

Canadian public libraries or school media centers or other libraries with significant Canadian collections may prefer to use derived records from the LAC database AMICUS than from LC for these subject areas. Figure 11.8 demonstrates the difference in classification schedules for Canadian history.

FIGURE 11.7

HE	TRANSPORTATION AND COMMUNICATIONS	HE
	Postal service	
	By region or country -- Continued	
6651-7496	Other regions or countries (Table H 10 modified)	
	Add country number in table to HE6500	
	Under each:	
	Apply Table HE6651/1 for 10 number countries	

	Table for postal service, by country (10 numbers)
1	*Periodicals. Societies. Serials*
3	*Guides. Directories*
	Biography
4.A 9-.A4	*Collective*
4.A5-.Z7	*Individual, A -Z*
5	*General works*
6.A-.Z7	*Local, A -Z*
	Colonies
6.Z8	*General works*
(6.Z9A-.Z9Z)	*By colony*
	see the colony
8	*Rates*
9.A -Z	*Other special topics, A Z*
9.A3	*Accounting. Auditing*
9.A4	*Air mail service*
9.A87	*Automation*
9. B34	*Balloon post*
	Branches and stations see HE6651/1 9.S68
9. C44	*Censorship*
	Cf. HE6 >84. P66, Postal censor stamps
	Certified mail
	see HE6651/l 9. R43
9. F5	*Finance*
9. F6	*Foreign mail*
9. M3	*Mail steamers*
9. M33	*Mailboxes*
9. M4	*Metered mail*
9. M6	*Mobile post offices*
9. P4	*Personnel. Postal service employees*
9. P5	*Pigeon post*
9. R2	*Railway mail service*
9. R43	*Registered mail. Certified mail*
9.S42	*Security measures*

FIGURE 11.8

This example is an illustration of:

- multivolume work with somewhat different authors
- publication date not listed, copyright date given
- descriptive illustration statement
- responsibility note
- publication note
- contents (bibliography and index) note
- two ISBNs qualified
- Library of Congress and Canadian subject headings the same
- personal name added entries
- corporate body added entry
- television program added entry
- title added entry
- difference between Library of Congress classification (LCC) and Library and Archives Canada's adaptation of LCC
- Canadian CIP data
- 2nd level cataloging

Gillmor, Don.
  Canada, a people's history / Don Gillmor. -- Toronto :
McClelland & Stewart, c2000-2001.
  2 v. : ill. (chiefly col.), maps, ports. ; 28 cm.

  Vol. 1 written by Don Gillmor and Pierre Turgeon, v. 2 by Don
Gillmor, Achille Michaud, and Pierre Turgeon. Foreword in v. 1
and afterword in v. 2 written by Mark Starowicz and Gene Allen.
  Published in conjunction with the series, Canada, a people's
history on CBC Television.
  Includes bibliographies and indexes.
  ISBN: 0-7710-3340-0 (v. 1). -- ISBN: 0-7710-3341-9 (v. 2).

  1. Canada -- History. 2. Canada -- Biography. I. Michaud,
Achille. II. Turgeon, Pierre. III. Canadian Broadcasting
Corporation. IV. Canada, a people's history (Television
program). V. Title.

Recommended LCC: F1026.G54 2000

Recommended Canadian LCC adaptation: FC164.G54 2000

Fig. 11.8—Continues

FIGURE 11.8 *(continued)*

(chief source of information)

(title page)

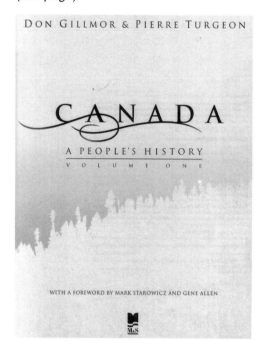

DON GILLMOR & PIERRE TURGEON

CANADA

A PEOPLE'S HISTORY
V O L U M E   O N E

WITH A FOREWORD BY MARK STAROWICZ AND GENE ALLEN

M&S

(information on verso of volume 1)

Canadian Cataloguing in Publication Data

Gillmor, Don
    Canada : a people's history

Includes bibliographical references and index.
ISBN 0-7710-3340-0

I. Canada – History. 2. Canada – Biography.
I. Turgeon, Pierre, 1947- . II. Title.

FC164.G54 2000   971   C00-931410-5
F1026.G54 2000

We acknowledge the financial support of the Government of Canada through the Book Publishing Industry Development Program for our publishing activities. We further acknowledge the support of the Canada Council for the Arts and the Ontario Arts Council for our publishing program.

Typeset in Janson by M&S, Toronto
Book design by Kong Njo

Printed and bound in Canada

McClelland & Stewart Ltd.
The Canadian Publishers
481 University Avenue
Toronto, Ontario
M5G 2E9
www.mcclelland.com

1 2 3 4 5   04 03 02 01 00

(title page 2)

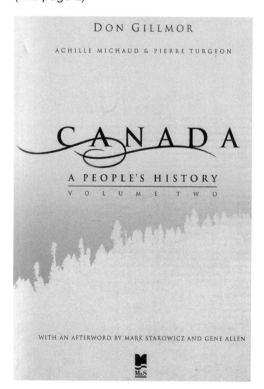

DON GILLMOR

ACHILLE MICHAUD & PIERRE TURGEON

CANADA

A PEOPLE'S HISTORY
V O L U M E   T W O

WITH AN AFTERWORD BY MARK STAROWICZ AND GENE ALLEN

M&S

(information on verso of volume 2)

National Library of Canada Cataloguing in Publication Data

Gillmor, Don
    Canada : a people's history

Published in conjunction with series, Canada, a people's history on CBC Television.
Vol. 2 written by Don Gillmor, Achille Menaud and Pierre Turgeon.
Includes bibliographical references and index.
ISBN 0-7710-3340-0 (v. 1).—ISBN 0-7710-3341-9 (v. 2)

1. Canada – History. I. Turgeon, Pierre, 1947-
II. Menaud, Achille III. Canadian Broadcasting Corporation IV. Title.

FC164.G54 2000   971   C00-931410-5
F1026.G54 2000

We acknowledge the financial support of the Government of Canada through the Book Publishing Industry Development Program for our publishing activities. We further acknowledge the support of the Canada Council for the Arts and the Ontario Arts Council for our publishing program.

Typeset in Janson by M&S, Toronto
Book design by Kong Njo

Printed and bound in Canada

McClelland & Stewart Ltd.
The Canadian Publishers
481 University Avenue
Toronto, Ontario
M5G 2E9
www.mcclelland.com

1 2 3 4 5   05 04 03 02 01

Conclusion

Although LCC is larger and more complex than DDC, and therefore more difficult to apply for original cataloging of materials, it has advantages that make it attractive to libraries, particularly those serving scholarly communities whose objectives are similar to those of congressional researchers (LC's primary patrons). They include the following:

- Some North American academic libraries that once used other classifications switched to LCC in the 1970s and 1980s, when catalog records containing LCC call numbers made up the lion's share of bibliographic network databases.

- The overall arrangement of subjects is more logical and better organized for contemporary use, particular in science, history, and languages and literatures.

- The schedules for different disciplines do not have to follow the same pattern, thus enabling each one to be arranged in the most "natural" order for the discipline.

- The close classification and larger amount of enumeration means original classifiers are likely to find the numbers they seek already established in the schedules, keeping number building at a minimum; also this feature makes it easy to arrange large collections easily.

- LCC schedules tend to be extremely stable, prompting very few large-scale shifts of materials.

- Greater flexibility afforded by LCC notation and pragmatic structure makes it unnecessary to revise related topics when a new topic is introduced.

At the same time, some of the same features of LCC make it less appealing for public libraries and school library media centers. For instance, close classification is less valuable for libraries that do not have large collections. Small collections tend to benefit from greater collocation, not greater dispersion. The added difficulty of original classification with LCC is not a trivial matter, particularly for libraries that may lack subject specialists. Moreover, at this writing, only a small proportion of U.S. and Canadian public libraries and school library media centers use LCC, so following the mainstream means not using it. The most important disadvantage of LCC for patrons of public libraries and school library media centers, however, is the loss of browsability that results from using a nonhierarchical system such as LCC, unless, of course, the system in use is even less browsable, such as an accession number system.

It is too early to tell whether globalization of cataloging, which the library world has experienced in the last four decades, will eventually result in widespread conformity to one type of classification practice—LCC practice—as appears to be happening with subject heading practice. Rather, the current division in the choice of classification by type of library (academic libraries using LCC and public libraries and school library media centers using DDC) seems likely to persist for the foreseeable future. Heightened awareness of the workings of each system and understanding their differences and implications for use are valuable for all librarians, media specialists, and their patrons.

Try your hand at assigning LCC numbers to the following sample problems in Figure 11.9. Answers are found in Appendix B.

FIGURE 11.9 Original Classification using LCC

Using the class Z schedule, assign a classification number to each of the following titles.

1. Item title: *The present state and future of the union catalog*

   Summary: Proceedings of an international conference

2. Item title: *Canadian fiction: a guide to reading interests*

   Summary: An annotated bibliography of the authors' suggestions

3. Item title: *Cataloging government documents*

   Summary: Manual that discusses rules and problems

4. Item title: *Private libraries in Brazil*

   Summary: A discussion about the growth of private libraries in Brazil

5. Item title: William Caxton's gift to modern society

   Summary: A description of the effect of Caxton's press* on his world and the ramifications for subsequent generations

*William Caxton was a 15th century printer

FIGURE 11.10
LC Rules for Creating Cutter Numbers

```
1. After initial vowels
        for the 2nd letter:  b  d  l,m  n  p  r  s,t  u,y
                use number:   2  3   4   5  6  7   8    9
2. After the initial letter S
        for the 2nd letter:  a  ch  e  h,i  m-p   t      u
                use number:   2   3  4   5    6   7-8     9
3. After the initial letters Qu
        for the 2nd letter:  a  e  i  o  r  y
                use number:   3  4  5  6  7  9
   for names beginning Qa-Qt
                    use:   2-29
4. After other initial consonants
        for the 2nd letter:  a  e  i  o  r  u  y
                use number:   3  4  5  6  7  8  9
5. When an additional number is preferred
        for the 3rd letter:  a-d  e-h  i-l  m  n-q  r-t  u-w  x-z
                use number:    2*   3    4   5   6    7    8    9
(*optional for 3rd letter a or b)
```

Recommended Reading

C. A. Cutter's Three-Figure Author Table [on CD-ROM]. Englewood, CO: Libraries Unlimited, 1995.

C. A. Cutter's Two-Figure Author Table [on CD-ROM]. Englewood, CO: Libraries Unlimited, 1995.

Chan, Lois Mai. *A Guide to the Library of Congress Classification*, 5th ed. Englewood, CO: Libraries Unlimited, 1999.

Cutter-Sanborn Three-Figure Author Table [on CD-ROM]. Englewood, CO: Libraries Unlimited, 1995.

Dershem, Larry D. *Cataloging Made Easy: A Concise Edition of Library of Congress Classification and Subject Headings*. Buffalo, NY: Hein, 2004.

Dick, Gerald K. *Author Numbers*. Englewood, CO: Libraries Unlimited, 1992.

Dittmann, Helena, and Jane Hardy. *Learn Library of Congress Classification*. Lanham, MD: Scarecrow Press, 2000.

Mann, Thomas. *Library Research Models: A Guide to Classification, Cataloging, and Computers*. New York: Oxford University Press, 1993.

Scott, Mona L. *Conversion Tables*, 3rd ed. Westport, CT: Libraries Unlimited, 2006.

Notes

1.   The Jeffersonian system had 44 classes divided into three groups: Memory, Philosophy, and Fine Arts. Memory included fifteen classes covering history, science, and technical arts; Philosophy had fifteen classes covering ethics, religion, law, politics, mathematics, astronomy, and geography; Fine Arts had fourteen classes covering architecture, fine arts, music, and literature. For more details, see "Introduction" in *Thomas Jefferson's Library: A Catalog with His Entries in His Own Order*," eds. James Gilreath and Doublas L. Wilson (Washington: Library of Congress, 1989, reproduced 2001), available at www.loc.gov/catdir/loc/becites/main/jefferson/88607928_intro.html (Viewed July 15, 2006).

2.   www.loc.gov/catdir/cpso/lcc.html (Viewed June 19, 2006).

3.   Generally, tables used with one number or a small span of numbers in the schedules will be printed together with those numbers. Back-of-the-book tables have more general application.

4.   www.loc.gov/cds/classweb.html (Viewed July 11, 2006).

5.   The new manual is to be titled *Subject Cataloging Manual: LC Classification and Shelflisting*. As of December 15, 2006, it had not been incorporated into *Cataloger's Desktop*.

6.   *Class FC: A Classification for Canadian History*, 2nd ed. (Ottawa: National Library of Canada, 1994), plus four *Additions and Changes* to 2006.

7.   *Class PS8000: A Classification for Canadian Literature*, 3rd ed. (Ottawa: Library and Archives Canada, 2003). Available at http://collections canada.ca/9/15/index-e.html

8.   Available at http://collectionscanada.ca/9/11/index-e.html

12

Computer Encoding

Introduction

Putting bibliographic records containing many different kinds of information (call numbers, main and added entries, subject headings, bibliographic descriptions, and more) into computers requires that the data be presented in a way that a computer can accept the data and identify the parts, and programs can be written instructing the processor to manipulate the data. This is called, generically, computer encoding (also known as computer markup) and the sets of instructions used to do it are called encoding protocols or markup languages. Encoding protocols are overlaid on the data but do not become an integral part of the contents. A simple example of overlaying protocols on data could be the identification of the parts of a bibliographic description by adding explanatory prefixes, as shown in Figure 12.1. The data do not change, but the way they are displayed does. The explanatory prefixes in Figure 12.1 demonstrate one possibility for doing this.

Careful examination of the display in Figure 12.1 reveals that two things have changed in the encoded version. First, as one would expect from the explanatory phrases used in the protocol, the AACR2 names of the descriptive elements have been added to identify the kind of data each part presents. Second, some of the ISBD punctuation mandated by AACR2, namely, the full stop–space–dash space required to divide one descriptive element from another, has been dropped.

Until the advent of the Internet and electronic transmission of bibliographic data via the World Wide Web, only one protocol for encoding bibliographic data was used by the library community: the MARC (MAchine-Readable Cataloging) format, initiated by the Library of Congress. At this writing, the MARC format remains the primary encoding or markup language for library data, but other protocols or markup languages are beginning to be used as well, especially for library-sponsored digital archives, such as the Dublin Core. This chapter will cover the MARC format in detail and generally describe the Dublin Core and a selection of other markup languages used by libraries.

FIGURE 12.1

This example is an illustration of:

- anonymous work entered under uniform title
- two other title information
- subsidiary responsibility
- edition statement
- distributor
- publishing date not listed, copyright date given
- detailed pagination
- edition and history statement in quoted notes
- two ISBNs
- Library of Congress subject headings
- added entry for translator
- Dewey decimal classification with prime marks and shelf mark
- Library of Congress CIP
- 2nd level cataloguing in protocol prefix style

Uniform title:	Frau in Berlin. English.
Main title:	A woman in Berlin : eight weeks in the conquered city : a diary / by Anonymous ; translated by Philip Boehm.
Edition:	1st American ed.
Published/created:	New York : Metropolitan Books/Henry Holt, c2005.
Description:	xxi, 261 p.; 23 cm.
Notes:	"First published anonymously in 1954 in an incomplete English translation in the United States"--Pref. This ed. "originally published in Germany 2003 under the title Eine frau in Berlin"--T.p. verso.
ISBN:	ISBN-13: 978-08050-7540-3. -- ISBN-10: 08050-7540-2.
Subjects:	World War, 1939-1945 -- Germany -- Berlin. World War, 1939-1945 -- Women -- Germany -- Berlin. World War, 1939-1945 -- Atrocities -- Germany -- Berlin. World War, 1939-1945 -- Personal narratives, German. Berlin, Battle of, Berlin, Germany.
Related names:	Boehm, Philip.
Call number:	940.53'43155 FRA

For Canadian libraries "Published/created" would be: New York : Metropolitan Books/Henry Holt: Distributed in Canada by H.B. Fenn, c2005.

Authors' note: Although the Library of Congress CIP does not give an uniform title to this book, a library that has different language editions of the book would enter it under a uniform title to bring all editions of the book together in the catalog.

Fig. 12.1—Continues

FIGURE 12.1 *(continued)*

(chief source of information)

(title page)

A WOMAN
IN BERLIN

(information on verso)

Metropolitan Books
Henry Holt and Company, LLC
Publishers since 1866
175 Fifth Avenue
New York, New York 10010
www.henryholt.com

Eight Weeks in the Conquered City

Metropolitan Books® and ⅲ® are registered
trademarks of Henry Holt and Company, LLC.

A DIARY

Originally published in Germany in 2003 under the title
Eine Frau in Berlin by Eichborn AG, Frankfurt am Main

BY ANONYMOUS

Library of Congress Cataloging-in-Publication Data

A woman in Berlin : eight weeks in the conquered city : a diary / Anonymous ;
translated by Philip Boehm.—1st American ed.
    p. cm.
ISBN-13: 978-0-8050-7540-3
ISBN-10: 0-8050-7540-2
1. World War, 1939–1945—Germany—Berlin. 2. Berlin, Battle of, Berlin,
Germany, 1945. 3. World War, 1939–1945—Women—Germany—Berlin.
4. World War, 1939–1945—Atrocities—Germany—Berlin. 5. World War,
1939 1945—Personal narratives, German. I. Boehm, Philip.
    D757.9.B4W66 2005
    940.53'43155—dc22   2005041984

Translated by Philip Boehm

Henry Holt books are available for special promotions
and premiums. For details contact: Director, Special Markets.

First American Edition 2005

Designed by Victoria Hartman

Printed in the United States of America
1 3 5 7 9 10 8 6 4 2

Metropolitan Books

Henry Holt and Company · New York

History of the MARC Format

In the 1960s, the first MARC format was designed at the Library of Congress under the supervision of Henriette Avram, who died in 2006, to enable bibliographic records for books to be entered into properly programmed computers and, once encoded and entered into a database, to be transmitted electronically to another computer programmed to receive them. MARC went through several versions before being published as a national standard by the National Information Standards Organization in the 1970s. Before long, a MARC format for serials was implemented and, later, formats for other types of materials cataloged by the Library of Congress, including motion pictures, musical scores, and sound recordings.

By the 1990s, the Library of Congress's MARC database had grown to millions of titles in multiple media. The proliferation of MARC formats for different material forms had become a problem. They were difficult to learn and, more importantly, difficult to use in programming. After several years of study and planning, an integrated MARC format was implemented in which all fields were made uniform across all the physical forms of materials collected by libraries. All MARC codes were not, and still are not, applicable to all types of material; but wherever they appear, they mean the same thing, simplifying the processes of learning and using the system.

The natural tension between uniformity and customization that led, first, to the development of individual MARC formats for different material forms and, then, to their integration, is reflected in other areas as well. Each major bibliographic network developed its own version of MARC, changing some of the displays and some of the protocols for its own users. Thus, the initial fields can appear in different forms on the screen depending on which database one searches (see Figure 12.2, fixed field displays in MARC 21 and OCLC). Some fields not part of the official standard were established by individual networks for use by their participants only; and individual computer systems reproduce certain codes differently (see Figure 12.3, displays of two different computer systems that use dollar signs or other symbols in place of delimiters, etc.).

Each nation in the original AACR2 group (Canada, the United Kingdom, and the United States) adapted the MARC format to fit the needs of its culture. Other nations also began

FIGURE 12.2

Fixed Fields for Monographs

MARC

008 Character Positions

- 18-21 – Illustrations
- 22 - Target audience
- 23 - Form of item
- 24-27 - Nature of contents
- 28 - Government publication
- 29 - Conference publication
- 30 – Festschrift
- 31 – Index
- 32 – Undefined
- 33 - Literary form
- 34 – Biography

007 Character Positions

00 - Category of material
01 - Specific material designation

OCLC

Type:	ELvl:	Srce:	Audn:	Ctrl:	Lang:
BLvl:	Form:	Conf:	Biog:	MRec:	Ctry:
	Cont:	GPub:	LitF:	Indx:	
Desc:	Ills:	Fest:	DtSt:	Dates:	

FIGURE 12.3   Examples of Different Computer Displays

```
                                     ¶ CAT                    SID: 09401        OL
Beginning of record displayed.


OLUC  ti "STANDARD CATALOGING FOR SCHOOL AND PUBLIC LI...  Record 2 of 2
   NO HOLDINGS IN OCL - 232 OTHER HOLDINGS
   OCLC:  33983358            Rec stat:     c
   Entered:    19951221       Replaced:    19970729     Used:     20000701
 ▶ Type:  a     ELvl:      Srce:       Audn:      Ctrl:       Lang:  eng
   BLvl:  m     Form:      Conf:  0    Biog:      MRec:       Ctry:  cou
                Cont:  b   GPub:       LitF:  0   Indx:  1
   Desc:  a     Ills:  a   Fest:  0    DtSt:  s   Dates: 1996,     ¶
 ▶   1   010     95-53186 ¶
 ▶   2   040     DLC ‡c DLC ‡d NLC ¶
 ▶   3   015     C97-10475-8 ¶
 ▶   4   020     1563083493 ¶
 ▶   5   043     n-us--- ¶
 ▶   6   050 00  Z693 ‡b .I56 1996 ¶
 ▶   7   055 02  Z693.3* ¶
 ▶   8   082 00  025.3 ‡2 20 ¶
 ▶   9   090     ‡b ¶
 ▶  10   049     OCLC ¶
 ▶  11   100 1   Intner, Sheila S. ¶
 ▶  12   245 10  Standard cataloging for school and public libraries / ‡c Sheila
S. Intner and Jean Weihs. ¶
 ▶  13   250     2nd ed. ¶
 ▶  14   260     Englewood, Colo. : ‡b Libraries Unlimited, ‡c 1996. ¶
 ▶  15   300     viii, 278 p. : ‡b ill. ; ‡c 27 cm. ¶
 ▶  16   504     Includes bibliographical references (p. 211-213) and indexes. ¶
 ▶  17   650 0   Cataloging ‡z United States. ¶
 ▶  18   650 0   Public libraries ‡z United States. ¶
 ▶  19   650 0   School libraries ‡z United States. ¶
 ▶  20   650 6   Catalogage ‡x Normes ‡z ´Etats-Unis. ¶
 ▶  21   650 6   Biblioth`eques publiques ‡x Normes ‡z ´Etats-Unis. ¶
 ▶  22   650 6   Biblioth`eques scolaires ‡x Normes ‡z ´Etats-Unis. ¶
 ▶  23   650 6   Catalogage ‡x Litt´erature de jeunesse ‡x Normes ‡z ´Etats-
Unis. ¶
 ▶  24   700 1   Weihs, Jean Riddle. ¶
```

Fig. 12.3—Continues

adopting MARC, but in doing so, also adapted it for their languages and cultures. Along with this local customizing work, national and international efforts to promote uniformity continued, with the goal of making it easier to share data originating in different national databases. As networking matured through the 1990s and into the 2000s, some of the "harmonization" efforts (that is, merging separate formats in a single version) succeeded, with the European nations developing a generalized UNIMARC format.

MARC 21, the current standard for the United States, and Canada, was the culmination of cooperative work done by U.S. and Canadian specialists to harmonize the two official versions used by their countries, USMARC and CAN/MARC, respectively. It was established in 1997 and has been updated several times since then. The United Kingdom adopted MARC 21 in 2004, abandoning UKMARC. Individual nations may have their own official versions of MARC, but the differences tend to be minor. The fundamental structure is the same and the identical principles apply to all versions.

FIGURE 12.3 *(continued)*

Bibliographic record from the Toronto Public Library

001: 000032356870
003: CaOOAMICUS
005: 20060912152532.0
008: 060306s2006 onc 001 0beng
016: $a 20069010919
020: $a 9780002006767
020: $a 0002006766 : $c $38.95
035: $a 9735660
040: $a CaOONL $b eng $c CaOONL
043: $a n-cn--- $a n-us---
055: 0 $a TK6143 B4 $b G73 2006
082: 0 $a 621.385092 $2 22
090: $a 621.38509 BEL GRA
100: 1 $a Gray, Charlotte, $d 1948-
245: 10 $a Reluctant genius : $b the passionate life and inventive mind of Alexander Graham Bell / $c Charlotte Gray.
250: $a 1st ed.
260: $a Toronto : $b HarperCollins, $c 2006.
263: $a 0608
300: $a 466 p. : $b ill., map.
500: $a "A Phyllis Bruce book".
500: $a Includes index.
600: 10 $a Bell, Alexander Graham, $d 1847-1922.
650: 0 $a Inventors $z Canada $v Biography.
650: 0 $a Inventors $z United States $v Biography.

Types of MARC Formats

Thus far, we have been describing the MARC format used to encode bibliographic data (MARC Bibliographic), but it is not the only format available. Five MARC formats have been developed, beginning with the one for bibliographic data. The others are for authority data, holdings data, classification data, and community information. Each format has fields, subfields, and content designators designed to identify and manipulate the kinds of information needed for its type. The MARC Authorities format has fields for authorized name and subject heading forms, "see" cross-references, "see also" cross-references, and the sources from which various name or word forms have been derived. Similarly, the MARC Classification format has fields for authorized classification numbers and terms, references, tracings, notes, and number buildings; the MARC Holdings format has fields for location and access, captions and publication patterns, enumeration and chronology data, textual holdings statements, item information, and so on; the MARC Community Information format can accommodate information about individuals, organizations, events, programs or services, and the like. Figures 12.4 through 12.8 illustrate these different types of MARC formats.

FIGURE 12.4   Personal Name Authority Record

```
ARN:    86904
Rec stat: c        Entered:        19800903
Type:        z     Upd status:   a    Enc lvl:    n    Source:
Roman:             Ref status:   a    Mod rec:         Name use: a
Govt agn:          Auth status:  a    Subj:        a   Subj use: a
Series:      n     Auth/ref:     a    Geo subd:    n   Ser use:  b
Ser num:     n     Name:         a    Subdiv tp:       Rules:    c
   1   010      n  50051972
   2   040      DLC   c DLC
   3   005      19840407101817.5
   4   100 10   Weihs, Jean Riddle.
   5   400 10   Riddle, Jean
   6   400 10   Weihs, Jean
   7   670      Her Non-book materials ... 1970.
   8   670      Her Accessible storage of nonbook materials, 1984:   b CIP t.p.
(Jean Weihs)
   9   678      Course Director, Library Techniques, Seneca College of Applied
Arts and Technology;   a b. 1930
```

FIGURE 12.5   Subject Authority Record

```
ARN:    2659069
Rec stat: c        Entered:        19891026
Type:        z     Upd status:   a    Enc lvl:    n    Source:
Roman:             Ref status:   a    Mod rec:         Name use: b
Govt agn:          Auth status:  a    Subj:        a   Subj use: a
Series:      n     Auth/ref:     a    Geo subd:        Ser use:  b
Ser num:     n     Name:         n    Subdiv tp:       Rules:    n
   1   010      sh 89006162
   2   040      DLC   c DLC   d DLC
   3   005      19940422110444.5
   4   150  0   IBM-compatible computers
   5   450  0   Clones of IBM computers
   6   450  0   Compatible computers, IBM-
   7   450  0   IBM clones
   8   450  0   IBM compatibles (Computers)
   9   550  0   Microcomputers   w g
  10   670      Work cat.: Pilgrim, A. Upgrade your IBM compatible and save a
bundle, c1990.
```

FIGURE 12.6   MARC Holdings Record

MARC holdings record

LEVEL 1   <Location Identifier> Main

LDR	*****nx###22*****1##4500
001	<control number>
852 ##	$a<location identifier>$bMain

LEVEL 2   <Location Identifier> Main 19870414 (0,ta,4,2,8)

LDR	*****nx###22*****2##4500
001	<control number>
008	8902202p####8###4001aa###0870414
852 ##	$a<location identifier>$bMain

FIGURE 12.7

MARC Classification Format: Dewey Decimal Classification

Scheme: **003.52 Perception theory**
Class computer vision in 006.37; class psychology of human perception in 153.7; class perception in animals in 573.87

See also 006.4 for computer pattern recognition

Record:
LDR   *******nw22*****n4500 01
001   <control number>
008   901001aaaaaaaa
084   0# $addc$c21
153   ## $a003.52$hGeneralities$hSystems$hTheory of communication and control$jPerception theory
685   00 $tPerception theory$iformerly located in$b001.534$d19890306$220 **753 ##** $aPerception theory

MARC Classification Format: Library of Congress Classification

Record: **LDR**   *****nw###22*****n##4500
001   <control number>
008   901001acaaaaaa
084 0   # $alcc
153 ## $aHE380.8$cHE560$hTransportation and communications$hWater transportation$jWaterways
680 0# $iClass here the transportation economic aspects of waterways

Record:
008   901001acaaaaaa
153 ## $aTC1$cTC1800$jHydraulic engineering
553 0# wjaHE380.8$cHE560$hTransportation and communications$hWater transportation $jWaterways$tengineering and construction

Governance of the MARC Formats

Ultimate authority over MARC 21 proposals rests with LC, the Library and Archives Canada (LAC), and the British Library. The national libraries each have their own consultative committees:

- In Canada, the Canadian Committee on MARC
- In the United States, the MARC Advisory Committee
- In the United Kingdom, the Book Industry Communication Bibliographic Standards Technical Subgroup

The MARC 21 formats are published by LC's Network Development and MARC Standards Office, and LAC's Standards section. LAC is responsible for the publication of the French translation of the MARC 21 formats.

Three stages in MARC development are typical: (1) proposal, discussion, study, and approval by national committees; (2) implementation by the governing bodies; (3) adoption and implementation by networks. Issues important to groups of librarians, who make propos-

FIGURE 12.8

MARC Community Information Format

Leader/06	q *[community information]*
Leader/07	o *[organization]*
001	\<control number\>
003	\<control number identifier\>
005	\<date and time of latest transaction\>
008	930917aaaaaaeng
040 ##	$a\<MARC code\>$c\<MARC code\>
041 0#	$aeng$aspa
110 2#	$aHaven House.
270 1#	$aP.O. Box 50007$bPasadenacCAe91115$j213-681-2626 (24 hour hotline)
307 ##	$a24 hours a day, 7 days a week.
520 ##	$aA residential shelter for women and their children who have been abused by alcoholic
partners.	
531 ##	$aWomen (18-64) with their children (0-18) who need shelter from physical and emotional abuse due to alcohol in family member;$bfrom $1.50/day (Residential) to $20.00/month (Group CNSL.);$ctelephone; no walk-ins.
546 ##	$aEnglish, Spanish.
574 ##	$aPublic transportation. Call RTD: 818-246-2593.
650 #0	$aBattered women.
650 #0	$aWomen's services.

━━━━━━━━━━

als and serve on the committees that consider and approve them, may not have high priority at LC and LAC, whose job it is to implement the changes, or to the networks that must adopt and implement them on behalf of their participants. Thus, although a proposed change is approved, it could take months or years before it becomes part of regular encoding practice "on the ground."

Elements of MARC Records

A MARC record is not a new type of cataloging. It is an encoded version of a catalog record prepared using the current standards accepted by North American libraries. It contains all the information included in a catalog record plus added information needed for computer processing. The cataloging data (main and added entries, title statements, edition statements, etc.) are the content of the record; everything else added to the content to identify individual records and their parts, is the encoding. Figure 12.9 shows a MARC record for a book in which the encoding is highlighted. The parts that are not highlighted comprise the record content.

MARC records are divided into parts called *fields*, which, themselves, are divided into smaller parts called *subfields*. Fields have names known as *tags* and subfields have names known as *subfield codes*. Fields also contain field-specific computer instructions called *indicators* and other symbols that identify specific record parts, including the start and end of each record, field, and subfield. Together, all the names and symbols used by the format to encode the record content—everything other than the content itself—are called *content designators*.

FIGURE 12.9   MARC Encoding highlighted in bold type

```
020      $a 0671042181
082 04  $a 793.734 $b Ed53 $2 22
100 1   $a Edley, Joe.
245 10  $a Everything Scrabble / $c Joe Edley and John D. Williams, Jr.
250      $a Updated and rev.
260      $a New York : $b Pocket Books, $c c2001.
300      $a xxii, 342 p. : $b ill. ; $c 24 cm.
500      $a "Only book authorized by the National Scrabble Association"
         --Cover.
650   0 $a Scrabble (Game)
700 1   $a Williams, John D., Jr.
710 2   $a National Scrabble Association.
```

Fields: As stated above, encoded catalog records are divided first into fields. Each element of the catalog record has a corresponding field, identified by a specific tag, into which the content for that element is put (12.10, Summary of MARC Bibliographic Field Tags). Tags are always three-digit numbers. Once catalogers using MARC format learn the tags for the elements, they soon refer to elements by their tags. For example, a cataloger might ask, "Does this score have a 250?" meaning "Does this score have an edition statement?" or, "Should the 300 [i.e., physical description] be 1 score or 1 miniature score?" When a computer programmed to accept catalog records in MARC format encounters the three consecutive digits "250" at the beginning of a field, it interprets the information that follows (up to the mark indicating the end of the field) as an edition statement.

FIGURE 12.10   Summary of MARC Bibliographic Field Tags

0XX	Includes fixed fields and control numbers.
1XX	Main entries, including personal author, corporate body author, conference names, and uniform title main entries.
2XX	Transcribed titles, editions, material specific details, and publication/distribution information.
3XX	Physical descriptions.
4XX	Transcribed series statements.
5XX	Descriptive notes.
6XX	Subject descriptors.
7XX	Added entries for names of contributors and titles other than main entry titles and titles proper (the latter are coded by different means, described later).
8XX	Series added entries traced differently than transcribed.
9XX	Intended for local data.

Subfields: Fields are further subdivided into subfields, which cover parts of a cataloging element. For example, field 245 contains the entire title statement for a document. Title statements can have several parts, which always include a title proper, but may also include other title information such as subtitles and a statement of responsibility. To accommodate these parts, field 245 is divided into subfields that can accommodate each of the parts into which a title statement can be divided. Each subfield has a name consisting of a delimiter symbol that identifies it as a subfield and a subfield code identifying which kind of subfield it is. Subfields are field–specific. For example, 245 subfield a is the title proper; 300 subfield a is the extent and specific material designation; 050 subfield a is the Library of Congress classification number.

Delimiters, which precede all subfield codes, may display differently in different computer systems, but usually are represented by either the double cross symbol (≠) or the dollar sign ($). Subfield codes are either single letters or numbers. For example, in field 082 (Dewey Decimal call number field), ≠a contains the classification number, ≠b contains the shelf marks, and ≠2 contains the number of the DDC edition used.

Indicators: Two character positions are available between the tag and the start of data in a field for field-specific instructions called *indicators* that tell a computer how to manipulate the data content of the field. Indicators are not defined for every field, but those that are defined are always specific to the field in which they appear. Fields can have no indicators, one indicator that can appear in either the first or the second position, or two indicators. For example, field 300 has none; field 100 has one indicator in the first position;[1] field 650 has one indicator in the second position; and field 245 has two indicators. Indicators can be added, deleted, or redefined by MARC's governing bodies.

Originally, indicators were a vital element in printing catalog cards from computerized data. They still be used for that purpose when cards are desired, but the instructions they convey are used today primarily to enable programmers to write programs for computers to display or suppress selected pieces of data as well as to index and file the data correctly and perform other database management tasks properly.

Content Designation: The process of encoding or marking up a catalog record in MARC format has several names. It is likely to be called plain "coding" not "encoding," which is not often heard. Library catalogers rarely use the term *marking- up* for MARC coding, perhaps, because the term and the idea of markup languages originated among computer specialists, not librarians. Because of the fact that MARC fields are known by tags, the process is often called *tagging,*"or both *coding and tagging*. The most formal name for the process is *content designation*, so called because the MARC protocols name (or "designate") elements of cataloging data (or "content") in the record. Thus, MARC protocols designate content and the process by which it is done is called content designation.

Content Designation Caveats: The MARC format, like other standards used in cataloging, is constantly being revised. As already described in this chapter, it has changed over the years, sometimes in major respects, such as occurred during format integration, and sometimes in minor respects, such as the establishment or deletion of an indicator for one or a few fields. It is wise to keep abreast of the MARC format's current specifications and examine older records with those specifications in mind. Sometimes, when a change in the format is officially approved, computer system managers are unable to revise all the existing records in their databases immediately to reflect the new rules. They assume knowledgeable catalogers will recognize and ignore the differences.

Figure 12.11 shows an item cataloged in a traditional format and also in a MARC format.

FIGURE 12.11

This example is an illustration of:
- other title information
- subsidiary responsibility
- edition statement
- descriptive illustration statement
- quoted note
- Library of Congress subject headings
- added entry for illustrator
- title added entry
- Dewey decimal and Library of Congress classifications
- catalog record in traditional format and in MARC format

Catalog record in traditional format

Wallis, Velma.
  Raising ourselves : a Gwich'in coming of age story from the
Yukon River / Velma Wallis ; illustrated by James L. Grant, Sr.
-- 1st ed. -- Kenmore, WA : Epicenter Press, 2002.
  212 p. : ill., geneal. table, map, ports. ; 24 cm.

  "Alaska book adventures."
  ISBN 0-9708493-0-3.

  1. Gwich'in women -- Alaska -- Fort Yukon -- Biography.
2. Gwich'in Indians -- Alcohol use -- Alaska -- Fort Yukon.
3.Alcholism -- Alaska -- Fort Yukon. 4. Fort Yukon (Alaska) --
Social life and customs. I. Grant, James L. II. Title.

Recommended DDC: 979.8'6

Recommended LCC:E99.K84 W34 2002

Catalog record in MARC format

```
020     $a 0970849303
050  0 $a E99.K84 $b W34 2002
082 04 $a 979.8/6 $2 22
100 1  $a Wallis, Velma.
245 10 $a Raising ourselves : $b a Gwich'in coming of age story
       from the Yukon River / $c Velma Wallis ; illustrated by
       James L. Grant, Sr.
250     $a 1st ed.
260     $a Kenmore, WA : $b Epicenter Press, $c 2002.
300     $a 212 p. : $b ill., geneal. table, map, ports. ; $c 24
       cm.
500     $a "Alaska book adventures."
650  0 $a Gwich'in women $z Alaska $z Fort Yukon $v Biography.
650  0 $a Gwich'in Indians $x Alcohol use $z Alaska $z Fort
       Yukon.
650  0 $a Alcholism $z Alaska $z Fort Yukon.
651  0 $a Fort Yukon (Alaska) $x Social life and customs.
700 1  $a Grant, James L.
```

Fig. 12.11—Continues

FIGURE 12.11 *(continued)*

(chief source of information)

(title page)   *(information on verso)*

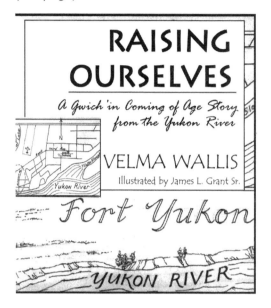

Epicenter Press is a regional press founded in Alaska whose interests include but are not limited to the arts, history, nature, and diverse cultures and lifestyles of the North Pacific and high latitudes. Epicenter seeks both the traditional and innovative in publishing high-quality nonfiction books and contemporary art and photography gift books.
Visit us at EpicenterPress.com.

Publisher: Kent Sturgis
Editor: Christine Ummel Hosler
Cover and Text design: Victoria Sturgis
Illustrations: James L. Grant Sr.
Proofreader: Sherrill Carlson
Printer: Transcontinental Printing

Text © 2002 Velma Wallis
Illustrations, maps © 2002 James L. Grant Sr.

All photos herein are from the Wallis family collection.
Family tree photograph © 2002 www.arttoday.com

Library of Congress Control Number: 2002111759
ISBN: 0-9708493-0-3

All rights reserved. No part of this publication may be reproduced, stored in a retrieval system, or transmitted, in any form or by any means, electronic, mechanical, photocopying, recording, or otherwise, without the prior written permission of the publisher. Permission is granted for brief excerpts to be published with book reviews in print or electronic publications.

To order extra copies of RAISING OURSELVES, mail $19.95 plus $4.95 to Epicenter Press, Box 82368, Kenmore, WA 98028. WA residents add $1.75 for state sales tax. You also may order via fax to (425) 481-8253, via phone to (800) 950-6663, or at our website, EpicenterPress.com.

Booksellers: Retail discounts are available from our trade distributor, Graphic Arts Center Publishing™, Box 10306, Portland, OR 97210.

PRINTED IN CANADA

First Edition
First printing September 2002

10 9 8 7 6 5 4 3 2

Other Markup Languages: Metadata

The generic term for the information librarians traditionally prepare about materials to make them available to those who want to read, view, and hear them is *cataloging*. Another term with a similar meaning is *metadata*, which means "data about data." However, metadata has a more precise meaning, referring solely to information added to electronic documents that identifies them and makes them retrievable. Library cataloging for electronic documents such as websites is a kind of metadata in which MARC is the markup language. MARC is a very complicated and sophisticated markup language, but it is not the only one currently being used. Projects initiated by libraries and nonlibrary groups employ different markup languages such as Dublin Core (DC), Metadata Object Description Schema (MODS), VRA (Visual Resources Association) Core, Encoded Archival Description (EAD), and so forth. Some are described in this section.

Dublin Core (DC): The Dublin Core Metadata Element Set originated in 1995 as a set of fifteen core elements for describing electronic documents. Later, a sixteenth element was added. The DC elements include the following:

Title	Creator	Subject	Description
Publisher	Contributor	Date	Type
Format	Identifier	Source	Language
Relation	Coverage	Rights	Audience (added last)

Intner, Lazinger, and Weihs[2] divide the original fifteen elements into three groups based on the type of information they cover: (1) content (title, subject, description, type, source, relation, coverage); (2) intellectual property (creator, publisher, contributor, rights); and (3) instantiation (date, format, identifier, language). Librarians sometimes think of DC as a kind of simplified MARC format, but, unlike MARC, it requires no special knowledge to learn and is easy to apply. Developed by a group that included experts from within and outside of the library community, DC has been widely used by libraries and adopted by digital library designers belonging to other communities as well.

Originally encoded using *HTML* (HyperText Markup Language), DC now can be encoded using *XML* (Extensible Markup Language), lending it greater flexibility. When early DC users complained the element set was not sufficiently precise, qualifiers were added to each element to define it further. Although DC is far below the level of complexity of MARC, it now can go beyond the initial fifteen elements known as Simple DC and continues to evolve.

Metadata Object Description Schema (MODS): Metadata Object Description Schema (MODS) was designed to be compatible with MARC, although it does not include all the MARC fields and subfields. Each basic MODS element has an equivalent MARC field, and the Library of Congress provides mapping between the two systems. Unlike MARC, MODS has language-based tags in an XML-based format. The MODS schema has nineteen top-level elements, which can be enriched with subelements and attributes to express more precise details. The top-level elements are as follows:

titleInfo	name	typeOfResource
genre	originInfo	language
physicalDescription	abstract	tableOfContents
targetAudience	note	subject
classification	relatedItem	identifier
location	accessCondition	extension
recordInfo		

MODS elements and attributes are optional.

VRA Core: The Visual Resources Association (VRA) developed its own set of elements to describe art works and the images that document art works. VRA Core consists of seventeen basic elements, as follows:

Record Type	Type	Title
Material	Technique	Creator

Date	Geographic	Rights
ID Number	Style/Period	Format
Culture	Subject	Relation
Description	Source	

VRA Core elements can be further qualified to add precision to the description. The order of elements is not predefined, and users can arrange the fields to suit the individual needs of their application.

Encoded Archival Description (EAD): First published in 1998, Encoded Archival Description (EAD), currently maintained at LC's MARC Editorial Office, is a standard used by the archives community for the description of archival materials. Archival materials differ considerably from library materials in that they often consist of unique groups of documents in a variety of media. EAD was intended to complement MARC, providing details of resource description and access that are not easily represented by MARC format. According to Intner, Lazinger, and Weihs: "EAD is intended primarily to accommodate registers and inventories describing the full range of archival holdings in various media."[3] EAD accommodates both simple and qualified markup, and permits individual users to determine both the level of detail desired and which elements they wish to use.

Examining the three lists of descriptive elements given above, only the following six elements seem to be common to all:

Title	Creator/Contributor/Name	Subject
Type/Type of Resource	Identifier/ID Number	Relation/Related Item

The meaning of some elements is not immediately obvious; for example, VRA Core's "Culture," MODS's "originInfo," and DC's "Format." Nevertheless, it is interesting that of the six common elements, three match the library catalog's traditional access points—title, "author," and subject—and a fourth, "Identifier/ID Number" is a logical element likely to be assigned to any compilation of documents.

Conclusion

This chapter explains the library community's basic computer encoding language, the MARC format, in some detail, exploring its history and background; the five types of MARC formats that LC, LAC, and its partners have developed; and its governance. The composition of MARC Bibliographic, the format used by library catalogers to prepare catalog records for online catalogs, is explored further.

Other markup languages, including the Dublin Core (DC), Metadata Object Description Schema (MODS), VRA Core, and Encoded Archival Description (EAD), are described briefly. Although these are not the only markup languages available, they are included here to illustrate alternatives to MARC format that are in current use. Librarians use non-MARC encoding systems to create metadata for digital libraries and other collections of electronic resources.

The following exercises ask readers to prepare a MARC record for the each of the figures indicated below using fields 020, 022, 050, 082, 100–899. Use the *MARC 21 Concise*

Format for Bibliographic Data (www.loc.gov/marc/bibliographic/) to complete these exercises. Answers are found on pages 251–253 in Appendix B.

Figure 12.12.   Prepare a MARC record for Figure 6.5 on page 104.

Figure 12.13.   Prepare a MARC record for Figure 8.5 on page 145 using the AC heading and add an appropriate DDC number from the abridged DDC.

Figure 12.14.   Prepare a MARC record for Figure 9.1 on page 158.

Figure 12.15.   Prepare a MARC record for Figure 9.2 on page 161 using Sears subject headings and the abridged DDC.

Figure 12.16.   Prepare a MARC record for Figure 10.6 on page 179.

Figure 12.17.   Prepare a MARC record for Figure 10.5 on page 175.

Figure 12.18.   Prepare a MARC record for Figure 11.3 on page 191.

Figure 12.19.   Prepare a MARC record for Figure 5.9 on page 80 adding appropriate Library of Congress subject headings.

Recommended Reading

Carlyle, Allyson. "Understanding FRBR as a Conceptual Model: FRBR and the Bibliographic Universe." *Library Resources & Technical Services* 50, no. 4 (October 2006): 264–273.

Ferguson, Bobby. *MARC/AACR2/Authority Control Tagging*. 2nd ed. (A Blitz Cataloging Workbook.) Englewood, CO: Libraries Unlimited, 2005.

Fritz, Deborah A. *Cataloging with AACR2 & MARC21 for Books, Electronic Resources, Sound Recordings, Videorecordings, and Serials*, 2nd ed. Chicago: American Library Association, 2004. Supplements are available at www.marcofquality.com

Furie, Betty. *Understanding MARC Bibliographic: Machine-Readable Cataloging*, 7th ed. Washington, DC: Library of Congress in collaboration with the Follette Software Co., 2003. Available at www.loc.gov/marc/umb

Jones, Wayne, Judith R. Ahronheim, and Josephine Crawford, eds. *Cataloging the Web: Metadata, AACR, and MARC 21*. Lanham, MD: Scarecrow Press in cooperation with the Association for Library Collections & Technical Services, 2002.

Library of Congress. Cataloging Directorate. Available at www.lcweb.loc.gov/marc/bibliographic

Smiraglia, Richard P., ed. *Metadata: A Cataloger's Primer*. New York: Haworth Information Press, 2005.

Notes

1.   At one time, field 100 had an indicator in the second position to show whether the name appearing in the field (the main entry) was also a subject heading. The coding was "0" when it was not also a subject heading and "1" when it was. If the second indicator of field 100 were "1," coders could skip re-entering the name as a subject heading.

2.   Sheila S. Intner, Susan S. Lazinger, and Jean Weihs, *Metadata and Its Impact on Libraries* (Westport, CT: Libraries Unlimited, 2006), pp. 32–34.

3.   Ibid., p. 90.

13

Managing the Catalog Department

Organization charts usually put catalog departments under the technical services division if libraries have such divisions, but catalog departments also may be combined with other database services in a unit responsible for all computer-based activities or may be stand-alone departments. Depending on the size, one librarian might manage the department as her or his sole responsibility or, if it is not large, might combine management with hands-on cataloging duties. Some libraries have self-managing catalog departments, in which no one is in charge and department members supervise themselves, but they are not typical.

Knowing how to catalog and classify materials purchased for the public library or school library media center is essential for managers to understand how to manage the work of the department, but it is just a start. Other skills come into play in managing the department, such as knowing how to communicate well in writing and speaking, motivating members of the department staff to work effectively, inspiring confidence in one's decisions, and doing a good job of representing the department to others within and outside of the library. Managers must deal with internal administrative matters such as overseeing budgets and staff deployment as well as with external issues involving interactions with representatives of the networks, companies, and other organizations on which their departments depend for needed products and services. Managers must navigate the library's internal organization successfully on behalf of the department so it can accomplish its work.

This chapter will explore department policies and procedures, management tasks, and current issues in managing catalog departments.

Department Policies and Procedures

Cataloging policies may seem obvious to those who work with them every day and have come to take them for granted, but every time a newcomer enters the department or a question about them arises in some nondepartmental context, one realizes the need to spell them out in some detail. Central among these policies are the choices of bibliographic level (fullness) for descriptive cataloging, subject authority list used as a source of subject headings, classification scheme used, and shelf marks to be added to classification numbers to create call numbers. In addition to making explicit choices about how to handle these basic matters are choices about how catalogers should respond to changes in cataloging rules, subject authorities, and classifications; the way that monographic series should be cataloged and classified; and what procedures should be followed to implement the policy decisions.

One way to make certain that everyone in and outside of the department understands and follows the same policies and procedures is to record them in writing in a departmental manual. Instead of leaving it to chance that different trainers will give the same advice to trainees about such things as assigning full or truncated classification numbers or using the designated bibliographic level, for example, consulting a policy manual to determine the answers ensures uniformity. What should this manual look like? What should it contain? It should begin with a brief description of the library's community or the media center's school, including its mission, goals, and objectives, to establish the context in which the policies operate. Next, the main body of the manual should contain sections for each type of operation in the bibliographic system, including descriptive cataloging, subject cataloging, and classification and call number decisions, as well as those covering how data are encoded and how changes in the cataloging rules and subject tools should be handled. Finally, provision should be made for reviewing and amending the manual on a regular basis, most likely once a year, and for obtaining formal approval from the library's or media center's governing body. No policy is enforceable without approval; therefore, even though some may think cataloging policies would be of little interest to boards of trustees, directors, and so on, their stamp of approval is needed.

Management Tasks

Setting Goals and Objectives: Deciding what the department needs to accomplish over a period of time (usually, though not always, a year) means setting goals—the kinds of work to be done and general guidelines about how it should be done—and objectives—measurable targets to be reached by the end of the period. Goals might include general aims such as permanently eliminating video backlogs. Objectives suggest specific strategies, numeric targets, and time limits. For example, two strategies that would eliminate video backlogs could be hiring a video cataloging specialist as a consultant for three months to complete the cataloging of an existing video backlog, and, afterward, having the consultant spend another month training the department's full-time catalogers to catalog videos as quickly and accurately as they currently catalog books, thus ensuring new backlogs do not develop. The objectives are measurable. To meet the first, a consultant must be hired and complete the job of working off the entire backlog within three months. (Specifying all backlogged materials implies a measurable number of items, not a percentage of the whole or a specific number of items, but "all" of them.) To complete the second, the consultant must teach the full-time catalogers to handle video cataloging as quickly and accurately as they currently handle books, and do it within a month.

The most important goal a department can adopt is to be backlog-free. If a static backlog exists, the goal should be to work it off. If a growing backlog exists, twin goals must address working it off and increasing production so it cannot develop again.

The biggest challenge to catalog department managers is being expected to absorb sudden changes in workflow caused by the loss of staff members, unforeseen increases in the volume of materials, and/or introductions of unfamiliar material types, especially the kinds that require sophisticated treatments, such as electronic resources. Wise managers will alert their supervisors about potential problems before they occur and turn into crises. Also, astute managers will resist agreeing to accomplish goals and objectives that department resources are clearly inadequate to support.

Staffing Issues: Computerization in the 1980s split catalog departments into two divisions: original and copy cataloging. Original cataloging, a small proportion of cataloging work in most public libraries and media centers, still had to be done by knowledgeable professionals. Copy cataloging, on the other hand, required different skills—searching, finding, and editing catalog records already part of bibliographic databases, and entering all the needed data quickly and accurately into computers. By 2000, departments that formerly had many librarians and a small number of support staff were replaced by departments that had many support staff (copy catalogers) and one or a few librarians to supervise them and complete whatever original cataloging still needed to be done.

Since 2000, the trend is to buy as many catalog records as possible from outside sources. Purchases often go beyond catalog records, including online public catalog displays (OPACs) and processing services as well as the catalog records. As a result, local public libraries and school library media centers need just a few catalogers to oversee purchases and incorporation of the records into local OPACs, be responsible for troubleshooting OPAC problems on-site, and do whatever cataloging work cannot be purchased, such as local history materials, unpublished materials, and other types of locally produced materials. In such minidepartments, the staff are likely to consist of a librarian serving as manager and cataloger, supervising a small number of support staff trained to work with bibliographic data and systems.

In departments large enough to have a number of catalogers, a large part of the manager's job is training. Two kinds of training need to be done: first, teaching new catalogers how rules and tools are applied locally and how local computer systems operate; second, updating veterans on changes to both the rules and the tools, and the computer systems used by the department. In departments divided into subunits, the overall manager might delegate training tasks to subunit heads, making them responsible for ensuring that staff members' skills are updated continuously.

Another important and time-consuming task is evaluating the department's personnel. Catalog department managers are expected to provide feedback about their performance to the members of their staff. Fortunate managers work in libraries and media centers that mandate regular staff evaluations and spell out how to do it. If a library or media center does not have an established procedure, the department manager should be guided by common sense in designing procedures to keep individuals apprised of their accomplishments and needed growth. Making sure that staff members know in advance how they are evaluated and applying the evaluative criteria objectively contribute to the success of the process. Keeping one's focus on evaluating the work, not the person, is important as well.

Managing the Budget: Some catalog department managers are expected to prepare budgets and oversee their implementation throughout the fiscal year. Others receive preset amounts annually as part of a larger technical services budget and are asked only to monitor and report on department-related expenditures. Either way, most managers bear some level of financial responsibility on behalf of the department.

Understanding how the department budget is prepared means learning about the types of expenses the department incurs, such as personnel, equipment, supplies, contract services (including services purchased from bibliographic networks, cooperatives, and other organizations), cataloging-related materials (such as AACR, LCSH, cataloging manuals, etc.), and so on. At the beginning of the year, each type of expense is allotted a total amount of money from which the purchases for that expense are deducted. The manager's job is to see that purchases are properly made and recorded, and that the total spent on each expense does not exceed its allotted amount. At the end of the year, part of a manager's annual report includes an accounting of how the money allotted to the department was spent.

Buying Products and Services: Known in recent years as *outsourcing*, buying cataloging products and services for the library from outside organizations goes back to the 1900s, when the Library of Congress began selling printed catalog cards. For more than a century, the ideal was for each book to be cataloged once, after which any library that bought the same book used the catalog record. In the twenty-first century, this goal is closer to being realized than ever before, thanks to the combined efforts of national libraries, networks, library automation companies, and individual libraries and media centers that contribute to growing bibliographic databases.

Small public libraries and school library media centers that buy mainstream materials whose catalog records are likely to be found in the major databases (LC's MARC database, OCLC's WorldCat, or LAC's AMICUS) before they reach their purchasers' doors may find it more advantageous to order catalog records together with the materials. Often, the same wholesalers that sell the materials can provide standard quality catalog records when they deliver the goods, for a price. The question catalog department managers must answer is whether that price is more or less economical than other methods of obtaining the data, which include joining a network or another shared cataloging group, or doing it in-house using CIP or "from-scratch" work. Managers must be vigilant that the catalog records they buy meet quality standards. Low-cost catalog records that fail to do so may prove more expensive in the long run if they have to be improved or redone.

Evaluating the Department: Managers need to establish departmental evaluation procedures and, then, supervise their implementation. This means developing evaluative criteria and data gathering methods, and setting up a regular schedule for measuring department activities. Typically, department managers keep track of the numbers of items cataloged and classified, and recataloged and reclassified. These are important measures of accomplishment. However, for staff evaluation purposes, individual productivity of department members is measured; and for vendor evaluation purposes, order turnaround times and discounts are tracked. Both of these more detailed measures should figure in the department's evaluation, if only to establish the ranges within which activities are accomplished and costs incurred. A department manager should know, for example, not only that 5,000 items were cataloged and classified by five staff members, but also that copy cataloging took between four and seven minutes to produce a record, and original cataloging took between twelve and seventeen minutes to produce a record. The manager should know the average weekly or monthly cataloging output for each person doing the work and whether there were explanations for exceptional production rates, high or low. Perhaps a staff member's productivity increased after the person attended a workshop or completed a course on how to catalog specialized materials. Turnaround time for important department activities such as establishing new headings for the catalog, cataloging new collections, and revising call numbers or subject headings, should be counted also, and quality norms for each product or type of output should be developed and measured in order to evaluate the department's work meaningfully.

Together, statistics showing how much output was produced (volume), how good the products were (quality), how long they took to produce (time), and how much they cost (price), establish how effectively the department has been operating. Comparing what it actually did over a period of time with what it set out to do in its goals and objectives for the period provides a definitive picture of departmental accomplishment.

Reporting, the Manager's Final Task: Why do all this work to establish how much work was done, how good it was, how fast it got done, and how much it cost? The answer is simple: to tell it to the department's supervisors, library or media center administrators, and institutional or community boards. Generally, department managers write annual reports describing and documenting the activities, both production and financial, of their departments. Often, their reports are combined with those from other departments into overall library/media center annual reports submitted by the directors to their supervisors and governing boards.

Reports about cataloging activities should emphasize both the quantity and the quality of outputs as well as the impacts of those outputs on library and media center services to patrons. Service is the ultimate objective of all bibliographic policies and procedures. Through their reports, department managers can explain how the work of their departments helps patrons do a better job of finding and locating the materials they need. Unless this connection is clearly made and properly documented, administrators may think the department has little to contribute to patron service and could easily be replaced by cheaper bibliographic products or services obtained from other sources. The most important result of good reporting is that it explains to people who may not know a great deal about cataloging activities and outputs or understand the implications of differences in their quality and quantity how much value the library or media center received for the money it allocated to the department.

Current Issues in Department Management

Metadata: The twenty-first-century trend in technical services and cataloging that is affecting departments more than any other is the one that puts metadata librarians under the catalog department's umbrella. Metadata refers to information used to locate and retrieve materials in electronic form from collections of such materials.[1] These collections of electronic materials may be part of locally owned and locally produced "digital libraries," or externally produced gatherings of electronic materials that local libraries and media centers do not own, but to which they have purchased access, or, in some instances, that they have gathered from among the many free offerings available through the Internet and World Wide Web. Because metadata resembles encoded cataloging more closely than any other kind of information known to librarians and school library media specialists, the catalog department seems to have become the logical "home" for its practitioners.

Differences between traditional cataloging and twenty-first-century metadata include the kinds of information covered in the records and the way the information is constructed and presented. Metadata almost always specifies comprehensive ownership and rights management information, which traditional cataloging never did, because libraries owned the traditional materials represented by catalog records. Electronic materials usually are accessed, not owned, making ownership and rights management information essential for potential users. Metadata records give far less detail for bibliographic elements such as authors, titles, and physical descriptions, and do not follow uniform rules (such as AACR2) in their construction. Metadata subject descriptors are unlikely to be derived from controlled vocabularies such as LCSH or Sears; instead, they are likely to be keywords automatically derived from the electronic documents being represented or provided by the authors of the documents. Metadata records are unlikely to bear subject-related classification numbers taken from library classifications, though they may be assigned control numbers of other kinds. Metadata encoding protocols, although they function in similar ways, do not look like MARC format protocols. Taken as a whole, despite the similarities, metadata protocols differ considerably from library cataloging.

Other differences from cataloging, seen in advertisements for metadata librarians, ask that the successful candidate demonstrate entrepreneurial skills, be able to interact successfully with nonlibrary communities, and develop their own job descriptions. Readers (and applicants) can imagine that successful metadata librarians not only will be able to create metadata records—which, despite their differences, traditional catalogers can visualize—but also will know how to develop salable products and marketing strategies geared for nonlibrary buyers, and implement them. Tasks such as these do not appear in advertisements for catalogers nor are they expected in the resumes of successful cataloging practitioners.

Just as libraries and media centers are still in the process of figuring out what metadata librarians' jobs will actually entail, catalog department managers supervising them are not certain of what the supervision involves other than providing space, equipment, and supplies for the person to do her or his work. Managers must develop the flexibility to grow with their metadata librarian(s), helping them develop appropriate, meaningful outputs.

Outsourcing the Department: Although not encountered as often in the twenty-first century as it was in the latter half of the 1990s, doing away with an entire catalog department by outsourcing all catalog work still happens. The motivation behind such decisions continues to be administrators' desires to gain more public services librarians without increasing the staff and to save money by buying cheaper products than are being produced in-house. The strategy, however, is extremely risky and may fail to accomplish either goal.

Librarians who are involuntarily reassigned can turn out to be ineffective in their new positions, mainly because they have had no say in the matter and believe themselves to have been badly or unfairly treated. They may have no experience in their new roles and find themselves at a disadvantage beside veteran public service librarians, who make them feel inadequate. In the past, veteran catalogers resigned or retired to avoid involuntary reassignment. Unless elimination of the department has been accomplished with the cooperation of its staff, it is likely to produce angry people who are unwilling and unable to perform well.

Similarly, unless the costs of in-house cataloging are unnecessarily high, buying cheaper catalog products, particularly if they are not consistent with current standards, might fail to provide good service and meet patron needs. If lower costs are attributable to a lack of authority control, inadequate subject analysis, and abbreviated or inaccurate descriptive cataloging, the library's or media center's catalog could quickly degrade and lose its effectiveness. Library directors need someone working in the library or media center who understands the implications of cataloging and classification decisions, knows about bibliographic standards, and can evaluate and supervise the purchased records. Careful thought should be given before making changes (or asking a commercial cataloger to make changes) to parts of the bibliographic record to suit what may be thought to be "better cataloging," such as changing gmds, eliminating dimensions, and the like. These changes are time consuming and costly even if a commercial firm does the cataloging. The cost might not show in the charge for cataloging, but the firm will make up the loss of time and money in other ways that the library will pay without knowing that these changes are actually costing it money.

Conclusion

Catalog department managers need management and leadership skills in addition to substantial knowledge of cataloging and classification to succeed in leading their departments. Planning to get the work done, motivating the staff to do good work, negotiating with vendors of online catalogs and other bibliographic products and services, overseeing department finances and personnel, evaluating department outputs, and reporting for the department on a regular schedule are tasks that knowing how to catalog and classify materials do not necessarily prepare one to do well. At the same time, having the management skills without the requisite cataloging knowledge can lead managers to make bad decisions that ultimately have poor results. Good catalog department managers need to understand means and ends, people and products. Excellent managers compete effectively with their peers and ensure that the contributions of the department to patron service are recognized, acknowledged, and appreciated.

Recommended Reading

Belcastro, Patricia. *Evaluating Library Staff: A Performance Appraisal System*. Chicago: American Library Association, 1998.

Evans, G. Edward, Sheila S. Intner, and Jean Weihs. *Introduction to Technical Services*, 7th ed. Englewood, CO [i.e., Westport, CT]: Libraries Unlimited, 2002.

Evans, G. Edward, et al. *Management Basics for Information Professionals*. New York: Neal-Schuman Publishers, 2000.

Gorman, Michael, and associates. *Technical Services Today and Tomorrow*, 2nd ed. Englewood, CO [i.e., Westport, CT]: Libraries Unlimited, 1998.

Intner, Sheila S., with Peggy Jonson. *Fundamentals of Technical Services Management*. Chicago, IL: American Library Association, 2007.

Intner, Sheila S., Susan S. Lazinger, and Jean Weihs. *Metadata and Its Impact on Libraries*. Westport, CT: Libraries Unlimited, 2006.

Larson, Jeanette, and Herman L. Totten. *Model Policies for Small and Medium Public Libraries*. New York: Neal-Schuman Publishers, 1998.

Ross, Catherine, and Patricia Dewdney. *Communicating Professionally*, 2nd ed. New York: Neal-Schuman Publishers, 1998.

Smiraglia, Richard P., ed. *Metadata, A Cataloger's Primer*. New York: Haworth Information Press, 2005.

Warner, Alice Sizer. *Budgeting*. New York: Neal-Schuman Publishers, 1998.

Woolls, Blanche. *The School Library Media Manager*, 2nd ed. Englewood, CO [i.e., Westport, CT]: Libraries Unlimited, 1999.

Note

1.   Technically speaking, metadata can be defined to include all cataloging, which also is information about informational materials. However, metadata specialists are generally in agreement that the term refers particularly to the discovery, retrieval, and use of electronic resources.

A

Dealing with Foreign Language Catalog Copy for a Library in an English-Language Community

Sometimes it takes a bit of work, with the help of a dictionary, to develop a useful English-language bibliographic record from a foreign language record, such as the French-language bibliographic record shown on page 234.

The music on the sound disc *Cordial* is sung in French, but many of the individual song titles listed on the jewel case liner are also given in English (probably to increase sales). The listing of these titles in the contents note may suggest to catalog users that these songs are also sung in English. To avoid this misunderstanding, it might be wise to eliminate the contents note, which is not mandatory. The words other than *Cordial* on the front part of the liner are humorous asides and should not be included in the descriptive cataloging. Capitalization in some languages differs from English, and capitalization of names and titles from foreign language records should be maintained.

FIGURE A.1
2nd level cataloging in the French language

```
110 2   $a Bottine souriante (Groupe musical)
245 10  $a Cordial $h [enregistrement sonore] / $c la Bottine souriante.
260     $a Joliette, Québec : $b Productions Mille-Pattes ; $a
        Mississauga, Ont. : $b Distribution EMI Canada, $c p2001.
300     $a 1 disque son. : $b numérique ; $c 12 cm.
500     $a Chansons et musique instrumentale.
505 0   $a Dans Paris y'a t'une brune = The brunette from Paris -- La
        grondeuse = The grumbling woman -- Le démon sort de l'enfer =
        The Devil comes out of hell -- Set à Ubert = Ubert's set -- En
        p'tit boggie = Giddy up -- Aimé -- Lune de miel = Honeymoon --
        Suède Inn -- J'ai fait une maîtresse = I got me a mistress -- À
        bas les rideaux = Out with the lies -- Les noces d'or = Golden
        wedding reel -- Viens-tu prendre une bière? = Come have a beer!
        -- Ma paillase = My straw mat -- Chant de la luette = The
        warbler's song -- Reel de Baie St-Paul = Baie St-Paul's reel --
        Et boucle le Bottine = And loop la Bottine.
546     $a Paroles avec trad. en anglais dans le livret.
650   6 $a Musique folklorique française $z Québec (Province)
650   6 $a Musiques du monde.
```

2nd level cataloging in the English language

```
110 2   $a Bottine souriante (Musical group)
245 10  $a Cordial $h [sound recording] / $c la Bottine souriante.
260     $a Joliette, Québec : $b Productions Mille-Pattes ; $a
        Mississauga, Ont. : $b Distribution EMI Canada, $c p2001.
300     $a 1 sound disc. : $b digital ; $c 3¾ in.
500     $a Songs and instrumental music.
546     $a Words with English translation on the liner.
650   0 $a Folk music, French $z Quebec (Province)
650   0 $a World music.
```

Fig. A.1—Continues

FIGURE A.1 *(continued)*

(chief source of information)

(information on CD)

(information on insert)

(information on insert)

B

Answers to Exercises

Answers to Examples in Chapter 5, Figures 5.11 Through 5.20

FIGURE 5.11
Completed description for figure 5.11 on page 85

This example is an illustration of:
- musical score
- uniform title
- general material designation
- musical presentation statement
- publication date not listed, copyright date given
- edition note taken from introductory text
- duration note
- title added entry not made for an nondistinctive uniform title
- two levels of cataloging

2nd level cataloging

Walton, William.
  [Concertos, viola, orchestra, A minor]
  Concerto for viola and orchestra [music] / William Walton. --
Full score. -- London : Oxford University Press, c1964.
  1 score (136 p.) ; 23 cm.

  The 1962 version rescored for a smaller orchestra.
  Duration: 23 min.
  ISBN: 0-19-368461-6.

1st level cataloging

Walton, William.
  [Concertos, viola, orchestra, A minor]
  Concerto for viola and orchestra [music]. -- Full score. --
Oxford University Press, c1964.
  1 score (136 p.).

  The 1962 version rescored for a smaller orchestra.
  Duration: 23 min.
  ISBN: 0-19-368461-6.

FIGURE 5.12

Completed description for figure 5.12 on page 86

This example is an illustration of:
- main entry under adapter/reteller
- subsidiary responsibility (in second level description)
- edition statement (in second level description)
- page numbers in square brackets because there are no page numbers on the last pages (gives a better picture of the length of the book)
- most illustrations are colored (in second level description)
- added entry for original author
- added entry for illustrator with optional designation (in second level description)
- added entry for title
- two levels of cataloging

2nd level cataloging

McCaughrean, Geraldine.
   The questing knights of the faerie queen / retold by Geraldine McCaughrean from the works of Edmund Spenser ; illustrated by Jason Cockcroft. -- 1st ed. - London : Hodder Children's Books, 2004.
   [144] p. : ill. (chiefly col.) ; 28 cm.

   ISBN 0-340-86621-7.

   I. Spenser, Edmund.   II. Cockcroft, Jason, ill.   III. Title.

1st level cataloging

McCaughrean, Geraldine.
   The questing knights of the faerie queen / retold by Geraldine McCaughrean from the works of Edmund Spenser. -- Hodder Children's Books, 2004.
   [144] p.

   ISBN 0-340-86621-7.

   I. Spenser, Edmund.   II. Title.

FIGURE 5.13

Completed description for figure 5.13 on page 87

This example is an illustration of:
* sound cassette
* general material designation
* program date
* optional omission of "sound" in extent of item (in 1st level description)
* information about sound channels not readily available
* quoted note (in second level description)
* accompanying materials note (in second level description)
* publisher's number
* title added entry
* two levels of cataloging

2nd level cataloging

McKhool, Chris.
  Earth, seas, and air [sound recording] / Chris McKhool. --
Ottawa : McKhool, p1996.
  1 sound cassette (42 min.) : analog.

  "Eco-songs for kids"--Cardboard wrapper.
  Lyrics on inside cover of wrapper.
  McKhool: MCK2001.
  ISBN 0-9680429-0-2.

  I. Title.

1st level cataloging

McKhool, Chris.
  Earth, seas, and air [sound recording]. -- McKhool, p1996.
  1 cassette (42 min.)

  McKhool: MCK2001.
  ISBN 0-9680429-0-2.

  I. Title.

FIGURE 5.14

Completed description for figure 5.14 on page 88

This example is an illustration of:
- publishing date not listed, copyright date given
- title information note
- contents (index) note (in second level description)
- additional title added entries
- two levels of cataloging

2nd level cataloging

Adams, Janine.
   You bake 'em dog biscuits cookbook / Janine Adams. --
Philadelphia : Running Press, c2005.
   128 p. : ill. ; 23 cm.

   At head of title: The National Dog Biscuit Baking Company.
   Includes index.
   ISBN 0-7624-2336-6.

   I. Title.   II. Title: National Dog Biscuit Baking Company.
III. Title: Dog biscuits cookbook.

1st level cataloging

Adams, Janine.
   You bake 'em dog biscuits cookbook. -- Running Press, c2005.
   128 p.

   At head of title: The National Dog Biscuit Baking Company.
   ISBN 0-7624-2336-6.

   I. Title.   II. Title: National Dog Biscuit Baking Company.
III. Title: Dog biscuits cookbook.

FIGURE 5.15
Completed description for FIGURE 5.15 on page 89

This example is an illustration of:
- videorecording
- title main entry
- general material designation
- no statement of responsibility
- publication date not listed, copyright date given
- accompanying material (in second level description)
- series statement
- language (closed-captioned and Spanish language track) notes
- source of title note
- physical description (duration) note
- intended audience note (in second level description)
- title added entry without ampersand
- series added entry
- two levels of cataloging

2nd level cataloging

Maps & globes [videorecording]. -- Wynnewood, PA :
  Schlessinger, c2004.
  1 videodisc : sd., col. ; 4¾ in. + 1 teacher's guide. -- (Map
skills for children)

  Closed-captioned.
  Spanish language track.
  Title from title screen.
  Duration: 23 min.
  Intended audience: Grades K-4.
  ISBN 1-57225-904-3.

  I. Title: Maps and globes. II. Series.

1st level enriched cataloguing

Maps & globes [videorecording]. -- Schlessinger, c2004.
  1 videodisc. -- (Map skills for children)

  Closed-captioned.
  Spanish language track.
  Title from title screen.
  ISBN 1-57225-904-3.

  I. Title: Maps and globes. II. Series.

Authors' note: The notes in the 1st level description are an example of notes that can be added if they are useful to a library's clientele.

FIGURE 5.16

Completed description for figure 5.16 on page 90

This example is an illustration of:
- bibliographic form of name from LC name authority file
- other title information (in second level description)
- detailed pagination
- edition and history note (in second level description)
- contents note (in second level description)
- title added entry
- two levels of cataloging

2nd level cataloging

Pritchett, V.S. (Victor Sawdon), 1900-1997.
   Mr. Beluncle : a novel / V.S. Pritchett ; introduction by Darin
Strauss. -- New York : Modern Library, 2005.
   xxi, 298 p. ; 20 cm.

   Original book published in 1951.
   Includes Reading group guide, p. [299-300].
   ISBN 0-8129-7379-8 (pbk.).

   I. Title.

1st level cataloging

Pritchett, V.S. (Victor Sawdon), 1900-1997.
   Mr. Beluncle. -- Modern Library, 2005.
   xxi, 298 p.

   ISBN 0-8129-7379-8 (pbk.).

   I. Title.

*Authors' note: Public libraries may want to add a subject heading
that will highlight the fact that this book is suitable for book
clubs because it has a Reading Group Guide.*

FIGURE 5.17

Completed description for FIGURE 5.17 on page 91

This example is an illustration of:
- musical score
- uniform title
- general material designation
- mark of omission shortening a long title
- musical presentation statement
- multiple places of publication; secondary place given for U.S. libraries (in second level description)
- publication date unknown
- title added entry not made for an nondistinctive uniform title
- two levels of cataloging

2nd level cataloging

Dvořák, Antonin.
  [Quartets, piano, strings, no. 2, op.87, E♭ major]
  Quartet E♭ major for piano, violin, viola and violincello, op. 87 ... [music] / by Antonin Dvořák. -- Miniature score. -- London : New York: Eulenberg, [19--].
  1 miniature score (77 p.) ; 19 cm.

1st level cataloging

Dvořák, Antonin.
  [Quartets, piano, strings, no. 2, op.87, E♭ major]
  Quartet E♭ major for piano, violin, viola and violincello, op. 87 ... [music]. -- Eulenberg, [19--].
  1 miniature score (77 p.).

Authors' note: Although required by AACR2-2005, the musical presentation statement has been omitted from the 1st level description as an unnecessary repetition of information.

FIGURE 5.18

Completed description for figure 5.18 on page 92

This example is an illustration of:
- joint authors
- authors not listed in prescribed source of information
- other title information (in 2nd level cataloging)
- subsidiary responsibility (in 2nd level cataloging)
- edition statement (in 2nd level cataloging)
- distributor
- publication date not listed; copyright date given
- index note (in 2nd level cataloging)
- joint author added entry
- optional designation of illustrator in personal name added entry (in 2nd level cataloging)
- added entry for abbreviated title
- two levels of cataloging

2nd level cataloging

Kilby, Janice Eaton.
  The book of wizard parties : in which the wizard shares the secrets of creating enchanted gatherings / [authors Janice Eaton Kilby, Terry Taylor] ; illustrated by Marla Baggeta. -- 1st ed. -- New York : Lark Books, c2002.
    144 p. : col. ill. ; 23 cm.

    Includes index.
    ISBN 1-57990-292-8.

    I. Taylor, Terry.   II. Baggetta, Marla, ill.   III. Title.   IV. Title: Wizard parties.

Authors' note: If catalogued for a Canadian library, publication, distribution, etc., area would read "New York: Lark Books : distributed in Canada by Sterling Pub., c2002."

1st level cataloging

Kilby, Janice Eaton.
  The book of wizard parties / [authors Janice Eaton Kilby, Terry Taylor]. -- Lark Books, c2002.
    144 p.

    ISBN 1-57990-292-8.

    I. Taylor, Terry.   II. Title.   III. Title: Wizard parties.

FIGURE 5.19
Completed description for figure 5.19 on page 93

This example is an illustration of:
- game
- title main entry with no statement of responsibility listed on the item
- general material designation
- copyright date only listed on item
- accompanying material given in the physical description area (in second level description)
- quoted note (in second level description)
- physical description note (in second level description)
- audience level (in second level description)
- two levels of cataloging

2nd level cataloging

Cool moves! [game]. -- Livermore, CA : Discovery Toys, c2000.
   12 penguins, 40 game cards, 1 game board : plastic and cardboard, col. ; in box 12 x 12 x 6 cm. + 2 instruction cards.

   "Strategy game that helps develop thinking and fine motor skills"--Container.
   Game board forms the lid of a container storing the game pieces.
   For children 8 years up.

1st level cataloging

Cool moves! [game]. -- Discovery Toys, c2000.
   12 penguins, 40 game cards, 1 game board + 2 instruction cards.

FIGURE 5.20

Completed description for figure 5.20 on page 93

This example is an illustration of:
- publication date not listed; copyright date given
- descriptive illustration statement (in 2nd level cataloguing)
- series statement
- contents (bibliography and index) note (in 2nd level cataloging)
- summary (in 2nd level cataloging)
- ISBN qualified
- title added entry
- series added entry
- Library of Congress CIP
- two levels of cataloging

2nd level cataloging

Ansary, Mir Tamin.
  Arctic peoples / Mir Yamin Ansary. -- Des Plaines, Ill. :
Heinemann Library, c2000.
  32 p. : col. ill., map ; 28 cm. -- (Native Americans)

  Includes bibliographical references and index.
  Summary: Describes various elements of the traditional life of
Arctic people including their homes, clothing, games, crafts, and
beliefs as well as changes brought about by the arrival of
Europeans.
  ISBN 1-57572-920-2 (lib. bdg.).

  I. Title. II. Series.

1st level cataloging

Ansary, Mir Tamin.
  Arctic peoples. -- Heinemann Library, c2000.
  32 p. -- (Native Americans)

  ISBN 1-57572-920-2 (lib. bdg.).

  I. Title. II. Series.

*Authors'note: Series is an optional addition to 1st level
cataloging because it might provide a useful series added entry.*

Answers to Exercises in Figure 7.5 on page 124

1. Subject heading: **Bed and breakfast accommodations—Scotland**

   Explanation: Use of a multiword heading with a geographic subdivision

2. Subject heading: **Precipitation (Meteorology)**

   Explanation: Use of a qualified heading

3. Subject heading: **Religion and society**

   Explanation: Use of a heading in which two concepts are connected (compare with answer 8.6, no. 3 on page 248)

4. Subject heading: **Lacrosse**

   Explanation: Use of the name of a sport not listed in Sears but allowed to be added as needed

5. Subject heading: **Bilingual education**

   Explanation: Use of a two-word phrase given in direct order (compare with answer 8.6, no. 5 on page 248)

6. Subject heading: **Chinese language – Business Chinese**

   Explanation: Use of a key heading using "English language – Business English" as the pattern

7. Subject heading: **United States – History – 1775–1783, Revolution**

   Explanation: Use of multiple subdivisions; use of a chronological subdivision (compare with answer 8.6, no. 4 on page 248)

8. Subject heading: **Retail trade – California—Directories**

   Explanation: Use of multiple subdivisions including a geographic subdivision and a form subdivision with broad application

9. Subject heading: **Toronto (Ont.) – Telephone directories**

   Explanation: Use of a geographic name with a subdivision using "Chicago (Ill.) – Telephone directories" as the pattern

10. Subject heading: **Homeless persons**
    Mental health services
    Industrial arts education

    Explanation: Use of three headings to express different aspects of the work (compare with answer 8.6, no. 10 on page 248)

Answers to Exercises in Figure 8.6 on page 147

Answers to Figure 8.6

Some of the exercises are the same for both Sears and Library of Congress subject headings to highlight the similarities and differences. Note answers to numbers 1, 2, and 8 in figures 7.5 on page XX and the same numbers in 8.6 below are similar. The answers that are dissimilar are noted below.

1. Subject heading: **Bed and breakfast accommodations — Scotland**
    Explanation: Use of a multiword heading with a geographic subdivision

2. Subject heading: **Precipitation (Meteorology)**
    Explanation: Use of a qualified heading

3. Subject heading: **Religion and sociology** (compare with answer 7.5, no. 3 on page 247)
    Explanation: Use of a heading in which two concepts are connected

4. Subject heading: **United States – History – Revolution, 1775-1783**
    Explanation: Use of multiple subdivisions; use of a chronological subdivision (compare with answer 7.5, no. 7 on page 247)

5. Subject heading: **Education, Bilingual**
    Explanation: Use of a two-word phrase given in indirect order (compare with answer 7.5, no. 5 on page 247)

6. Subject heading: **Political satire**
    Explanation: Use of a two-word phrase given in direct order

7. Subject heading: **Wheat – Biological control**
    Explanation: Use of a subdivision using Corn as the a pattern heading

8. Subject heading: **Retail trade – California — Directories**
    Explanation: Use of multiple subdivisions including a geographic subdivision and a form subdivision

9. Subject heading: **World War, 1939-1945 – Personal narratives, Canadian**
    Explanation: Use of a type of pattern subdivision that allows the substitution of a nationality other than American

10. Subject heading: **Homeless persons**
                     Mental health services
                     Industrial arts – Study and teaching (compare this heading with answer 7.5, no. 10 on page 247)

11. Subject heading: **Breast – Cancer – Diagnosis – Illinois – Chicago — History**
    Explanation: Use of a pattern heading based on the heading for Heart; use of a geographic subdivision and a free-floating subdivision

Answers to Exercises in Figure 10.8 on page 185

1.   Classification: **641.6'521**

    Explanation: Use of a pattern number drawn from instructions to add numbers to a base number; in this case, the base number is 641.6 and 521 is added for potatoes.

2. Classification: **929.7'481**

    Explanation: Use of a geographic subdivision (-481 means Norway).

3. Classification: **326.'022'2**

    Explanation: Use of the number for pictures and related illustrations (-022 2).

4. Classification: **600**

    Explanation: Use of general number for all types of mechanical and technical de-
    vices.

5. Classification: **727.6**

    Explanation: Example of an item containing two subjects, each given equal empha-
    sis; the number assigned is the number that comes first in the schedules.

6. Classification: **290**

    Explanation: Example of an item containing three or more subjects, all given equal
    emphasis; the number assigned covers all of the subjects.

7. Classification: **340.'0922**

    Explanation: Use of a biographical subdivision (-0922 means biographical infor-
    mation about a group of persons, not just one person); if this work contained
    collected biographies of only American lawyers, the number would be
    340.'0922'73 (-73 means United States).

8. Classification: **327.'44'042**

    Explanation: Example of a number drawn from instructions to add numbers to a
    base number; in this case –042, the number for England, is added to -44, the
    number for France.

9. Classification: **398.204'61**

    Explanation: Use of language subdivision (-61 means Spanish language).

10. Classification: **917.321**

    Explanation: Use of the number for Bruce County where Port Elgin is located.

Answers to Exercises in Figure 11.9 on page 204

1. Classification: **Z693.A15**
    Explanation: A cutter number indicating a congress

2. Classification: **Z1377.F4**

    Explanation: A cutter number indicating a special topic

3. Classification: **Z695.1.G7**

    Explanation: A cutter number indicating specific subject

4. Classification: **Z994.B7**

    Explanation: A cutter number indicating a specific region or country

5. Classification: **Z232.C38**

    Explanation: A cutter number for Caxton taken from the list of individual printers and printing establishments

Answers to Exercises in Chapter 12, Figures 12.12 through 12.19

FIGURE 12.12
MARC Encoding for figure 6.5

```
020      $a 0385659792
100  1   $a Haddon, Mark.
245 14   $a The curious incident of the dog in the night-time / $c
         Mark Haddon.
260      $a [S.l.]: $b Doubleday Canada, $c c2002.
300      $a 226 p. : $b ill. ; $c 22 cm.
650   0  $a Autism $v Fiction.
650   0  $a Savants (Savant syndrome) $v Fiction.
651   0  $a England $v Fiction.
```

FIGURE 12.13
MARC Encoding for figure 8.5

```
020      $a 0871569175 (alk. paper)
082 14   $a 591.9866 $2 14
100  1   $a Heller, Ruth.
245 10   $a "Galápagos" means "tortoises" / $c written and
         illustrated by Ruth Heller.
250      $a 1st ed.
260      $a San Francisco : $b Sierra Club Books for Children,
         $c c2000.
300      $a 41 p. : $b col. ill. ; $c 24 x 27 cm.
520      $a Rhyming text and illustrations present the
         characteristics and behavior of animals found on the
         Galápagos Islands, including the giant tortoises, blue-
         footed boobies, and land iguanas.
650   1  $a Zoology $z Galápagos Islands.
```

FIGURE 12.14

MARC Encoding for figure 9.1

```
020      $a 1550379399 (bound)
020      $a 1550379380 (pbk.)
050   0 $a LB1048 $b R48 2005
082 04 $a 371.3/028/1 $2 22
245 00 $a Research ate my brain : $b the panic-proof guide to
         surviving homework / $c Toronto Public Library ; art by
         Martha Newbigging.
260      $a [Toronto] : $b Annick Press : Firefly Books
         [distributor], $c c2005.
300      $a 96 p. : $b ill. ; $c 22 cm.
504      $a Includes bibliographic references and index.
650   0 $a Homework $v Handbooks, manuals, etc.
650   0 $a Research $x Methodology $v Handbooks, manuals, etc.
700 1  $a Newbigging, Martha.
710 2  $a Toronto Public Library.
```

FIGURE 12.15

MARC encoding for figure 9.2

```
020      $a 1896973043 (pbk.)
082 14 $a 305.4/09713 $2 14
100 1  $a Macdonald, Jeanne.
245 10 $a Toronto women : $b changing faces, 1900-2000 : a
         photographic journey / $c photographic research by Jeanne
         MacDonald and Nadine Stoikoff ; text by Randall White.
260      $a Toronto : $b Eastendbooks, $c 1997.
300      $a 144 p. : $b chiefly ill., ports. ; $c 28 cm.
504      $a Includes bibliographical references and index.
650   7 $a Women $z Toronto (Ont.) $x History $y 20th century
         $v Pictorial works. $2 sears
700 1  $a Stoikoff, Nadine.
700 1  $a Randall White.
```

FIGURE 12.16
MARC Encoding for figure 10.6

```
020     $a ISBN 0679422714
082 04 $a 951.05/092 $b MAO CHA $2 22
100 1  $a Chang, Jung.
245 10 $a Mao : $b the unknown story / $c Jung Chang, Jon Halliday.
246 13 $a Unknown story.
260     $a New York : $b Knopf, $c 2005.
300     $a vii, 814 p., [32] p. of plates : $b ill., maps ; $c 24 cm.
500     $a At head of title on paper jacket: The unknown story.
504     $a Includes bibliographical references and index.
600 10 $a Mao, Zedong.
650  0 $a Heads of state $z China $v Biography.
651  0 $a China $x Politics and government $y 1949-1976.
700 1  $a Halliday, Jon.
```

FIGURE 12.17
MARC Encoding for figure 10.5

```
082 04 $a 611.12 $2 22
245 00 $a Pumping heart $h [model].
246 13 $a Visible pumping heart.
260     $a Skokie, Ill. : $b Lindberg, $c [19--].
300     $a 1 model (various pieces) : $b plastic ; $c 29 cm. high in
        container 31 x 24 x 7 cm.
440  0 $a Natural science series
500     $a Assembly instructions (4 p.) has title: The Visible
        pumping heart.
500     $a "Life-like continuous action pumps blood thru the
        visible heart chambers"--Container.
521     $a Intended audience: for use by doctors, educators,
        students and schools for study demonstration purposes.
500     $a Library's copy unassembled.
650  0 $a Heart $x Anatomy
```

FIGURE 12.18
MARC Encoding for figure 11.3

```
020     $a 0671042181
050   4 $a E161.5$b.S77 1998
082 04 $a 910.8996073 $2 22
245 02 $a A stranger in the village : $b two centuries of
        African-American travel writing / $c edited by Farah J.
        Griffin and Cheryl J. Fish.
260     $a Boston : $b Beacon Press, $c c1998.
300     $a xvii, 366 p. ; $c 23 cm.
504     $a Bibliography: p. 357-62.
650   0 $a African-Americans $x Travel $x History $x Sources.
650   0 $a Travelers' writings, American $x African-American
        Authors.
651   0 $a United States $x Description and travel.
700   1 $a Griffin, Farah Jasmine.
700   1 $a Fish, Cheryl J.
```

FIGURE 12.19
MARC encoding for figure 5.9

```
022     $a 1492-4676
130  0 $a Bulletin (National Library of Canada). $l English.
245 10 $a Bulletin $h [electronic resource] / $c National Library of
        Canada.
246 13 $a National Library of Canada bulletin
260     $a Ottawa : $b National Library of Canada, $c 2002-2004.
310     $a Bi-monthly
362     $a Vol. 27, no. 6 (June 1995)-vol. 36, no. 2 (Mar./Apr. 2004).
538     $a Mode of access: World Wide Web.
500     $a Title from contents page (viewed Jan. 10, 2007).
500     $a Issues from 1995 to May 2000 have title: National Library
        News.
530     $a Also issued in print ed. previous to 2003.
530     $a Also issued in French-language ed.
500     $a Ceased publication.
610  2 $a National Library of Canada $v Periodicals.
650   0 $a Libraries $z Canada $v Periodicals.
710  2 $a National Library of Canada.
740  0 $a National Library news.
856     $u http://www.collectionscanada.ca/bulletin/index-e.html
```

Glossary

This list of acronyms and cataloging terms includes those defined in the text compiled here in one place for convenience as well as for readers who encounter a term or acronym subsequent to its first mention (the definition of a term appears only at its first mention). The list also includes some terms not used in the text, but often encountered in the cataloging literature.

A&C. *Additions & Changes,* quarterly publication of the Library of Congress used to update the Library of Congress Classification.

AACR. *Anglo-American Cataloguing Rules*. Cataloging rules cooperatively developed by the library associations and national libraries of the United States, United Kingdom, Canada, and, beginning in 1981, Australia. *See also acronyms beginning with the initials AACR.*

AACR1. *Anglo-American Cataloging Rules,* 1967. The first edition of AACR, published in two versions, one for North Americans and one for the United Kingdom.

AACR2. *Anglo-American Cataloguing Rules,* 1978. The second edition of AACR, this time published in one version for all the participating nations.

AACR2R. *Anglo-American Cataloguing Rules,* second edition, 1988 revision. This edition was the standard until 1998, when an updated revision was published.

AACR2–98. *Anglo-American Cataloguing Rules,* second edition, 1998 revision.

AACR2–2002. *Anglo-American Cataloguing Rules*, second edition, 2002 revision.

AACR2–2005. *Anglo-American Cataloguing Rules*, second edition, 2002 revision, with updates issued in 2003, 2004, and 2005. This is the current version of descriptive cataloging rules at this writing.

AALL. American Association of Law Librarians.

AAT. *Art & Architecture Thesaurus.*

AC heading. Annotated Card heading. Subject heading from a special list of terms created by the Library of Congress for juvenile materials. *See also* Annotated Card Program.

Access. The process of choosing and formulating headings for bibliographic records. Also refers to the larger processes of providing bibliographic access (that is, cataloging), intellectual access (that is, classification and indexing), and physical access to material.

Access point. Any name, word, or phrase by which a catalog record can be retrieved from the catalog, known also as an *Entry, Heading,* or *Retrieval point.*

Added entry. A secondary access point; any heading by which a catalog record can be retrieved other than the first (or *main)* entry.

A-G Canada Ltd. The Canadian bibliographic utility formerly known as ISM.

ALA. American Library Association.

ALCTS. Association for Library Collections & Technical Services. A division of the American Library Association called the Resources and Technical Services Division before 1989.

Alphabetico-classed catalog. A semiclassified catalog in which principal headings are in classified order, but headings at the same level of hierarchy are arranged alphabetically.

Alternative title. A title following title proper and preceded by the word *or,* in any language. For example the underlined data in the operetta by Gilbert and Sullivan titled *Trial by jury, or, The lass who loved a sailor.*

AMICUS. The resource-sharing database of the Library and Archives of Canada.

Analytic(s). Catalog records or access points for a work that is part of a larger bibliographic unit; for example, one song on a sound recording containing several songs.

Annotated Card Program. Program initiated by the Library of Congress for cataloging juvenile materials that includes adding specialized subject headings and summary notes to the catalog records.

ANSCR. Alpha-Numeric System for the Classification of Recordings.

Area of description. One of the eight parts of a bibliographic description designated by ISBD and AACR2; for example, the Edition area (area 2) or the Series area (area 6).

ARLIS/NA. Art Libraries Society of North America.

ASTED. Association pour l'avancement des sciences et des techniques de la documentation. The professional association for French-speaking librarians in Canada.

Authority file. A file containing the official forms of names, uniform titles, series titles, subject headings, or all of these, used as access points in a library catalog, and citations to sources used to establish them as well as cross-references to variant forms.

Authority record. One record in an authority file. *See also* Name authority, Subject authority.

Auxiliary table. In classification, a separate table of subdivisions intended to be used with numbers from the main schedules.

BALLOTS. Bibliographic Automation of Large Library Operations using a Time-sharing System. The forerunner of RLIN®.

Bibliographic description. The part of a catalog record that identifies the item it represents, exclusive of access points, call numbers, and control numbers other than the ISBN and the ISSN.

Bibliographic identity. The name used on an item to identify the creator. One who uses more than one name on his or her works is said to have multiple bibliographic identities.

Bibliographic level. 1. One of three standard styles of description prescribed by AACR2–2005, each containing varying amounts of bibliographic information from the least (level 1) to the most (level 3). 2. In OCLC's MARC format, a fixed field identified by the prefix "BLvL," that indicates whether an item is monographic or serial.

Bibliographic network. A group of libraries that shares a computerized database of bibliographic information or whose individual bibliographic databases are electronically linked.

Bibliographic record. A catalog record.

Bibliographic unit. A cataloging unit; an entity capable of being cataloged, indexed, and classified, such as a book, a videorecording, a game, etc.

Bibliographic utility. A group of electronically linked libraries that generates new catalog records.

Blind reference. A cross-reference used in a catalog that leads searchers to a term having no entries under it.

Book mark. *See* Cutter number, Shelf mark.

Book number. *See* Cutter number, Shelf mark.

Boolean operators. The words *AND, OR, NOT*, etc., used in combining subject terms for retrieval.

Boolean retrieval. Computer programs based on Boolean algebra that permit retrieval for combinations of search terms.

Call letter. *See* Shelf mark.

Call number. The shelf address of an item, usually consisting of its classification number and shelf marks.

CAN/MARC. CANadian MAchine-Readable Cataloguing. Superseded by MARC 21.

Carrier. For selected nonbook materials, the container that carries the material on which the intellectual content of an item is recorded, such as a cartridge, cassette, disc, reel, etc.

Cast. In some nonbook media such as videorecordings, the performers. Also, a note naming the performers. *See also* Credits.

CCC. The Canadian Committee on Cataloguing, responsible for monitoring issues and standards in cataloging for the Canadian cataloging community.

CC:DA. Committee on Cataloging: Description and Access, a committee of the Cataloging and Classification Section of the Association for Library Collections & Technical Services, a division of the American Library Association. This committee is responsible for monitoring issues and standards in descriptive cataloging for the U.S. cataloging community.

CCM. Canadian Committee on MARC.

CD-ROM. Compact Disc–Read Only Memory. A storage device for computerized information; data are read from the disc by a scanner.

CDS. Cataloging Distribution Service. The marketing agency for the Library of Congress's bibliographic products.

Chartered Institute of Library and Information Professionals. Formerly known as the (British) Library Association, a professional association for librarians and information specialists in the United Kingdom.

Chief source. In descriptive cataloging, the main location from which bibliographic data are taken, such as the title page of a book, title screens of an electronic resource, etc. *See also* Prescribed source.

CILIP. Chartered Institute of Library and Information Professionals.

Citation order. In classification and indexing, a prescribed order in which the components of a topic are given; for example, Topic-Location-Period *versus* Location-Topic-Period.

CLA. Canadian Library Association.

Classed catalog. A catalog in which records are filed by subject, such as a shelflist. *See also* Dictionary catalog, Divided catalog.

Closed entry. Catalog record previously containing open dates, etc., for a publication in progress, that has been completed or "closed," presumably because the title is completed. *See also* Open entry.

CODEN. An internationally recognized identifier for a serial title, administered by the Chemical Abstracts Service.

Coding. The act or process of assigning MARC content designators to bibliographic data. Sometimes called *coding and tagging. See also* Tagging.

Coextensive. Exactly matching. In indexing and classification, an index term or a class that is neither broader nor narrower than the topic being represented, but exactly matches its breadth and depth.

Collocate. To bring related items together, such as titles written by the same author, editions and versions of the same title, or materials on the same topic.

Colophon. A page at the end of a printed item on which bibliographic information is given.

Command-driven. A computerized system requiring the entry of commands for operation. *See also* Menu-driven.

COMPASS. A computer-assisted system of indexing library materials used at one time in the United Kingdom and elsewhere. Originally developed by the British Library's Classification Research Group in the 1970s and named PRECIS, the system subsequently was simplified and renamed COMPASS. *See also* PRECIS.

CONSER. CONversion of SERials. A program originally administered at the Library of Congress but later shifted to OCLC, whose objective is to build a national database of catalog records for serials and holdings.

Content designators. In the MARC formats, all of the characters or combinations of characters identifying specific parts of bibliographic, authority, or holdings records, and the kinds of data held in them.

Continuation. A publication such as a serial, series, or frequently revised monographic title to which a library or information center subscribes on an ongoing basis.

Continuing resource. A publication issued in parts, often numbered and/or dated, that is intended to continue indefinitely. *See also* Integrating resource, Serial.

Control field. A field in the MARC format identified by a tag beginning with the number zero. Control fields contain information such as call number, ISBN, LCCN, etc. *See also* Fixed field, Variable field.

Controlled vocabulary. A list of terms authorized for indexing, such as a subject heading list or thesaurus. *See also* Subject authority, Uncontrolled vocabulary.

Conventional title. *See* Uniform title.

Copy cataloging/classification. A method of cataloging or classifying library materials in which a source record is copied or edited instead of creating a new record. Also called *Derived cataloging/classification. See also* Original cataloging/classification.

CORC. Cooperative Online Resource Catalog. A project sponsored by OCLC to compile a database of metadata for Internet resources.

Core record. A catalog record standard containing less data than that required for full-level status by national bibliographic input standards, but more than that required for minimal level status. Core records include, in addition to minimal level data, selected descriptive fields and access points that conform fully to national authority control requirements. *See also* PCC.

Corporate body. A named group of people that acts as an entity.

CPSO. Cataloging Policy and Support Office at the Library of Congress.

Credits. For some nonbook items such as videorecordings, a statement naming participants in the creation of the item. Also a note naming those participants. Credits can be divided into technical credits (those responsible for taping, filming, editing, etc.) and artistic credits (writers, directors, producers, etc.). *See also* Cast.

Cross-reference. A message in the catalog that links two or more related access points. For example, a message at *Clemens, Samuel Langhorne* referring searchers to *Twain, Mark*.

CSB. *Cataloging Service Bulletin*. A Library of Congress periodical publication providing news of cataloging policy decisions, new subject authorities, etc.

CSH. *Canadian Subject Headings*.

Cutter letter(s). Alphabetic device similar to a cutter number in which one or more letters are used in place of combined letters and numbers to arrange items in alphabetical order. *See also* Cutter number, Shelf mark.

Cutter number. An alphanumeric code originated by Charles A. Cutter, designed to arrange items in alphabetical order. Sometimes called *Book mark* or *Book number*. *See also* Shelf mark.

Cuttered, cuttering, cutters. Forms of the word *cutter* used as a verb, meaning the act of assigning cutter numbers.

DC. *See* DDC, Dublin Core.

DDC. Dewey Decimal Classification. Sometimes referred to as "Decimal Classification" and abbreviated "DC."

De facto. Literally meaning "in fact" or "in practice." A term applied to the Library of Congress functioning in the role of national library of the United States even though no legislation designates it as such.

De jure. Literally meaning "in law." A term that can be applied to the National Library of Medicine and the National Agricultural Library functioning in the role of national libraries of the United States, because legislation legally designates them as such.

Delimiter. In the MARC format, a symbol identifying the start of a subfield. Delimiters can print variously as double daggers (‡), dollar signs ($), or "at" symbols (@). *See also* Subfield code.

Derived cataloging/classification. *See* Copy cataloging/classification.

Descriptor. A term consisting of one or more words indicating subject matter, often taken from a list of terms known as a thesaurus or subject heading list. *See also* Subject authority, Subject heading.

Dictionary catalog. A catalog in which all records are filed alphabetically. *See also* Classed catalog, Divided catalog.

Direct entry. 1. An access point in which the desired name or word is the first part of the heading, without naming a larger unit of which it is part. For example, OHIO, not UNITED STATES—OHIO. 2. A multiword heading given in the order in which it would be spoken (that is, "natural order") without reversing the order of the words. For example, LIBRARY CATALOGS, not CATALOGS, LIBRARY. *See also* Indirect entry. 3. A corporate body name heading for a part of a larger body that is entered under its own name, not the name of the large body. For example, LIBRARY OF CONGRESS, not UNITED STATES. LIBRARY OF CONGRESS.

Distinctive title. A title consisting of words in addition to those naming a compositional or publication type, such as "Scottish symphony," or "Bulletin of healthy living." *See also* Generic title.

Divided catalog. A catalog in which different types of records are gathered into separate files; for example, author headings in one file, title headings in a second file, and subject headings in a third file; or author and title headings in one file, topical subject headings in a separate file. *See also* Classed catalog, Dictionary catalog.

Downloading. The act of transmitting data electronically from a large computer database to a smaller local computer system. *See also* Uploading.

Dublin Core. A set of fifteen identifying elements used to create metadata for electronic resources similar to the much larger number of elements used in library catalog records. Abbreviated *DC*.

Dumb terminal. A video display monitor that does not contain a central processing unit.

Dumping. Automatic entry of data in a computerized system. Also called *loading* or *mounting* data.

EAD. Encoded Archival Description; a set of protocols for editing text for computer input and communication.

Emanate/emanation. To issue/issuing items by a corporate body.

Entry. Narrowly defined, an access point; broadly defined, a bibliographic record.

Enumerative. A classification or subject authority in which all topics, both simple and compound, are listed (or enumerated) for the cataloger, who merely selects the appropriate one(s) for each item. *See also* Faceted, Precoordinate, Postcoordinate, Synthetic.

Extent. The total amount of an item's physical manifestation; for example, the pages of a book, reels of microfilm, cassettes of a videorecording, disks of an electronic resource, etc. Data given in the extent can also include the number of frames, duration, etc., for some materials.

Faceted. A classification or subject heading list in which topical components (that is, facets) are listed and the cataloger builds an appropriate class number or heading by combining the appropriate components. *See also* Postcoordinate, Synthetic.

Field. In the MARC formats, one part of a record corresponding to one area of description, one subject heading, one call number, etc. *See also* Control field, Fixed field, Variable field.

Fixed field. 1. Any field containing data of fixed length and in fixed format. For example, the 043 field contains codes representing geographic data given in eye-readable form elsewhere in the record: "na us ca" in the 043 field stands for "North America–United States–California." 2. In OCLC and RLIN records, this refers also to special formatting of the 008 field in which specially designed prefixes identify subfields in place of the usual subfield codes. *See also* Control field, Variable field.

Form subdivision. In subject cataloging or indexing, a term used as a subdivision that describes the form or genre of an item, such as -DICTIONARIES; in classification, a number or span of numbers assigned to materials having specific forms or genres; for example, in DDC, standard subdivision -05 means Serials.

Format integration. In the MARC formats, the process by which individual formats for books, serials, maps, and other material forms, each developed separately, were compiled into one unified group of protocols called an integrated format. *See also* Integrated format.

Free-floating subdivision. In subject authorities, a term that can be added to authorized subject terms as a subdivision without a specific listing or instruction.

Full stop. British term for the mark of punctuation called a "period" by North Americans.

General material designation. *See* gmd.

Generic title. A title consisting of words naming a type of composition or publication, such as "Symphony," or "Bulletin." *See also* Distinctive title.

gmd. General material designation. Part of the first area of description naming the media group to which an item belongs.

Heading. *See* Access point.

Help screen. A feature of computer systems in which an instructional screen (help screen) can be requested by the user.

Host/host system. A larger computer system to which a smaller computer system is linked.

HTML. HyperText Markup Language; a set of protocols for editing text for computer input and communication.

ICCE. International Conference of Cataloging Experts, held in Toronto in 2000.

ICCP. International Conference on Cataloguing Principles, held in Paris in 1961.

IFLA. International Federation of Library Associations and Institutions.

Imprint. Publishing data for a book, including the location and name of the publisher, and date of publication. In AACR2, these data were expanded and renamed "Publication, distribution, etc., information."

Indicators. In MARC format fields, special values that instruct the computer to manipulate data in a particular way. For example, in the 245 field, the first indicator value controls making an added entry for title proper, and the second indicator value controls indexing of title proper.

Indirect entry. An access point—often a geographic or corporate body name—in which the desired name is not the first part of the heading. For example, the desired name is REFERENCE AND ADULT SERVICES DIVISION, but the heading is AMERICAN LIBRARY ASSOCIATION. REFERENCE AND ADULT SERVICES DIVISION. *See also* Direct entry.

Indirect subdivision. A subdivision of an access point in which the subdividing term is expressed indirectly. For example, to show agriculture in Canterbury, England, indirectly, the subdivision is AGRICULTURE—ENGLAND—CANTERBURY, not AGRICULTURE—CANTERBURY.

Input standards. Standards dictating the amount of data that must be included in catalog records that can be entered into the database of a bibliographic utility.

Integral label. A label permanently affixed to the carrier of a nonbook material by its publisher or distributor.

Integrated format. In the MARC format, the unified set of protocols applicable to all types of library materials now in use for encoding bibliographic data. *See also* Format integration.

Integrating resource. An ongoing bibliographic resource that is updated by means of additions or changes incorporated into the resource as a whole, such as computer system documentation that is updated when changes occur and websites that are updated.

Interactive multimedia. The gmd proposed by CC:DA for a media group consisting of computer files combined with other media such as video, sound, graphics, text, etc., in which the user of the item is able to manipulate it to produce unique results. The term is not included on the lists of gmds in AACR2–2005.

International Serials Data System. *See* ISDS.

International Standard Bibliographic Description. *See* ISBD.

International Standard Book Number. *See* ISBN.

International Standard Music Number. *See* ISMN.

International Standard Recording Code. *See* ISRC.

International Standard Serial Number. *See* ISSN.

ISBD. International Standard Bibliographic Description. An international standard promulgated by IFLA for describing materials, which mandates sources for the descriptive data, the data elements, the order in which they are to appear, and punctuation to identify them.

ISBN. International Standard Book Number. An internationally used unique identifier for each title issued by publishers participating in the program.

ISDS. International Serials Data System. A program for identifying the world's serials using an individual symbol (CODEN) and title (key title) identifier for each unique title.

ISMN. International Standard Music Number. An internationally used unique identifier for each musical publication issued by publishers participating in the program.

ISRC. International Standard Recording Code. An internationally used unique identifier for each recording issued by publishers or distributors participating in the program.

ISSN. International Standard Serial Number. An internationally accepted unique identifier for each serial issued by publishers participating in the program.

Joint Steering Committee for Revision of AACR. An international body consisting of representatives of the library associations and national libraries of the United States (that is, the Library of Congress), Canada, the United Kingdom, and Australia, charged with determining the contents of the *Anglo-American Cataloguing Rules.* Also called "Joint Steering Committee" and abbreviated *JSC*.

JSC. *See* Joint Steering Committee for Revision of AACR.

JSCAACR. *See* Joint Steering Committee for Revision of AACR.

Key heading. In *Sears List of Subject Headings,* a designated subject heading whose subdivisions can be applied to any similar subject heading; for example, "Chicago" is the key heading for all cities. *See also* Pattern heading.

Key title. In the ISDS program, a title assigned to an individual serial to identify it uniquely.

Keyword. 1. A significant word in a title or subject heading. 2. A searchable word, such as a significant word in a title or subject heading. 3. Colloquially, any searchable subject word or term.

Keyword index. An index in which significant words from titles, subject headings, or other areas of a catalog record are access points. *See also* KWIC index, KWOC index.

KWIC index. KeyWord In Context index. An index of title or subject words in which the titles are given in natural word order.

KWOC index. KeyWord Out of Context index. An index of title or subject words in which the titles are given in indirect order, bringing the keyword to the filing position.

LA. Library Association. *See* Chartered Institute of Library and Information Professionals.

LAC. Library and Archives Canada. Formerly known as National Library of Canada.

LACRI. Library and Archives Canada Rule Interpretation. A policy decision for the application of a rule appearing in AACR2–2005 made by the Library and Archives Canada for its catalogers.

LCC. Library of Congress Classification.

LCCN. Library of Congress Control Number. A unique number assigned by the Library of Congress to each catalog record it creates and by which its customers order cataloging on cards or in computer-readable format. Before the advent of computerized cataloging products, the acronym stood for Library of Congress Card Number.

LCRI. Library of Congress Rule Interpretation. A policy decision for the application of a rule appearing in AACR2–2005 made by the Library of Congress.

LCSH. *Library of Congress Subject Headings.* A subject authority produced by the Library of Congress.

Linearity. A feature of library classification in which all subjects are perceived as being placed in a straight line (that is, in two dimensions) from beginning to end, as on library shelves.

Loading. *See* Dumping. *See also* Downloading, Uploading.

Local system. A computer system entirely within the control of a single library or library system. A local system can be shared by a small group of libraries.

LSP. Linked Systems Project. A program linking the Library of Congress's computer system with the computer systems of other program participants.

Main class. In classification, the primary categories into which knowledge is divided.

Main entry. 1. The first and most important descriptive access point assigned to a catalog record by which the item can be retrieved. 2. In a single entry catalog, the access point for a record.

MARA. MAchine Readable Accessions.

MARBI. Committee on Representation in MAchine-Readable Form of Bibliographic Information. An interdivisional committee of the American Library Association comprised of representatives from three of its divisions: Association for Library Collections & Technical Services, Library and Information Technology Association, and Reference and User Services Association.

MARC. MAchine-Readable Cataloging. A group of identifying codes used to communicate bibliographic and other types of data using computers, originally devised by the Library of Congress.

MARC format(s). The compilation(s) of codes used for identifying data for computer communication. Formats have been established for bibliographic data, authorities, holdings, classification, and community information. *See also* MARC.

MARC 21. A version of the MARC format that merges previously separate formats used by Library of Congress (USMARC) and National Library of Canada (CAN/MARC).

Material specific details. The third area of description. Also called *Mathematical details*.

Mathematical details. *See* Material specific details.

Menu-driven. A computer system that operates by presenting a list of options (menu) to the user from which a selection must be made. *See also* Command-driven.

MeSH. *Medical Subject Headings*. A thesaurus of terms for indexing medical information issued by the National Library of Medicine.

Metadata. 1. Data identifying other data, such as citations to documents. 2. Data identifying electronic resources, particularly Internet resources.

METS. Metadata Encoding and Transmission Standard.

Minimal level cataloging. Catalog records containing less information than the minimum required by currently accepted standards.

Mixed notation. In classification, a system of symbols representing the subjects composed of more than one type of character; for example, numbers and letters of the alphabet. *See also* Pure notation.

Mixed responsibility. An item created by differing contributions of more than one responsible party, such as a book having an author, an editor, and an illustrator.

MLA. 1. Medical Library Association, 2. Music Library Association.

MODS. Metadata Object Description Schema.

Module. In a computer system, a program segment or package designed to perform one function in a multifunction system.

Monograph. An item published or produced in full within a finite time period. *See also* Continuing resource, Serial.

Monographic series. *See* Series.

Mounting. Batch loading electronic data. *See* Dumping.

Multimedia. British gmd for multipart items in which the parts belong to more than one medium and no one part predominates, but not a synonym for and not to be confused with interactive multimedia.

NACO. Name Authority Cooperative Organization.

NAF. Name Authority File.

NAL. National Agricultural Library [U.S.].

Name authority. An official record of the establishment of a name form for use as an access point in library catalogs, with its cross-references and data sources. *See also* Authority record.

NLC. *See* LAC.

NLM. National Library of Medicine [U.S.].

NLMC. National Library of Medicine Classification.

Notation. In classification, the system of symbols used to represent subjects. *See also* Mixed notation, Pure notation.

OCLC. Online Computer Library Center. A bibliographic utility headquartered in Dublin Ohio, formerly known as the Ohio College Library Center.

OCLC/WLN. A bibliographic utility headquartered in the state of Washington, originally called Washington Library Network, then renamed Western Library Network, and subsequently merged with OCLC.

Ohio College Library Center. *See* OCLC.

OLUC. OnLine Union Catalog. Former name of OCLC's bibliographic database, now known as WorldCat. *See also* WorldCat.

Online Computer Library Center. *See* OCLC.

OPAC. Online Public Access Catalog. *See also* PAC.

Open entry. Catalog record for a publication in progress in which selected elements are left incomplete, such as dates and extent of the item. *See also* Closed entry.

Original cataloging/classification. The process of creating a new catalog record for an item without the use of a previously created record for the same or related item. *See also* Copy cataloging/classification.

Other physical details. Data relating to the physical properties of an item being cataloged other than its extent, dimensions, and accompanying materials. For example, for a book, it includes illustrations; for an electronic resource, it includes the presence of sound, color, etc.

Other preliminaries. *See* Preliminaries.

Other title information. Title information other than the main title (title proper), alternative title (a title following title proper preceded by the word *or*), and parallel title (title proper in another language or script).

Outsourcing. The practice of contracting with an organization outside the library or media center, often but not always a commercial organization, for operations or services typically performed within the library or media center, such as cataloging.

PAC. Public Access Catalog. *See also* OPAC.

Parallel title. The main title of an item in another language or script.

Parenthetic qualifier. *See* Qualifier.

Paris principles. A statement of descriptive cataloging principles adopted by participants in the International Conference on Cataloguing Principles held in Paris in 1961.

Pattern heading. In *Library of Congress Subject Headings,* a set of subdivisions for a subject heading designated to be applied to all other subject headings of the same type without additional instruction. *See also* Key heading.

PCC. Program for Cooperative Cataloging; promulgator of the core record standard.

Periodical. 1. A serial title issued on a regular schedule, generally more frequently than once or twice a year. 2. Journal, magazine, or newspaper.

Postcoordinate. A classification or subject heading list in which class numbers or headings for topical components are given in the schedule or list to be assembled by the cataloger or searcher as needed. *See also* Faceted, Synthetic.

PRECIS. PREserved Context Indexing System. A computer-assisted system of indexing library materials once used in the United Kingdom and elsewhere, developed by the British Library's Classification Research Group in the 1970s. The system was later simplified and renamed COMPASS. It was discontinued in the 1990s.

Precoordinate. A classification or subject heading list in which topical components are already preassembled (precoordinated) and given in the schedule or list. *See also* Enumerative, Postcoordinate.

Preliminaries. Pages in a book beginning with the cover and concluding with the verso of the title page. Also called *Other preliminaries* to exclude the title page recto from the definition.

Prescribed source(s). In description cataloging, location(s) authorized by AACR2 for obtaining bibliographic data for a particular area of description. The locations vary by type of material. *See also* Chief source.

Primary entry. *See* Main entry.

Pure notation. In classification, a system of symbols representing subjects that use only one type of character; for example, only digits (as in DDC) or only letters of the roman alphabet (as in the Bliss Bibliographic Classification). *See also* Mixed notation.

PURL. Permanent Uniform Resource Locator; permanent address for an Internet resource that is maintained over time, eliminating retrieval problems caused by changing Internet addresses. *See also* URL.

Qualifier. A word or phrase that removes ambiguity from an access point, usually given in parentheses; for example, Cambridge (Mass.) and Cambridge (England), or Kiss (Performing group).

Recto. The right-hand page of a book, always bearing an odd number. *See also* Verso.

Research Libraries Group. The parent organization of RLIN.

Research Libraries Information Network. *See* RLIN.

Retrieval point. *See* Access point.

RLG. *See* Research Libraries Group.

RLIN. A bibliographic utility headquartered in Mountain View, California, established to serve the needs of research libraries. At this writing, RLIN has merged with OCLC, Inc.

RTSD. Resources and Technical Services Division of the American Library Association. Former name of the division known since 1990 as Association for Library Collections & Technical Services (ALCTS).

Rule of three. A library rule of thumb using three as the cutoff point for differing treatments; for example, if one, two, or three authors are equally responsible for an item, choose the first named as the main entry, but if there are more than three, choose the title as the main entry.

SAC. Subject Analysis Committee of the Cataloging and Classification Section of the Association for Library Collections & Technical Services. This committee is responsible for monitoring issues and standards used in subject analysis.

SACO. Subject Authority Cooperative Organization.

Search key. In computer systems, a combination of characters representing parts of access points (for example, letters from an author's surname and the first significant title word) used in place of the full access points. Search keys minimize the storage space used by indexes and minimize the number of characters searchers must enter.

Secondary entry. *See* Added entry.

Separate bibliographic identity. *See* Bibliographic identity.

Serial. An item published or produced in parts intended to go on without end. Should not be confused with *Series*. *See also* Continuing resource, Integrating resource, Monograph.

Series. A group of discrete items having, in addition to their own titles, a common title identifying them as part of the group. Also called *Monographic series*. Should not be confused with *Serial*.

Set. A group of related materials that can be cataloged as a group.

SGML. Standard General Markup Language; a set of protocols for editing text for computer input and communication.

Shared responsibility. Applies when an item is created by more than one responsible party sharing the same type of contribution; for example, a book with multiple authors.

Shelflist. A catalog of items owned by a library arranged by call number.

Shelf mark. Any code or system of marks designed to arrange items on shelves, excluding the classification numbers. Also called *Book mark, Call letter. See also* Cutter letter, Cutter number.

SLA. Special Libraries Association.

smd. Specific material designation. Part of the fifth area of description, naming the physical manifestation of the item.

Specific material designation. *See* smd.

Specificity. The degree of broadness or narrowness of a term used for indexing materials; or the degree of broadness or narrowness of a subject catalog.

Standard number. *See* ISBN, ISMN, ISRC, and ISSN.

Standard subdivision. In DDC, a number from auxiliary Table 1 that can be added to a number from the schedules without a specific instruction to do so.

Statement of responsibility. Part of the first area of description naming those with overall responsibility for the creation of the item.

Subfield. Part of a field in the MARC format.

Subfield code. A character identifying the subfield and the data it contains. *See also* Delimiter.

Subject authority. A record documenting the establishment of an acceptable subject term containing the term, the cross-references established with it, and the sources of the information. *See also* Controlled vocabulary.

Subject cataloging. The act of assigning subject headings to an item being cataloged.

Subject heading. 1. A word or phrase identifying the intellectual content of an item being cataloged and used as an access point. 2. A term from an authorized list of terms to be used as access points. *See also* Descriptor.

Subject heading list. A list of terms, usually including cross-references, for indexing items being cataloged. Subject heading lists usually cover all branches of knowledge unless they explicitly state otherwise. *See also* Thesaurus.

Symbolic notation. *See* Notation.

Syndetics. The structure of cross-references that link related terms.

Synthetic. A classification or subject heading list in which components of class numbers or headings are given to be assembled (synthesized) by the cataloger or searcher. *See also* Faceted, Postcoordinate.

Tag. The three-digit code identifying a field in the MARC format.

Tagging. The act of assigning codes to bibliographic data in the MARC format. Also known as *coding and tagging. See also* Coding.

TEI. Text Encoding Initiative; a set of protocols for editing text for computer input and communication.

TGN. *Thesaurus for Geographic Names.*

Thesaurus. A list of terms, with cross-references that clarify the relationships among terms used for indexing. Thesauri often are limited to a single discipline or group of disciplines. *See also* Subject heading list.

Title proper. The main title of an item.

Truncation. A feature of computerized retrieval in which searches can be performed on word roots; for example, LIBR- would retrieve records for LIBRA, LIBRARIAN, LIBRARIES, LIBRARY, etc.

Turnkey system. A computer system package that includes hardware, software, installation, training, and (usually) ongoing maintenance, support, and development.

UBC. Universal Bibliographic Control. A program of IFLA.

UDC. Universal Decimal Classification. An international classification system based on the Dewey Decimal Classification.

UKMARC. United Kingdom MAchine Readable Cataloguing. Superseded by MARC 21.

Uncontrolled vocabulary. A system of indexing in which any terms, not just those on an authorized list, are used for retrieval, such as a title keyword index. *See also* Controlled vocabulary, KWIC index, KWOC index.

Uniform title. A title created and assigned by catalogers to collocate editions and versions of a work that appear under different titles proper. The uniform title assigned to an item may be the title by which it is commonly known, the original title of a work published in translation, or a title constructed by the cataloger.

UNIMARC. UNIversal MAchine Readable Cataloguing.

Uploading. The act of transmitting data electronically from a small local computer system to a larger computer database. *See also* Downloading.

URL. Uniform Resource Locator. Address for an Internet resource. *See also* PURL.

USMARC. United States MAchine-Readable Cataloging. Superseded by MARC 21.

Utility. *See* Bibliographic utility.

UTLAS. University of Toronto Libraries Automated Systems. The original name of the Canadian bibliographic utility currently known as A-G Canada Ltd.

Utlas International. Name of the Canadian bibliographic utility originally known as UTLAS when it was purchased by the Thomson Corporation. *See also* A-G Canada Ltd.

Variable field. A field in the MARC format containing data that varies in length and format. *See also* Control field, Fixed field.

Verso. 1. Left-hand page of a book, always bearing an even number. 2. Back of the title page.

Washington Library Network. *See* OCLC/WLN.

Western Library Network. *See* OCLC/WLN.

WLN. *See* OCLC/WLN.

WorldCat. Name of OCLC's online shared bibliographic database. *See also* OLUC.

Indexes

The three indexes that follow provide a detailed guide to the contents of the book. The first index is a topical guide to the text followed by an index of both personal and corporate names. The third index accommodates those who wish to study the figures and examples more systematically, and is divided into four subsections: Type of Media, Access Points, Description, and Classification. Problems encountered in normal cataloging and rule interpretations can be checked across figures and examples using these indexes. This should provide valuable additional practice in learning the rules.

TOPICAL INDEX TO THE TEXT

273

INDEX TO NAMES

INDEX TO FIGURES AND EXAMPLES

TYPE OF MEDIA

Art original, 46
Art reproduction, 45
Atlas, 64–65
Audiocassette. *See* Sound recording
Audiodisc. *See* Sound recording

Book, 7, 9, 29–30 & 32, 42–43, 52–53, 54–55, 66,
    67–68, 69–70, 71–72, 73, 85–86, 88, 90,
    92–93, 104–5, 141–42, 145–46, 158–59,
    161–62, 179–80, 191–92, 201–2, 208–9,
    216, 218–19, 238, 240, 242, 244, 246

Cartographic material, 39–40, 49–50, 64–65
Cassette. *See* Sound recording; Videorecording
Chart, 182
Compact disc, 78–79
Computer file. *See* Electronic resource
Continuing resource
    integrating resource, 45–46
    serial, 41–42, 51, 80

Disc/disk. *See* Electronic resource; Sound recording
Dominant component. *See* Multicomponent item

Electronic resource
    serial, 41–42, 51, 80

Film. *See* Motion picture
Flip chart. *See* Chart

Game, 34, 93, 245

Integrating resource. *See* Continuing resource

Kit, 36–38

Map, 39–40, 49–50
Medium not obvious, 34–35
Microform, 11
Model, 175
Multicomponent item
    dominant part, 36–38
    one part only, 42–43
Music, printed, 85, 91, 237, 243

Overhead transparency. *See* Transparency

Naturally occurring object, 47

Picture, 110–11
Printed music. *See* Music, printed

Realia, 47

Sample. *See* Realia
Score. *See* Music, printed
Serial. *See* Continuing resource; Electronic resource
Software, computer. *See* Electronic resource
Sound recording
    cassette, 31, 36–38, 87, 239
    disc, 32, 78–79, 112–13, 234–35
Specimen. *See* Realia

Videorecording, 82–83, 89, 241

ACCESS POINTS

Author/Creator Main Entry
Adapter/reteller, 238
Bibliographic form of name. *See* entries in first
    index to figures and examples
Composer and uniform title, 78, 237, 243
Corporate body, 64
Conference. *See* Named conference
Conventional title. *See* Uniform title
Full form of given names added, 191
Musical group, 234
Named conference, 54
Personal author, item emanating from a corporate
    body entered under, 66

Single author/creator, 9, 11, 34, 36–38, 42, 44, 46,
    69, 104, 110, 112, 145, 201, 218, 239, 240,
    242, 246
Two authors/creators, 52, 66, 161, 179, 216, 244
Three authors/creators, 71, 32

Title Main Entry
Anonymous work, 208
Collective title, 82–83, 191
Conventional title. *See* uniform title
Corporate body, emanating from, 39,41, 45, 49, 51,
    67, 82, 158
Edited/ compiled work, 7, 141, 191

DESCRIPTION

CLASSIFICATION

About the Authors

SHEILA S. INTNER is Professor Emerita in the Simmons College Graduate School of Library and Information Science. She was the founding director of Simmons' MLIS program at Mount Holyoke College, established in 2001, and is currently adjunct professor at the College of Library and Information Science at the University of Maryland. She has been teaching library organization and collections management since 1980 and retired from Simmons College in 2006. She has been involved in the development of organizational standards since 1989, when she was simultaneously elected an American Library Association Councilor-at-large and president of the Association for Library Collections & Technical Services, the association most closely associated with metadata and cataloging standards. She has received numerous awards, including the prestigious Margaret Mann Citation Award for outstanding contributions to education for cataloging and classification, and the Online Audiovisual Catalogers' Annual Award for excellence in promoting standards in online cataloging. She is the author or principal editor of twenty-two books, including *Electronic Cataloging* (2003), *Cataloging Correctly for Kids* (American Library Association, 2006), *Metadata and Its Impact on Libraries* (Libraries Unlimited, 2006), and the first three editions of *Standard Cataloging for School and Public Libraries* (Libraries Unlimited, 1994, 1998, and 2001).

In her long career, **JEAN WEIHS** has worked in university, public, school, and special libraries as a reference librarian, a bibliographer, and a school librarian. Most of her career, however, she has been involved in cataloging, as both a practitioner and a teacher of librarians, library technicians, and school librarians in Canada, where she served as Director of the Library Techniques Program at Seneca College of Applied Arts and Technology until her retirement in 1986. Subsequent to this, she taught as a visiting professor at UCLA and Simmons College and acted as a consultant. She represented the Canadian Committee on Cataloguing for nine years on the Joint Steering Committee for Revision of AACR, five of these as JSC Chair. She has held forty-five positions on national and international committees. Among the many publications for which she is a principal author or editor are four editions of *Nonbook Materials: The Organization of Integrated Collections* (one of the books that was used as the basis for formulating rules in AACR2 for these materials; published 1970, 1973, 1979, and 1989); *Accessible Storage of Nonbook Materials* (1984) and its second edition, *The Integrated Library* (1991); *The Principles and Future of AACR: Proceedings of the International Conference on the Principles and Future Development of AACR* (1998); and three editions of *Standard Cataloging for School and Public Libraries*. She is the recipient of many honors, including the prestigious Margaret Mann Citation Award sponsored by the Cataloging and Classification Section of the Association for Library Collections & Technical Services, University of Toronto Faculty of Library and Information Science 60th Anniversary Award for outstanding contributions to the field of library and information science, the Queen's Jubilee Medal (given by the Governor General of Canada, nominated by the Canadian Library Association), the Online Audiovisual Catalogers' Nancy B. Olson Award for lifetime achievement in the development of access to media collections, and the Canadian Association of College and University Libraries' Blackwell's Award for Distinguished Academic Librarian.